User Participation in Health and Social Care Research

Voices, Values and Evaluation

User Participation in Health and Social Care Research

Voices, Values and Evaluation

Edited by

Mike Nolan, Elizabeth Hanson,
Gordon Grant and John Keady

 Open University Press

Open University Press
McGraw-Hill Education
McGraw-Hill House
Shoppenhangers Road
Maidenhead
Berkshire
England
SL6 2QL

email: enquiries@openup.co.uk
world wide web: www.openup.co.uk

and Two Penn Plaza, New York, NY 10121-2289, USA

First published 2007

A catalogue record of this book is available from the British Library

ISBN-10 0 335 22205 6 (pb)   0 335 22206 4 (hb)
ISBN-13 978 0 335 22205 6 (pb)   978 0 335 22206 3 (hb)

Library of Congress Cataloging-in-Publication Data
CIP data applied for

Typeset by RefineCatch Limited, Bungay, Suffolk
Printed in Poland by OZ Graf. S.A.
www.polskabook.pl

*The **McGraw·Hill** Companies*

For Will Nolan 1955–2006
'Nothing compares to you'

Contents

List of figures

List of tables

List of contributors

Fredrik Arvevik is an Assistant Nurse with a long experience of working with older people living at home and their family carers in Borås municipality, Sweden. Over the past seven years Fredrik has worked in the ACTION (Assisting Carers using Telematic Interventions to meet Older people's Needs) call centre, together with Paul Svensson, where he has developed expertise in partnership working with elders with chronic illness and their family carers. Today, Fredrik also has a lead role in further developing family carer support services in Borås municipality together with a group of practitioners and carers. He is actively involved with colleagues in implementing COAT (Carers' Outcome Agreement Tool) into everyday practice.

Lewis Atkinson is a retired Canon of the Church of England. He and his wife, Connie, have been married 49 years and she is now in full-time care at Birch Avenue suffering from Alzheimer's disease. Lewis is a member of the Support 67 Group. He is also deeply involved with the Sheffield Care Trust User and Carer Council and Chairs both the Older Adult Mental Health Sub-Group, and the Sheffield Older Persons' Empowerment Network which seeks to strengthen the voice of older adults, particularly the weak and vulnerable in society.

Barry Aveyard is a Lecturer at Sheffield Hallam University. He has worked with older people for most of his nursing career. He has been involved in a number of research projects around older people's mental health and has published widely on the subject.

Jo Booth has been Senior Research Fellow in the Centre for Gerontological Practice, Glasgow Caledonian University since 2004. Prior to this she gained extensive experience in a number of clinical roles working with older people in both acute and community services, the most recent as a Consultant Nurse for Older People's Services. She has directed the development of nursing practice throughout her career and is a lead researcher in the Gerontological Nursing Demonstration Programme. Her research interests focus on stroke rehabilitation nursing and promoting urinary continence in older people.

Lauren Clark is Associate Professor and Associate Dean for Research and Extramural Affairs, University of Colorado at Denver and Health Sciences Center School of Nursing, USA. She teaches qualitative research, public health nursing, and a course in cultural competence for advanced practice nurses. Her research with Mexican immigrant and Mexican American families explores childhood feeding and nutrition, particularly the cultural aspects of early childhood obesity.

Jane Coad is a Senior Research Fellow (postdoctoral) in the Centre for Child and Adolescent Health, the University of the West of England, Bristol, UK and Honorary Senior Research Fellow in Family Talk; Communicating Genetic Information across families at the University of Birmingham, UK. Jane undertakes participatory research in Child Health and Children's Nursing using art-based research methods both locally in Bristol and Birmingham, but also nationally. Her current research projects include engaging children and families in research in acute and community health settings, young people's perceptions of health and the effects of the arts on young children's health.

Jonathan Crichton is a Research Fellow in the Research Centre for Languages and Cultures Education in the School of International Studies at the University of South Australia, where he teaches courses in Applied Linguistics. He is interested in the place of language in people's lives, particularly in situations which affect their life chances. His research includes the role of language in interactions within medical, health, legal and educational settings.

Monica Curran is a Sociologist with over 15 years' experience of carer-related research. She has a postgraduate degree from Manchester University in applied social research, and a particular interest in how research partnerships are built between research participants and researchers. Her previous research includes the involvement of older people and carers in key decisions about how services can be provided: complex needs assessment, discharge from hospital and entry into care. Her most recent work was for the Partnership in Carer Assessment Project at the University of Sheffield, studying carer assessment for carers of people with mental health problems.

Sue Davies worked as a health visitor and as a senior nurse within a unit providing services for older people in London before moving into higher education. She recently completed a Department of Health postdoctoral fellowship exploring quality of life and quality of care for older people living in care homes and their families. Sue now holds an Honorary Readership at the University of Sheffield and lives in Minnesota.

Gordon Grant is Research Professor in the Centre for Health and Social Care Research, Sheffield Hallam University, and also Research and Innovation Lead, Doncaster and South Humber Healthcare NHS (National Health Service) Trust.

His main research interests centre on contributions and human capital in vulnerable groups, family caregiving across the life-course and the inclusive research agenda. Gordon is an editor of the *British Journal of Learning Disabilities*. Ever the eternal optimist, he is a lifelong supporter of the other Manchester football team (City not United).

Elizabeth Hanson is a Senior Lecturer at ÄldreVäst Sjuhärad (ÄVS) Research Centre, University College of Borås (UCB) and the University of Kalmar, Department of Humanities, Sweden. She acts as scientific leader in elder care at ÄVS and of ACTION (Assisting Carers using Telematic Interventions to meet Older people's Needs), Department of Health Sciences, UCB. Elizabeth is a Visiting Reader at the University of Sheffield. She is a nurse and currently a steering board member and research representative for Carers Sweden. Her research interests include family care support, palliative care needs of older people and empowerment in research and practice.

John Hughes-Roberts is a Nurse Specialist, Division of Psychology, Mental Health and Learning Disability, Conwy and Denbighshire NHS Trust, Wales. His current role is leading the development of a memory clinic service across the counties of Conwy and Denbighshire in North Wales. The aim of memory clinics is to provide a service for people with early memory problems to include assessment and diagnosis along with post diagnostic support and interventions. His current interests include the subjective experience of early dementia, in particular how individuals and their families adapt and cope with a diagnosis of dementia.

John Keady trained as a Registered Mental Nurse in Warley Hospital, Brentwood, Essex between 1983 and 1986 before moving to North Wales and working as a community mental health nurse in a community dementia team. From this time John has maintained an active research, publication and teaching profile in dementia care, and in October 2006 he took up the appointment of Professor of Older People's Mental Health Nursing, a joint appointment between the University of Manchester and the Bolton, Salford and Trafford Mental Health NHS Trust. John is founding and co-editor of *Dementia: The International Journal of Social Research and Practice* and the first edition of this quarterly Sage journal was published in February 2002.

Timothy B. Kelly is currently the Head of the Division of Social Work at Glasgow Caledonian University (GCU). Previously he was a Senior Research Fellow within the Centre for Gerontological Practice at GCU and he maintains active membership within the centre. His publications include articles on gerontological practice in health and social care settings, groupwork practice, involving service users and practice development. He is the Vice-President of the Association for the Advancement of Social Work with Groups and a member of the editorial board for *Groupwork*.

In July 2005 **Tina Koch** was appointed in a Clinical Chair as a joint initiative between Hunter New England (NSW) Health and the University of Newcastle, Australia. An Older Person Research Program is being established with a strong research team. The focus of recent research is storytelling with older people within a participatory action approach. This has involved researchers in listening to the voices of frail older people with respect to their choices for future care. Older people want to be involved in decisions that affect their lives. Development of proactive strategies is critical in helping frail older people maximize their potential, even when their life and decision-making options are reduced.

Ann Macfadyen has been a Senior Lecturer in Childhood and Family Studies at Northumbria University in Newcastle since 1993. She has worked as a nurse in both adult and children's services in Glasgow, London and Newcastle. Over the past 13 years she has been involved in a number of projects which have aimed to promote children's rights to be involved in decisions about their care. More recent projects have focused on accessing children and young people's views in service evaluation and development.

Lennart Magnusson is a Senior Lecturer in the Department of Health Sciences, University College of Borås and the Department of Humanities, University of Kalmar, Sweden. He is an engineer, nurse and founding director of ÄldreVäst Sjuhärad Research Centre. Lennart is manager of ACTION and his doctoral thesis 'Designing a responsive support service for family carers of frail older people using information and communication technology' was based on research carried out within the European Union (EU) and Swedish projects. He has a long-standing interest in innovative ways of working to improve elder care, family care support and to enhance job satisfaction for practitioners.

Gene W. Marsh is an Associate Professor and Chairperson, Division of Health Experience and Technology at the University of Colorado at Denver and Health Sciences Center, School of Nursing, USA. She also holds an Honorary Professorship at the University of Sheffield School of Nursing and Midwifery, UK. She teaches advanced public health nursing and research methodology. Her current research focuses on determining appropriate hospice admission criteria and care for Alzheimer's disease patients and their families.

Una Martin is a retired Legal Executive specializing in Criminal and Matrimonial law. She has been married to her husband, Ernest, for 50 years and he is now in full-time care at Birch Avenue suffering from Alzheimer's disease. She is a founder member of the Support 67 Action Group and also a representative of the group at Team Governance meetings at Birch Avenue. She is also a member of the Older Adults' Mental Health Sub-Group of the Sheffield Care Trust User and Carer Council.

Scott McCaffrey completed his nurse training at Napsbury Hospital in London Colney, Hertfordshire. He has 21 years' experience of nursing in mental health in the fields of acute psychiatry, continuing care and rehabilitation, older adults and forensic psychiatry. He has also worked in the capacity of clinical risk adviser within a Health Care Trust. Scott has been the Registered Manager at Birch Avenue for the past three years.

Alex McClimens is a Senior Research Fellow in the Centre for Health and Social Care Research, Sheffield Hallam University. A career in care preceded an academic involvement in learning disability nurse education and a subsequent move to research in health and social care. Alex's research is aligned with the scope of advocacies and emancipatory paradigms. In his current work he is exploring the potential of narrative and drama to unlock meaning for people labelled with learning disability. A keen student of Oriental Studies, Alex devotes much of his spare time to an exchange scheme designed to promote Sino-Scots relations.

After training as a teacher **Mike Nolan** gained qualifications in general and psychiatric nursing and has worked with older people and their family carers in a variety of clinical, educational and research roles for over 25 years. He has particular interests in creating partnerships between older people, family and professional carers. He is currently Professor of Gerontological Nursing at the University of Sheffield, and has a Visiting Chair at the University College of Health Sciences, Borås, West Sweden.

Ann Powell is currently Team Leader for the Assisted Discharge Dementia Team based within Sheffield Care Trust. Previously she managed 67 Birch Avenue, a care home for older people with dementia, which was jointly managed by a mental health trust and a housing association. She has a strong interest in practice development approaches.

Mo and **Pat Quinn** were born and raised in Liverpool. Mo was the youngest of seven children, two boys and five girls. Mo and Pat have been married for 49 years. Mo was diagnosed with Alzheimer's disease in January 2003 at the age of 64 years. Her mother and three of her sisters had Alzheimer's disease. Mo still lives a normal life; she enjoys life and takes each day as it comes. Mo and Pat feel that it is important to be given the opportunity to be actively involved in research studies, as their experience of Alzheimer's disease may be beneficial to future generations.

Paul Ramcharan is a Lecturer in Disability Studies in the School of Health Sciences at the Royal Melbourne Institute of Technology (RMIT). His research in relation to people with learning disabilities spans two national strategies in Wales and England. Paul has undertaken formal research around services for people with learning disabilities and their carers, as well as participatory and emancipatory research with people with learning disabilities. Most recently Paul was, with Gordon Grant, an academic coordinator of the Learning Disability Research Initiative designed to support the implementation of the White Paper *Valuing People*.

Julie Repper has worked as a mental health nurse, lecturer and researcher. Over the past 15 years she has developed a programme of research into the unintended effects of mental health policy and the experiences of people who are marginalized within mental health services: women, prisoners, gypsies and travellers, 'unpopular patients' and, most recently, carers of people with mental health problems. She has co-written and edited a number of books including, with Rachel Perkins, *Social Inclusion and Recovery: A Model for Mental Health Practice*.

Kristine Morgan Reimer earned a Nursing Doctorate from the University of Colorado at Denver and Health Sciences Center School of Nursing, Denver, Colorado, USA, and a Master of Nonprofit Management from Regis University, Denver, Colorado. Her primary areas of interest include public health nursing, mental health nursing, nursing theory, and ethics. She is currently adjunct faculty for Colorado Mountain College and Adams State University, in Alamosa, Colorado. Dr Reimer served four years as Director of Public Health in Chaffee County, Colorado. She was a leader in assessing health needs of the community and instrumental in implementing changes in community health services.

Irene Schofield is a Research Fellow in the Centre for Gerontological Practice, Glasgow Caledonian University. She has worked clinically with older people in a range of settings prior to moving into education and research. Irene has worked on research projects related to the caring attributes of nurses who work with older people, service use and choices of people with chronic obstructive pulmonary disease, and the Gerontological Nursing Demonstration Project. Her current research activity focuses on delirium, and cognitive assessment of patients admitted to emergency care. She has written a number of book chapters and articles in clinical and academic nursing journals.

Graham Shields is 43 years of age and lives in Driffield, East Yorkshire, having been born in Hull: 'I remain single, never having been married mostly due to the long interjection of my illness which I have suffered for some 17 years.

I am a Christian seeking the equilibrium of the antimony between political liberalism and fundamentalism. My time is occupied with helping to run an allotment, assisting children with learning disabilities at Mencap, working part-time for the mental health trust and writing a book which may end up being called *101.5 Things to Do whilst Psychotic* . . . as well as being ill of course!'

Paul Svensson is an Assistant Nurse with extensive experience of working with frail older people and their family carers in home care and long-term care settings in Borås municipality. Paul works with Fredrik Arvevik in the ACTION call centre where he has gained expertise in partnership working with older people with chronic illness and their family carers. Recently, in addition, Paul has begun working with disseminating ACTION to other municipalities in Sweden. He currently acts as an expert facilitator and role model for other practitioners working with ACTION across Sweden, providing regular supervision and ongoing support.

Veronica Swallow is a Senior Lecturer in Children's Nursing at the University of Manchester. She is a paediatric nurse and has 13 years' experience of leading and conducting research in child health and professional learning in the NHS. She recently completed a PhD at Northumbria University. This study investigated the way children and families learn to participate in chronic childhood disease management. Her current research includes an investigation into fathers' and mothers' reported views of their own and their partner's roles in self-managing their child's chronic renal condition.

Debbie Tolson is a Professor of Gerontological Nursing and the founding Director of the Interdisciplinary Centre for Gerontological Practice based at Glasgow Caledonian University, Scotland. She has over 20 years' experience of working with older people and their families in a variety of clinical and academic roles. Her interest in the potential to work collaboratively with users stems from practice experiences and a curiosity about the impact of policy and care guidance on the quality of nursing care. Current research interests include inclusive approaches to the construction of care guidance, working with communities of practice to develop care, age-related hearing disability, and supporting individuals and families with dementia.

After graduating in Applied Biology in 1973, **Ray Wainwright** has worked as a schoolteacher, British Rail signalman and part-time lecturer. Having experienced several episodes of mental illness since 1967, his condition worsened in 1994 resulting in permanent disability. However, he has recovered sufficiently to volunteer first as an advocate in Darlington and continues to act as a befriender. He also participates in user research in the North East. In 2001 he began part-time PhD research into the possible impact of phenomena diagnosed as mental illness upon sense of personal identity. His 'home' interests are walking in Teesdale, watercolour painting and DIY.

Sion Williams is a Lecturer in Nursing in the School of Healthcare Sciences at the University of Wales, Bangor. He is currently engaged in an RCBC (Research and Capacity Building Collaboration) Wales postdoctoral fellowship examining later-stage adjustment in people with Parkinson's disease. This contributes to an ongoing collaborative programme of constructivist grounded theory studies in North Wales, centred on examining adjustment to life with Parkinson's disease, Alzheimer's disease, stroke and rheumatoid arthritis. He has a particular interest in seeking to understand adaptation and coping in long-term conditions through participatory approaches, using grounded theory, narrative research and testimony.

Acknowledgements

The editors would like to thank warmly all the countless user researchers whose expert input over many years has been the inspiration for this book.

We are indebted to all the contributors who produced drafts on time, and to the team at Open University Press for their patience in waiting for the final manuscript.

Most importantly, our sincere appreciation goes to Helen Mason, whose dedication, skill and determination ensured that this book progressed from idea to reality.

1 Introduction: what counts as knowledge, whose knowledge counts? Towards authentic participatory enquiry

Mike Nolan, Elizabeth Hanson, Gordon Grant, John Keady, Lennart Magnusson

> The creation and use of knowledge are inherently the motivating force behind all research.
>
> (Wallerstein and Duran 2003: 35)

> Consumer involvement in health research is required in order to develop and incorporate compelling and different forms of knowledge; such knowledge cannot be considered to be knowledge or capable of incorporation without involvement; but involvement cannot proceed unless different kinds of knowledge come to be considered knowledge.
>
> (Hodgson and Canvin 2005: 39)

As Hodgson and Canvin's conundrum (2005) suggests, the answer to the question 'What counts as knowledge, and whose knowledge counts?' is crucial to realizing user participation in health and social care research. For if the creation and use of knowledge is the motivating force behind all research (Wallerstein and Duran 2003), then how we define what 'counts' as knowledge and whose knowledge we value, largely determine what we see as being the *raison d'être* for involving users in health and social care research. Addressing such concerns is far more than an academic exercise, for 'user participation' in its many forms impacts significantly on the lives and experiences of all those involved in health and social care, be they users or carers, practitioners, service providers, policy-makers or researchers.

The issues involved are complex and opinions often polarized, for user participation in research is still in its infancy (Hulatt and Lowes 2005), with many practical, ethical, moral, methodological and philosophical questions unanswered.

Despite this the political rhetoric, promoting the value of user participation is 'unrelenting'. It is suggested that it currently occupies a 'morally
impervious' position and is increasingly 'resistant to criticism' (Hodgson and
Canvin 2005). Consequently, the inherent danger is that 'user participation'
will join the ranks of 'motherhood' and 'apple pie'.

Our aim in this book is to explore some of the contradictions and tensions
that surround user participation in research, particularly whose voices are
being heard (or silenced), what values drive the enterprise, and how we evaluate the processes and outcomes involved in order to know if we are doing
'good work' (Bradbury and Reason 2003). The bulk of the book comprises ten
case studies providing accounts of differing approaches to user participation
in research. These are diverse and vary considerably in their scope, ranging from the individual to the level of the community and the user group
involved, including children, older people, people with dementia and their
family carers, people with mental health problems and their family carers, and
people with learning disabilities. We also include the voices of practitioners, as
we see these as being 'users' of research with differing, but no less important,
concerns and experiences. In several of these case studies users are co-authors,
their voices being left to speak largely for themselves. In others, academic
researchers have worked closely with users in 'co-constructing' an account,
whereas in some the main voice is that of the academic researcher. Moreover,
case studies come from several countries including the UK, USA, Sweden and
Australia. We feel this diversity is a strength and a witness to the worldwide
momentum for inclusivity in research design and conduct.

In this chapter we outline the emergence of user participation in research
and then consider some of the literature and published accounts of the varying
models of user involvement with a particular emphasis on whose voice is privileged and the way that knowledge is defined, the sorts of values that either
implicitly or explicitly underpin user involvement in research, and, finally,
we turn attention to how such efforts might be evaluated, with particular
reference to an approach that some of us have been involved in co-creating
and applying with older people in Sweden.

In the final chapter we distil the key messages emerging from the case
studies, and provide a framework that might help others interested in user
participation in research to do so in a considered and reflexive way.

User participation: an idea whose time has come?

Despite user participation in research being a relatively recent phenomenon
(Hulatt and Lowes 2005), user participation in research is of relevance to
health and social care systems throughout the Western world (Nicholson
and Burr 2005). However, as Beresford (2005) suggests, it is not possible to

consider its impact fully without reference to the wider literature on user involvement more generally. We would go further and argue that three distinct but closely related trends help to inform an understanding of the issues currently surrounding user participation in research. These are:

- the emergence of participatory and emancipatory research approaches which preceded the current focus on user participation/involvement in service design and evaluation
- the political drive for greater user participation/involvement in health and social care
- the recent emphasis on evidence-based practice or evidence-based care.

Realization that the complex health and social care problems facing modern society could not be adequately addressed using an 'outside expert' approach to research saw the emergence of more participatory models in the 1950s and 1960s (Minkler and Wallerstein 2003). These have since diversified considerably and the 'multiplicity' of terms used can be daunting (Wallerstein and Duran 2003). However, there is agreement that such models are not simply about applying different methods, but rather represent differing 'orientations to research' (Minkler and Wallerstein 2003), sharing the common goal of forging closer connections between research, action and learning, and thereby raising questions about knowledge defined by whom, about whom, and for what purpose (Wallerstein and Duran 2003).

Whilst participatory research may share common goals, there is a continuum of participation, with studies primarily led by an outside researcher at one end, to truly emancipatory research at the other (Minkler and Wallerstein 2003). Driven by the disabled people's movement, emancipatory research gained momentum in the 1960s and 1970s with the primary aim of empowering disadvantaged groups, both personally and politically (Beresford 2005). As will become apparent, emancipatory models continue to exert considerable influence on user participation in research by explicitly promoting user-controlled approaches.

The concept of greater user involvement in health and social care built on debates about empowerment in the 1980s (Beresford 2005) but gained greatest momentum in the 1990s (Hanley et al. 2004; Hodgson and Canvin 2005; Warren and Cook 2005). From a UK perspective the main driver was political (Hanley et al. 2004), forming part of new Labour's modernization agenda (Warren and Cook 2005), with the initial emphasis being placed on the health service (Hodgson and Canvin 2005). The result was Labour's vision for the 'new NHS' (DoH 1997), and developments such as the 'expert patient' initiative (DoH 2001a), whereby the knowledge and expertise of people living with long-term conditions were increasingly recognized as a valuable resource to inform the development of better and more appropriate services. Further momentum was provided by a series of adverse events that resulted in the launch of the National Service Frameworks for Mental Health, Cardiovascular Disease and Older People's Services (Hodgson and Canvin 2005). Subsequently the principles of user involvement and participation have rapidly influenced several areas including the education and training of professionals, the development of quality standards, occupational and professional practice, and user controlled services and support (Beresford 2005), but the emphasis on user participation in research has been a rather more recent development. Nevertheless, infrastructure to support such participation and guidance for researchers have been formalized in structures such as INVOLVE (Hanley et al. 2004). As a result of these initiatives the language of participation and partnership have become 'part and parcel of social policy and provision' (Humphries 2003).

The 1980s also saw the emergence of the evidence-based medicine (later evidence-based practice) movement, which originated in Canada (Jennings and Loan 2001) and arrived in the UK in the early 1990s (Rolfe 1999). This marked a shift in the rhetoric away from research-based practice and, in theory at least, signalled the acceptance of a broader view of what constitutes evidence (Rolfe 1999). However, in reality, research evidence still predominates, and the resultant hierarchy of evidence privileged one particular form of research, the Randomized Controlled Trial (RCT) (Kitson 2002; Grypdonck 2006) above all others. Therefore, although service users are considered by advocates of participatory research to be 'active shapers' of knowledge (Clough 2005), the reality remains different.

Indeed, commentators in the fields of both health (Kitson 2002) and social care (Humphries 2003) suggest that evidence-based practice is incompatible with other major ideological movements such as patient-centred health services (Kitson 2002), as the former is primarily a 'practitioner engineered' development serving practitioner interests (Humphries 2003). Therefore, despite the rhetoric of actively involving users in research, their role, it is claimed, remains largely confined to being sources of data (Kitson 2002; Humphries 2003).

Whilst Owen (2005) suggests that there are both tensions and convergences between user involvement and debates about evidence-based practice, Hodgson and Canvin (2005) are swingeing in their critique of user involvement, seeing it as little more than tokenistic. They argue, as have others (Owen 2005; Steel 2005), that users lack the 'insider' knowledge to truly participate in research, which is still dominated by the scientific method whose language, discourse and practice is alien to 'lay' people (Hodgson and Canvin 2005). Therefore, without a shared understanding of key principles and techniques, users are effectively excluded, and, consequently, the user involvement movement simply maintains the status quo (Hodgson and Canvin 2005). Beresford

(2005) contends that the 'politics' of knowledge creation are such that practice may never be truly evidence based, and in so doing he poses several very pertinent questions:

- Can user knowledge ever have equal status?
- What status does user knowledge have as evidence?
- How can we move from individual to collective knowledge?
- How can knowledge claims be resolved?
- Who is best placed to interpret the experience and knowledge of service users?

Such questions essentially raise issues to do with voice, power and control. It is to here that we now turn.

'They who shout the loudest'

In the present context two issues capture the tensions within the user participation movement particularly well; these are to do with the level of participation that is seen as desirable and the increasingly contentious question of what 'counts as evidence/knowledge'.

There is little consensus in the literature about the optimum level or degree of participation. Many commentators (Minkler and Wallerstein 2003; Hanley et al. 2004; Reed et al. 2004; Hulatt and Lowes 2005) suggest that a continuum exists ranging, for example, from the user as a source of data, through a partnership model, to users as independent researchers (Reed et al. 2004), or from consultation to collaboration to user-controlled research (Hanley et al. 2004). In thinking of respective roles for users and researchers Hulatt and Lowes (2005) suggest two continua as follows:

User role	Subject	Partner	Investigator
	↕	↕	↕
Researcher role	Investigator	Partner	Mentor

In seeking to impose some order on the many models that exist, Beresford (2005) suggests that user participation falls into one of two broad categories:

- managerialist/consumerist – where the main goal is to modify/improve service systems with no real intention of redistributing power
- democratic – where the aim is to improve people's lives, with the ultimate goal being emancipatory research whereby people are empowered to take greater control over their situation.

Minkler and Wallerstein (2003) suggest that emancipatory research should be the 'gold standard' and, in reviewing the literature on user involvement, Turner and Beresford (2005) conclude that users themselves make important distinctions between involvement and emancipatory approaches, with the former being viewed 'unfavourably' by users as they are seen to 'embody inequalities of power which work to the disadvantage of service users' (p. 3). The key question is one of control, with, for some, user controlled researcher being the only legitimate aim (Turner and Beresford 2005).

However, there is far from universal agreement with such a stance. Hanley et al. (2004), for example, argue that there is a place for consultation, collaboration and user control, with none being inherently superior to the other. Others go further and contend that privileging user-controlled research is itself potentially a form of oppression as it assumes that all users want to exercise this degree of control, when in fact there is evidence to suggest the opposite (Dewar 2005; Clough et al. 2006). Clough et al. (2006: 60) note that 'important as power and control are to understand the research process, to judge the quality of older people's involvement in research primarily in relation to these attributes runs the risk of missing other factors'.

Dewar (2005) is highly critical of the de facto assumption that empowerment is the 'gold standard', believing that more attention needs to be paid to reciprocity and shared learning in the process of user involvement in research and development. This sentiment is mirrored by Steel (2005: 21) as follows: 'Ownership and empowerment need not always involve total control of a process. It can mean an interest, will and ability to participate and share control and responsibility with others for a mutual purpose. This is interdependence.'

Pawson et al. (2003) consider that one of the key questions is whether participation in research is really about user control or a full and equal partnership. Several authors talk about creating 'real' (Hulatt and Lowes 2005), 'equal' (Dewar 2005), 'active' (Hanley et al. 2004) or 'collaborative' (Marsh et al. 2005) partnerships between service users and researchers, based on mutual trust and respect (Reed 2005). Such partnerships are participatory (Humphries 2003) and involve users at all stages of the research process (Marsh et al. 2005), from design to dissemination. Partnerships result in 'co-learning' between users and researchers (Minkler and Wallerstein 2003; Faulkner 2004; Dewar 2005) by paying particular attention to the relational and social dimensions of working together (Bradbury and Reason 2003; Faulkner 2004; Morgan and Harris 2005). Within such a model participation is a defining characteristic of the 'new world' in which the quality of our 'relational practices' are a key consideration (Bradbury and Reason 2003). We return to the question of user control or relational partnerships in the concluding chapter.

The other dimension to 'voice' that we consider here concerns the nature and status of differing forms of evidence/knowledge.

What counts as knowledge?

> The modernization of Britain's health and social care services inevitably calls attention to the quality of the knowledge base than can underpin change and development. Research evidence forms a cornerstone of this knowledge base.
>
> (Marsh et al. 2005: 1)

Philosophers have reflected on the nature of knowledge for centuries and researchers have long debated the role that differing types and levels of theory play in better understanding the world in which we live. Over the past 50 years or so various practice disciplines have entered the fray, challenging the supposed superiority of theoretical knowledge, promoting instead the value of practical, tacit and experiential forms of knowing (see, for example, Ryle 1949; Benner 1984; Schön 1987; Eraut 1994).

In the present context the most recent debates have been stimulated by the growing interest in evidence-based practice. As noted earlier, this was initially seen to mark a move towards a wider view of what comprises evidence (Rolfe 1999), but in reality traditional forms of scientific evidence generated using the techniques of the hard sciences, modified slightly to accommodate the less highly controlled settings of 'real-world medicine', still predominate. However, the emphasis now placed on greater involvement has once again challenged the ascendancy of certain types of knowing and called for a reconsideration of what constitutes knowledge (Fleming 2005; Hodgson and Canvin 2005; Morgan and Harris 2005) and how it is created and used (Wallerstein and Duran 2003).

This raises questions about the power and authority of the 'scientist' to define knowledge (Hodgson and Canvin 2005) and represents an implicit challenge both to universities (Bradbury and Reason 2003) and to professional knowledge and expertise (Stevens et al. 2005).

Within the field of health and social care both practitioner and user knowledge have traditionally been marginalized (Beresford 2005), but user involvement requires recognition of 'consumer experts' as authoritative voices (Hodgson and Canvin 2005), both about their own experience (Fleming 2005) and the use of that experience to contribute to theory-building (Hodgson and Canvin 2005). This requires that debates about the types and purpose of knowledge are not confined to the 'institutions of normal science and academia' (Bradbury and Reason 2003), with more attention being given to the creation of 'living' knowledge, whereby knowledge is seen as a verb rather than a noun (Bradbury and Reason 2003).

There are several typologies which characterize different forms of knowledge but two will serve our purpose here.

Based on their extensive work in the field of participatory action-based research Bradbury and Reason (2003) define four interdependent ways of knowing:

Experiential knowledge – arising from direct encounters with the world.
Presentational knowledge – growing out of experience and being concerned with how we 'tell' our story.
Propositional knowledge – drawing on concepts, ideas and theories.
Practical knowledge – which uses the above three to chart action in the world.

Therefore, whilst not undermining the importance of 'conceptual' knowledge, Bradbury and Reason (2003), as others, call for the widespread acceptance of differing ways of knowing (Merighi et al. 2005; Gould 2006), or 'extended epistemologies' (Bradbury and Reason 2003). Such debates are also increasingly apparent in the policy literature (see, for example, Pawson et al. 2003; Marsh et al. 2005), which gives wider recognition of all forms of research and calls for 'citizens' to be 'directly involved in determining what sort of evidence should be sought, what research processes should be used, and what outcomes matter' (Marsh et al. 2005: viii). Such approaches have no implied hierarchy of evidence but rather see differing types of knowledge as suiting differing purposes, so that we should not 'privilege the viewpoints of any particular stakeholder or of any one strategy for generating knowledge. But neither should we assume that all standpoints are of equal merit on all occasions, on all issues, and for all purposes' (Pawson et al. 2003: 3).

In their overview of the types of knowledge that should inform social care Marsh et al. (2005) draw on the work of Janet Lewis (2001) in suggesting that:

Knowledge = evidence + practitioner wisdom + service user and carer experiences and preferences.

They, however, note that research is of little use unless it is relevant, derives from practice concerns, and is potentially translatable into applicable ideas. They therefore add that:

Evidence = research findings + the interpretation of these findings.

For us this simple equation properly locates research findings as integral to, but not dominant over, other forms of knowledge.

Taking a slightly differing approach Pawson et al. (2003) analysed the varying ways that knowledge for social care policy and practice could be categorized, and concluded that it should be most usefully considered by its 'source'. Five sources were identified:

Organizational knowledge   – to do with governance and policies.

Practitioner knowledge   – personal, context specific, often tacit.

User knowledge   – first-hand experience and reflection, often unspoken and undervalued.

Research knowledge   – the most 'plausible' source but requiring a 'broad church' interpretation of research.

Policy community   – concerning societal and political drivers determining the issues of significance.

The point here is that none of the above ways of categorizing knowledge is necessarily 'right' or 'better than' the other. What is significant is that there is growing acceptance (in most, but by no means all, quarters) of a wider definition of knowledge, and at least some indication that Barnes's (2002: 329) call to 'transform the rules by which the game is played' is being heeded.

What do we value?

Traditional 'scientific' research is viewed as being 'value neutral' with the researcher adopting a distant and detached stance. Such a viewpoint has long been seen as irrelevant to most researchers who adopt qualitative and participatory approaches. The subtitle to this book 'voices, values and evaluation' clearly indicates our position on this subject. User participation is obviously highly value-laden. However, as we have indicated, sometimes these values differ, particularly concerning the degree of involvement and the 'value' accorded to user-controlled research for instance. Despite such variation, Table 1.1 summarizes the range of values that commentators typically use when debating user participation. Such values should inform the way that user participation is evaluated, and it is here that we now turn.

How do we know we are doing 'good work'? (Bradbury and Reason 2003)

> The culture of the research community is generally one of academic rigour that is measured by the complexity and nuance of language, as well as ideas, and not its transparency and parsimony.
>
> (Brehaut and Juzwishin 2005: 5)

Gauging the extent to which you are doing 'good work' depends in large measure on the purpose of the enterprise, a far from straightforward consideration in participatory research. Those who subscribe to a user-controlled model

Table 1.1   Typical values informing user participation in research

Minkler and Wallerstein 2003	Beresford 2005	Turner and Beresford 2005	Dewar 2005
• Participation • Cooperation • Co-learning	• Support to get people together • Equal opportunity to participate regardless of age, gender, race, disability, and so on • Ensuring good access and support • Addressing ethical issues	• Empowerment • Emancipation • Participation • Equality • Anti-discriminatory	• Equality • Fairness • Clear sense of purpose and roles • Commitment to learning • Shared values and beliefs

view anything else 'unfavourably' (Turner and Beresford 2005), whilst some argue that user involvement is no more than tokenism (Hodgson and Canvin 2005). Others take a more measured stance and suggest that the characteristics of 'good' involvement comprise the following:

- the opportunity to have some influence and control
- the opportunity to take the lead and be proactive
- the opportunity to work in partnership with others
- to be clear about intended outcomes
- to have realistic expectations (Clough et al. 2006).

As noted earlier, several commentators suggest that at the very least user involvement should not be a 'one-way street' but rather as a process of 'co-learning' (Minkler and Wallerstein 2003; Faulkner 2004; Dewar 2005; Owen 2005), whereby everyone involved comes away with a differing perspective. In respect of user participation in health and social care research there should also be some 'action' taken, with the bottom line being improved services and/or experiences of services (Beresford 2005; Warren and Cook 2005) that potentially make a 'discernable difference to people's lives' (Beresford 2005). Beyond this it is also suggested that user participation may lead to new theoretical understandings (Beresford 2005; Hodgson and Canvin 2005), which have the potential to result in change by stimulating action in the 'overtly quietist' tradition of knowledge generation (Bradbury and Reason 2003).

There is considerable debate about the need for specific 'criteria' by which to judge the outcomes of participatory research (see, for example, Bradbury and Reason 2003). But, as the quote above suggests, if criteria are to be applied then they need to be 'transparent', for one way in which voices can be controlled and power retained by certain groups is through the 'complexity and nuance of language' (Brehaut and Juzwishin 2005). Several commentators have argued that if users are genuinely to participate, then research must use more accessible concepts and language (Hodgson and Canvin 2005; Owen 2005; Steel 2005). Unfortunately even the writings of emancipatory researchers often effectively preclude full engagement by those who lack the relevant 'insider knowledge' (Hodgson and Canvin 2005): 'It is important to develop accessible materials about user controlled research. From undertaking the literature review it becomes apparent that some of the writings on the subject can be as difficult to understand as literature on traditional research' (Turner and Beresford 2005: 8). It was the desire to make the conduct and evaluation of participatory research more transparent and accessible that led to the development of the ÄldreVäst Sjuhärad Research Centre in Borås, Western Sweden (Magnusson et al. 2001; Nolan et al. 2003a).

ÄldreVäst Sjuhärad, established in 2001, is supported by the Department for Social Affairs for Sweden, by six municipalities in West Sweden (Bollebygd, Borås, Mark, Svenljunga, Tranemo and Ulricehamn), the county council of West Sweden and the University College of Borås. Its main aims are:

- to promote cooperation and partnerships in shaping the direction and quality of health and social care and medical treatment
- to enhance the sharing of perspectives and experiences between older people and their families, professionals, voluntary organizations, health and social care providers and researchers
- to increase the opportunities for older people and their families, together with professionals working with older people to initiate, participate in and evaluate new research-based interventions and service developments
- to raise the awareness and competence of care professionals to ensure the future quality of health and social care and medical treatment through their involvement in programmes of research, development and education.

In pursuing the above aims the research centre adopted a philosophy which sought to create an environment which facilitated a genuine dialogue between the 'factual knowledge' of service providers and the more 'situated' and 'personal' knowledge of those receiving services and participating in research (Barnes 1999). This decision was underpinned by the belief that there are many forms of 'expertise', with none being inherently superior to the other, but with each contributing to a fuller and more complete understanding (Magnusson et al. 2001).

One of the dilemmas the research centre faced was how to judge its effectiveness in order to know that we were 'doing good work' (Bradbury and Reason 2003). The 'authenticity' criteria proposed by Guba and Lincoln (1989) were attractive but there were concerns that they were not fully true to their own principles, for the manner in which they were presented, and particularly the language used, meant that they were neither accessible nor easily understandable to a non-academic audience. This seemed to belie the fundamental criterion of 'fairness' (Nolan et al. 2003a). Efforts were therefore made to see if these limitations could be overcome without losing the principles upon which the criteria were based.

Authenticity criteria for constructivist research

Fairness	–	Are the voices of all the major interest groups heard (that is, are all their opinions listened to and valued)?
Ontological authenticity	–	Does the study provide participants with new insights into their own situation?
Educative authenticity	–	Does the study help participants to better understand the position of other interest groups?
Catalytic authenticity	–	Does the study stimulate or identify areas for change?
Tactical authenticity	–	Does the study facilitate, enable or empower change?

(After Guba and Lincoln 1989)

In developing the authenticity criteria further, the aim was, as far as possible, to present them in a way that could be understood by all those who might have an interest in using them. They were therefore modified and re-labelled using the terms below, each beginning with the letters EA:

Original criteria	*Renamed*
Fairness	Equal Access
Ontological authenticity	Enhanced Awareness of the position/views of self/own group.
Educative authenticity	Enhanced Awareness of the position/views of others.
Catalytic authenticity	Encouraging Action by providing a rationale or impetus for change.
Tactical authenticity	Enabling Action by providing the means to achieve, or potentially achieve, change.

(After Nolan et al. 2003a)

	Planning	Process	Product
Equal Access			
Enhanced Awareness – Self			
– Others			
Encourage Action			
Enable Action			

Figure 1.1 Applying the authenticity criteria: the ÄldreVäst Sjuhärad approach.

As will be seen, the original intention of the authenticity criteria remain largely unchanged but experience in applying them suggests that re-labelling has ensured that they now 'speak to' older people, family carers and practitioners, and potentially promote their more widespread usage. In other words, the criteria are now far more readily understandable and therefore should enable everyone to contribute more fully to informed debate about their relative merits (or otherwise) (Nolan et al. 2003a).

Furthermore, rather than applying the 'authenticity' criteria primarily to the interpersonal processes of research, as was their original intent (Rodwell 1998), at ÄldreVäst Sjuhärad they are applied to all stages, as indicated in the matrix in Figure 1.1. This approach has served the centre well (see Hanson et al. 2006a) and is something we return to in the concluding chapter.

Conclusion – where to from here?

In setting the scene we have reflected on some of the issues concerning voices, values and evaluation that, for us, seem important in the context of participatory research. We now let other voices speak, in the form of ten case studies that describe very differing approaches to participatory research. Our original intention was for each case study to be followed by a commentary but, on reflection, this seemed unnecessarily intrusive as it is important to let you, the reader, reach your own conclusions. We therefore reserve our own thoughts for the concluding chapter, when we attempt to address some key questions needed to take the debate forward.

2 ACTION (Assisting Carers using Telematic Interventions to meet Older people's Needs): practitioners' reflections on a Swedish innovation

Elizabeth Hanson, Paul Svensson, Fredrik Arvevik, Lennart Magnusson

Introduction

This case study focuses on the implementation of an innovative technology-based service, ACTION, designed to support frail older people and their carers at home. Building on an initial EU-funded research and development project, ACTION was further tested in Sweden and subsequently has been introduced as a mainstream service in Borås municipality in West Sweden, and other municipalities throughout the country.

The story of how ACTION became a reality is told in the words of Paul and Fredrik, two experienced assistant nurses from Borås municipality who have worked in the ACTION call centre since 2000. They compare their prior experiences of working with older people and their relatives in the community with their work over the past six years with ACTION. In particular, they focus on how the service works in everyday practice and how it has enabled them to form partnerships with families. They also consider how ACTION evolved from an idea into a mainstream service, and reflect on their potential work in the future. This chapter therefore consolidates the key lessons learned from ten years of working together with frail older people and their family carers.

An overview of ACTION

ACTION is an information and communication technology (ICT)-based support service for older people and their family carers which originated from an

EU-funded project (1997–2000) involving England, Northern Ireland, the Republic of Ireland, Portugal and Sweden. After this initial project, additional funding was secured in Sweden from the Ministry of Health and Social Affairs to further develop and test the ACTION services. ACTION is designed to help families to readily access education, information and support about family caregiving, empowering and enabling them to make informed decisions about their situation throughout their caring career (Magnusson et al. 2005). Families have been involved in all stages of the design and evaluation process using a variety of methods such as user working groups, focus group interviews, individual interviews, user trials, questionnaires, log diaries and field testing (Magnusson and Hanson 2005).

The core components of the ACTION service are illustrated in Figure 2.1. The multimedia educational programmes are based on carers' needs identified from the empirical literature and extensive user consultation in the two projects, namely: caring skills in daily life; planning ahead; respite care services; financial and economic support; and coping strategies. These are accessed over the Internet via a personal computer (PC) with broadband connection which is installed in each family's home. Families also have access to Internet and email facilities. Internet videophone facilities are provided via a small camera

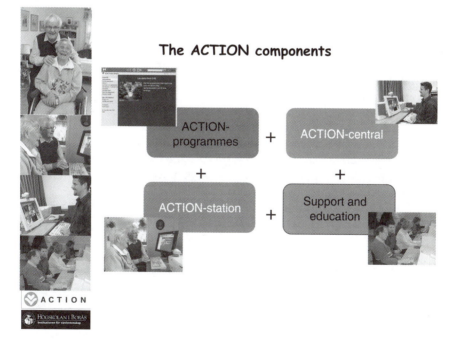

Figure 2.1 The ACTION service.

placed on top of the PC and an integrated user-friendly videophone pro-gramme installed in the computer. This enables families to have visual and oral contact with other participant families, as well as with professional carers at a dedicated call centre. Families are invited to take part in an initial edu-cational programme to learn how to use ACTION as the majority of users are predominantly computer novices.

Evaluations have demonstrated that ACTION helps to reduce families' social isolation due to the informal support networks that develop amongst participant families. Many carers also feel both better prepared for their caring situation and an active part of the 'information society' (Magnusson 2002; Magnusson et al. 2005). In addition to increasing the quality of everyday life for most participant families, there are also cost savings for the municipality due to a reduction in the number of public services used (Magnusson and Hanson 2005). Following these evaluations Borås municipality took the deci-sion to make ACTION part of their support services available to frail older people in need of care and their family carers. Subsequently a further eight municipalities across Sweden, and one in Norway, have also decided to implement ACTION.

A partnership approach to working with older people and their families

ACTION is one of several projects undertaken by the authors at the ÄldreVäst Sjuhärad Research Centre, University College of Borås in Sweden, together with Mike and Janet Nolan at the University of Sheffield, England, using participa-tory approaches to working with older people, their families and practitioners (for more details see Nolan et al. 2003a; Magnusson et al. 2005; Hanson et al. 2006a).

An account of how the families have been involved has been provided elsewhere. Here our focus is on the story of Paul and Fredrick, who have worked in ACTION for over seven years. It charts their personal and professional growth and development over this period.

However, before turning to Paul and Fredrick's story, a case study provides an indication of how ACTION works in practice.

Case study example of an ACTION family: Karl and Inga

The following highlights the multiple roles Paul and Fredrik employ in their support of a couple who have had the ACTION service for approximately two years, particularly their openness to new ideas enabling them to develop true partnerships.

Inga cares for her husband who has had a severe stroke; he has aphasia and requires help with all activities of daily living. Consistent with their prior relationship, Karl expected his wife to be the sole carer, and Inga considered it entirely natural to do so. Karl has a son who lives in the same town, and Inga's daughter and family live in the south-west of Sweden. Inga initially rejected ACTION but, almost a year later, she changed her mind. By this stage Inga had begun to realize that she was a carer and needed help and support, so Paul and Fredrik worked with Inga in a variety of ways, whilst at the same time building up a trusting relationship with Karl.

Initially they supported Inga by providing more information about care-giving via the ACTION educational programmes:

> We led her into the programmes, now she knows everything ... Sometimes though she says she needs to go back and have another read and it can also take on another meaning, she can understand it better. This is a strength of ACTION, that it's always there. The first time you read it perhaps you don't have need of it but the next time you perhaps do. ACTION is a service that works as a knowledge bank or an educational platform.
>
> (Paul)

Together with Inga, Paul and Fredrick were able to arrange for the necessary support to be available:

> Inga saw about the different assistive aids that are available in the programme, in particular, a stair lift so she could come out with Karl. 'I don't want to be a nuisance' she said, so we rang to the occu-pational therapist and we said there should be a lift there and they came and assessed the situation and arranged for a lift to be installed ... So it was much easier for them to get out, as she likes him to be able to get out each day, that feels good, to be able to help in this way.
>
> (Fredrik)

Paul and Fredrik acknowledged that a major part of their work was providing ongoing emotional support which included an exploration of the satisfactions of caring which help to sustain Inga in her caring role:

> A lot though is about psychological support, listening to her talking about how difficult it is and how she feels ... 'I think if Karl could just once say that he appreciated it'. She also takes up small things that make her happy, he can stroke her cheek, sometimes it's a feeling of togetherness. They look at photos together in an album

and he points and remembers and she thinks that it's so great. So she alternates between the difficult times and the happy times so we talk about the positive things, also the difficult things and afterwards she says that it feels better. She thanks us so much, and really we have just sat and listened and perhaps asked a few follow-up questions.

(Paul)

Having built up a trusting relationship they are able to actively encourage her to accept help to manage her caring situation, as well as to consider alternative care options for the future. Paul and Fredrik also help to boost her self-esteem by reaffirming her caring efforts and skills: 'She feels she is useless . . . but I say to her that she does everything right that she can do, you're so skilled and we're really impressed with what you do. It's so tragic that she can't get that feedback from her husband, think what this would give to her, she does everything right and yet it's still wrong' (Paul).

Fredrik illustrated how they would constantly use new ideas to help them in their work with families. For example, they have used the Carers Outcome Agreement Tool (COAT – Hanson et al. 2006b) as a means of facilitating more open discussion and debate with Inga, by empowering her to have a life outside of caring, and by involving others more:

COAT has helped recently with her. We've come to many practical solutions that she can work with and think about, to involve her son more, she's done that, he is there more now and gives support. She is beginning to see that she can dare to go to the theatre. It isn't often, but she can go away for a short while now and do her exercises and take it easy and have a coffee, and she goes with Berit and with Greta (other ACTION carers) so they build up a support network. Most recently, this last half year, its come more and more her greatest wish to go out and go birdwatching again, it wouldn't surprise me if she did this. This would never have happened without ACTION, I'm sure she'd have been burned out by now otherwise. All of these things that she can start with having respite care, in the beginning this was impossible but now it is possible.

(Fredrik)

Whilst working in partnership with older people and their carers is now 'second nature' to Paul and Fredrick, this was not always the case, and in order to understand the magnitude of the work required Paul and Fredrick describe their prior pattern of working.

Paul and Fredrik's story

Before becoming involved with the ACTION service both Paul and Fredrik worked in home care for a number of years. Despite home care being viewed as enabling a greater degree of autonomy for care practitioners than a long-term care setting (Olsson and Ingvad 2001), for novice practitioners it can be a daunting and isolating experience, as Paul explains:

> In home care, it was more demanding as you were more often alone, you couldn't discuss back and forth with colleagues and get advice. It was tougher and I had no education to fall back on. We didn't have discussions. We should have had more supervision when we worked alone. At that time there was no nurse to talk with and no mobile phones, you perhaps met your colleagues the next day and you took up the issue then.
>
> (Paul)

Paul and Fredrik explained that their attempts to work collaboratively with older clients and their relatives often resulted in conflict with colleagues who tended to work in more traditional hierarchical ways:

> I feel we met their [older people and carers] needs as we were able to listen, but sometimes we'd fall between two stools, like I'd go out to a home to do cleaning but when I got there they'd set the table ready for a cup of coffee and cake, they'd say 'I don't want you to clean, I'd much rather we have a cup of coffee instead' and you did that but then you got into an argument with your older colleagues.
>
> (Paul)

Their early attempts to work in partnership with older clients and their relatives could lead to dilemmas about whose view to focus on, the older person's or their relative's. As Fredrik notes, they lacked an appropriate framework to guide their work with families:

> It's always difficult to go into a family for the first time where there's a wife, for example, and she's used to talking over the head of the cared for person. It's difficult to manage this as you don't know what relationship they have. Sometimes you listened to the relative and other times it was the other way round so there were conflicts. You tried to do the best you could but at times you made the decision to go with the routine.
>
> (Fredrik)

Comparing their previous experiences with their work in ACTION

Reflecting on their earlier experiences, Paul and Fredrik explained how the theoretical background to family care and partnership working underpinning ACTION, and their direct experiences of working with ACTION families, had helped them change their views of their role. As Paul explained:

> I feel we've built up knowledge about how it is to be a relative in a family. The family carer is expert, perhaps we didn't always see that, we perhaps thought as care staff that we knew best . . . We've learnt a lot from relatives and also, thanks to the university and research, the theoretical part that has also helped us to understand and to see the whole picture in what we do, so it's a big difference. If we go back to the example with the family carer and cared for person, we try to listen to both of them and it's not always to go with the family carer's view. The problem can often be that the relative and cared for person have never talked about it together before so that you can be the link so that they can talk together . . . I think we're much better now at listening to both.
>
> (Paul)

Fredrik reinforced the importance of seeing the family carer as an expert, but also recognizing that they needed help occasionally:

> I really realized about the family carer being an expert for the first time when Karin cared for her husband who had aphasia. I can't give the nursing care she does, she knows her husband and knows exactly how he thinks and feels, knows what he likes and doesn't like. It's difficult for me to take all that in. All relatives are expert in their own situation but it's not always that they do the right thing, sometimes they make mistakes but that's something else . . . That's when I understand that they have a wealth of knowledge; we can only be there and be a complement.
>
> (Fredrick)

Paul also saw it as their role to help equip the carer with the right tools: 'We've come to understand that family carers are the most central person in the cared for person's life.'

Fredrik highlighted the delicate balancing act that carers need to achieve in being 'experts':

Expert family carers are those relatives who want to take care of their nearest and dearest, they often have empathy and they really respect their relative's views and thoughts and that you don't take over too much . . . That you can plan your day and plan ahead and can understand that as a carer you have the right to your life, to have respite care sometimes, to be able to take that step and can live with and work with the guilt feelings they have. A lot have the skill to be able to look back and reflect.

(Fredrik)

As well as supporting family carers Paul and Fredrik feel that ACTION has helped them to deal with difficult emotional situations:

In ACTION we're not isolated as Fredrik and I sit so close to each other and we can act as a sounding board for each other, but also we have other good contacts with Needs Assessors and nurses who we can bandy ideas with and refer to if you don't have the competence, it's better for the relatives and cared for person if the nurse goes in or the Needs Assessor. We have such a good relationship with the Needs Assessors here so it's a security I feel.

(Paul)

Ways of working in partnership with ACTION families

For Paul and Fredrik working in partnership with the families is about developing meaningful reciprocal relationships, as Fredrik elaborated:

It's about opening up, to come into the life of someone. So if you feel that they need to talk about something you must give of yourself, you don't have to share something very personal but share something. It's so important to know about their background to help and support the whole family, but you must give something of yourself, otherwise there's no exchange.

(Fredrik)

This required good interpersonal skills that Paul and Fredrick used in their videophone contact:

It's about listening, show that you can listen, ask follow up questions, show you're interested in their lives, then you get good contact, you gain trust, you can work more with it.

(Paul)

> If they call us they want something, they might not say it straight out, you must listen and be sensitive, it can take a long time before it comes out what they really want to talk about. That's why the videophone is so good because you see their body language . . . when you know them . . . that there's something there.
>
> (Fredrik)

Initial contacts were very important, as carers had often not had the chance to talk about their situation before:

> In ACTION you raise their awareness of their situation with both of them. Many relatives don't see themselves as a family carer . . . they don't like to use the word family carer. ACTION can help . . . it can help them to understand what it means to be a family carer.
>
> (Fredrik)

> If it's the first time that this awareness has been raised then there are a lot of discussions about how they experience their situation. There are many carers who explain how their situation is, how difficult it is as there's no one who's asked them before, so we try to raise the subject and listen a lot. I think this is where ACTION plays a significant role . . . a lot with the videophone communication.
>
> (Paul)

This requires flexibility and spontaneity, as well as the time to listen and the understanding that comes with continuity:

> You can never have a finished packet that you go from when you meet people . . . they're so different. You can't sit down and prepare for a videophone call and know which strategy you're going to use today . . . it doesn't work.
>
> (Paul)

> You have such a close relationship that you can talk openly a lot. You can't do this in a short space of time. It wouldn't be the same if you hadn't had such a long time with someone.
>
> (Fredrik)

Paul and Fredrik now see their roles largely as facilitators and enablers rather than direct 'doers'.

> We enable them to solve things themselves. For instance, there was a carer whose husband had dementia and he rapidly became worse so

that he became a totally different person to the one she had married. It was tragic but we came into the 'End of Life' programme where she learnt about grieving, even whilst her husband was still alive. Those sorts of things . . . it was a support to her, but I could never have guided her to the programme if I hadn't known the carer so well.

(Fredrik)

A family carer can say one day that she wants to care and then the next day she says she can't manage. We don't say that she must carry on, we say 'yes perhaps it is so' . . . We discuss perhaps it is time to solve it in another way, to think about other options and support her in this. We're much better at that now.

(Paul)

It is clear that Paul and Fredrik have both grown, developed, and learnt a great deal from working closely with families over a six-year period, with the carers themselves often acting as 'mentor':

We started with five users, we didn't have such a lot of knowledge at that time about how to support the families. We supported them and we grew as staff and we saw, especially with Barbro, how much ACTION helped her (a family carer in the original EU project in 1997). She was a very intelligent lady and was skilled socially. She was our first mentor, you didn't just ring up and chat with her . . . the discussions always gave you something.

(Fredrik)

The families you meet and the in-depth discussion you have together, you have it with you and can use it in the future and use it again . . . For every family we've got to know we've learnt something new.

(Paul)

Despite their considerable experience, such learning is ongoing: 'Each day you become more aware of how you work. I think you learn something new every day you come here' (Fredrik).

Adding a further layer of complexity Paul and Fredrik also tried to stimulate informal networks amongst the ACTION families:

Our job can be seen as a spider in the web, we link people together. For example, we had a family who wanted to get away from home for a while and both had had a stroke, and I asked them if they'd heard of a rehabilitation centre called Sommarsol, 'no they hadn't'. Usually (as a professional) you'd have told them about it but in this case I knew of an ACTION family who'd been there who'd got the same illness and I asked if it was alright if she rang them up and they said that was OK. So she rang them up and told them how they'd experienced it and how they'd applied. Now the family have got to go there for several weeks and they've also got to know a good friend in the process too. This is why it's incredible to work with something like this, to link people together.

(Paul)

Further, they recognize now the unique strength and value of families developing informal support networks to reduce their isolation: 'The fantastic thing about ACTION is the security net provided by the other families, that are available for the relatives and the cared for person too. They can talk with others who are in a similar situation, you're not alone in the whole world, it's an enormous relief' (Fredrik).

Paul and Fredrick now feel very comfortable in working as partners with older people and their family carers, but they also recognize that working in this way is not always easy, and that they have been on a steep learning curve over the past few years.

Exploring the challenges of partnership working

Paul and Fredrik acknowledge that working so closely with families is not always easy, and that they have learned a number of skills and strategies, particularly if the carer and cared for person did not have good channels of communication. This often means working separately with the carer and cared for person prior to them being able to work together:

When you come to a family where they haven't talked about the situation, the family carer can't talk openly when the cared for person is sitting there, or they talk over their head, that's not easy. Sometimes the family carer opens up more when we sit on our own, but you feel yourself you want the cared for person there, but perhaps you must take the family carer first and work with the cared for person in the next stage. It's difficult when it's a new family; it's to get to know the situation. You try to take every opportunity to talk. You get them to read together in the programmes as this is the key for them to start to talk together, this is something we work on in the education sessions. It's easier to read about each other's situation in the education programme, it's not like coming home to them and formally talking with them about their respective roles.

(Paul)

They both highlight that working in partnership does not happen overnight and that it can take a long time before the benefits are visible. This requires patience:

> Sometimes you feel inadequate. With some families you cannot help straight away, you must take it easy. For example, there was a family who had ACTION and didn't really find it useful and now, a year later, they want it back again – ACTION is a partnership. We can take a step back. We're calmer now, we know we can wait and see. You wonder if so and so couldn't benefit from each other. You can see it from another perspective when you're calm and let families try the service.
>
> (Fredrik)

In difficult situations it is important for them to have support from each other:

> Of course you always want to help families to make it easier for them and when you don't succeed you don't feel good, heck, I don't know anything. It sometimes happens. We must always discuss with someone, back and forth, this is very important. It's important that we're two; it's good that we can work together.
>
> (Fredrik)

Exploring sources of satisfaction from partnership working

Although at times difficult, Paul and Fredrik readily identified several major sources of satisfaction as a result of working together with the ACTION families.

First, they spoke of being part of a caring community in which everyone helps and genuinely cares for one another:

> Even if they have it really hard, they have time to support others. Which I think is marvellous. There's a warmth, it's a feeling of thoughtfulness for others and a sense of humanity/community. A lot is to do with being seen as a person with needs and you can also help others when you yourself see that you have needs.
>
> (Paul)

They also explained that their way of working enables them to promote the autonomy and independence of families:

> You feel that with this service, you work at another level. We go from their needs, instead of going from a menu that they can choose between, they feel that we leave the ball with them. I can influence but they manage the situation themselves with help. We don't go in and take over, there's continuity in what we do.
>
> (Paul)

This in turn can directly empower families in their daily lives as Fredrik highlighted:

> This is the most satisfying thing. For example, Mona thought it was so difficult to lift and I thought it would be good for her to read in the programme about how you lift, and she got confirmation that she should use her legs more, so she did that and she felt much better and didn't need more help. So you feel yeah!
>
> (Fredrik)

They both talked openly of the immense satisfaction they gain from working in this way, and the gains they experience too:

> Every family that benefits from ACTION, it's a big plus for us, that's what we live for, that's what we work for. You feel that you help families. ACTION is a tool which makes it a bit better for families to go forward.
>
> (Paul)

> You get so much back, a lot of thanks. You get to know some families so well it also affects you. It's that that gives so much.
>
> (Fredrik)

Reflecting on the factors promoting ACTION as a mainstream service

Paul and Fredrik noted a variety of reasons why ACTION had become a mainstream service within the municipality, especially its user-centred and participatory approach:

> Number 1, the service was built upon the family carers' and older people's needs and views, that carers and older people experience support from the service in different ways at different phases of their life and caring situation. To have recently become a family carer, to being able to continue caring to the day you stop being

a carer and there is after support too, this makes the service so good.

(Paul)

The families have always been able to have their views heard. They've been involved in different ways, they've been together and developed the service, they've been in the education sessions, in the presentations. I think our user focus has enormous significance. Without them there'd have been no reality, it would have stayed as an idea only.

(Fredrik)

They also acknowledged that the fact that ACTION is underpinned by sound theory, and has been properly evaluated, is also essential: 'The university, the research is important. The results show what the users think and feel about the service, it's an important foundation from which to go further on. To show that it gives an increase in their quality of life and, at the same time, it can lead to cost savings to the municipality is very important' (Paul).

Notwithstanding the strengths of ACTION, the support of managers and practitioners in the municipality are also instrumental in its success:

Also competent people in leadership positions in our municipality, we've had a very strong municipality manager. During 2002–4, when we felt like we were treading water, Borås weren't sure whether they'd continue. Without her support, we wouldn't be sitting here. We've had managers who really believed in it, from our direct manager, to the manager for care for older people, to the manager of Borås municipality. So we're thankful, they believed in it and had patience during those two years when we weren't sure if it would continue. Also, the politicians took the decision about ACTION being a mainstream service. Without them being on board it would've been very difficult.

(Paul)

Such support was reinforced by the innovative application of ICT in ACTION:

The service is still something new, even if the technology is 10 years old, the service is still innovative. Also our way of thinking about family care support, we think back to 1996/97 when ACTION started and it's sad to say, but it's still innovative to think about family care support. If you think that not all municipalities see family care support like we do.

(Paul)

There are many people who talk about how you should work with

> family carers, but to actually do it is a very different thing. It's also innovative, there's research there. We have a foundation, we don't follow the development, we're first, we lead.
>
> (Fredrik)

Finally, they noted that commercialization also had an impact, as it increased the possibility to make the service more widely accessible:

> Telia [Swedish Telecom] have had a bigger role to play than you would think. A company makes it possible to spread it to more people, there are limits obviously to this co-operation, but I think there must be a commercial company that steers a model to make it possible to sell and make it more available.
>
> (Paul)

When they were asked to reflect on the significance of it being an information technology (IT)-based service they both felt that it was a crucial factor. Most importantly they considered it enabled sick older people to be part of the information society, and thereby opened up several new opportunities for them:

> It's important, this with it being an information society, it's not often that older people are involved and with this service they're the ones who can have the greatest benefit from this service. It's very important to show that older people can use new technology.
>
> (Paul)

> I don't think there's any other IT-based service that focuses on older people with chronic illness, and enables them to be actively part of the information society. There are many older people who go on courses to learn how to use the Internet, but they're the healthy ones, the sick older people can't manage to take part. This is a strength, to really be able to manage one's daily life, and, in turn, ACTION leads to other things. They learn how to use email and communicate with their children and grandchildren, and several chat on MSN. I don't think a frail pensioner would have gone into that without ACTION.
>
> (Fredrik)

They also highlighted the flexible nature of IT-based support services compared with more traditional carer support services, especially its availability 24 hours a day, seven days a week (24/7):

> Of course there are family carer circles [support groups], some are

super and they meet each other outside of the meetings but some circles are only once a month. With ACTION you always have support when you need it, that's a strength with IT, it's there 24 hours. Okay we aren't there (24 hours) but they can send me an email at 12 midnight and know that I'll answer it the next morning, that's security. I don't think this would ever have worked if the medium hadn't have been IT, it's so flexible. We could have used a book instead, but just think how thick that book would have been, we could have used a normal telephone but how personal would that really have been?

(Paul)

Even if we've worked with it for a number of years, it's just now that it starts to bear fruit. More users, more municipalities thinking about family care support, it takes time.

(Paul)

Recent developments in partnership working

Paul and Fredrik also described recent developments in their work, especially their role in helping to support those staff working in other municipalities who are implementing ACTION. They provide ongoing informal advice and support, and regular supervisory sessions via the videophone:

Supervising/guiding other municipalities is a big responsibility that's very interesting. It's been important to have had the experience of working in ACTION for a number of years. I can see all the things they experience, that we also experienced in the beginning, and it feels good to be able to guide them. When they encounter the same happiness and satisfaction amongst the families, you see how it gives them a boost and it gives me a kick too. The same as when there are things that are difficult or don't work or . . . it's also difficult for me.

(Paul)

They both acknowledged that their way of working with the families mirrors their current approach with practitioners: 'Sometimes the supervision with municipalities reminds me of the support we give to the families, to listen, discuss, guide, support, exactly as we do with the families. We support by putting our hands behind our backs so they solve things themselves and this works well actually' (Paul). This also helped to form reciprocal relationships with peers, both locally and further afield:

Others have more competence in areas than we have (specific case knowledge, rehabilitation). We have experience of how we can support the families. We feel humble with regards to the other municipalities. They have a lot of competence in their area so you learn a lot from them too. It's great to have different competences, to work together will be fantastic.

(Fredrik)

They increasingly recognized that a larger caring community with a shared philosophy and approach to working was being created: 'If we look at the people who work with ACTION (in the other municipalities) they think the same as we do. It's so great to be able to see other municipalities grow and see other families benefiting from the service' (Paul).

Table 2.1   A proposed ACTION virtual platform for families and practitioners

---

Potential developments for families
- Individual web pages for each family to present themselves with pictures and text such as interests, hobbies to facilitate contact amongst the families
- Entertainment, exercises, group discussions, lectures, conferences, study circles to families simultaneously via a videophone bridge
- More medically related services such as direct consultations with a physician, taking your own vital signs, reading your medical history, booking a doctor's visit electronically
- Playing games with another family online
- Access to different expertise across the different call centres, such as current information and advice about assistive aids, rehabilitation, dementia
- An electronic forum for frequent questions relating to the technology and what to do
- Links to other relevant sites, for example, a link to a recent television programme of interest

Potential developments for practitioners
- A bulletin board for each ACTION call centre to highlight weekly events, to describe the staff who work at the call centre and their roles, information about education sessions and local events of interest including upcoming social events for families
- A bulletin board for local voluntary organizations, current information about their organization and the services they offer, online access to their weekly newsletter, details about their opening hours and availability
- A discussion forum for practitioners to discuss issues together in a supportive, secure environment; download education sessions, lectures, seminars, films
- Group supervision of practitioners from different municipalities across Sweden via a videophone bridge facility
- A more in-depth version of ACTION for staff, for example, for home care workers to use the videophone to ring and see the client and do an assessment of the situation; access short instruction films via the mobile phone to prepare for a procedure immediately prior to a home visit

---

Looking to the future with regards to partnership working

Looking to the future they are both enthusiastic about the possibilities to further extend their partnership approach harnessing a range of IT-based solutions to create a virtual ACTION platform for families and practitioners to enable an ongoing exchange of experiences and knowledge transfer to take place, which are summarized in Table 2.1. They also acknowledged that the ACTION concept could be further extended to address actively the needs of other groups of families, such as parents caring for children with learning difficulties.

Conclusion

It is now over ten years since the ACTION concept emerged, over that time it has evolved from an 'idea' to a mainstream service provided in growing numbers of municipalities in Sweden and beyond. It is still evolving. It is now no longer a 'research and development project' but rather a major force in improving the quality of lives of numerous people. Few projects can make such claims. We have written elsewhere about the technical and theoretical approaches underpinning ACTION (Magnusson 2002; Magnusson and Hanson 2005; Magnusson et al. 2005; Hanson et al. 2006a), but here our goal has been to capture the essential interpersonal dimensions that are critical to the success of partnership working. We have therefore let the voices of Paul and Fredrik speak largely for themselves, without undue analysis and interpretation. This was not required, for their own account eloquently captures the complex, subtle but essentially human qualities required in 'making things work' in the real world. Table 2.2 (overleaf) summarizes some of the key learning points and, might we suggest, serves as a template for all those interested in participative enquiry in which working together and co-constructing better shared realities are important aspirations. We have learned much, but there is still a long way to go.

Table 2.2 Ways of working in partnership with families: key benefits and challenges

Ways of working in partnership with ACTION families	Challenges of working in partnership with families	Sources of satisfaction of working in partnership
• Developing meaningful reciprocal relationships by use of listening and sensitive questioning and sharing personal information • Getting to know the families via the use of biography • Awareness raising amongst families via in-depth discussions • Being adaptable and sufficiently flexible to meet the needs of individual families • Being facilitators and enablers rather than direct 'doers' • Being patient and giving sufficient time to establish a solid relationship • Being continuously open to new learning and ideas • Acknowledging and supporting the unique value of families developing informal support networks with one another	• It is more difficult to achieve in situations where family members do not talk openly about their situation • In some cases it can take a long time before the benefits are made visible • Being extremely patient and allowing time to pass rather than taking over the situation • In situations where ACTION has not proved beneficial, it is essential to have support from trusted co-worker(s)	• Being part of an active caring community • Being able to promote the autonomy and independence of families • Being able to help to empower families in their daily lives • Learning and developing as practitioners due to the in-depth relationships developed with families • Immense intrinsic satisfaction and feeling privileged to get to know the families so well

3　Partnerships in best practice: advancing gerontological care in Scotland

Debbie Tolson, Irene Schofield, Jo Booth, Timothy B. Kelly

Introduction

This chapter reflects on the first five years of a longitudinal action research study designed to promote evidence-based gerontological nursing across Scotland (Tolson et al. 2006; www.geronurse.com). The project arose in response to the national strategy for nursing and midwifery, which called for partnerships in promoting best practice (SEHD 2001).

The study known as the Gerontological Nursing Demonstration Project (GNDP) sought to establish collaborative partnerships to enhance and improve the care of older people across all care environments within the National Health Service (NHS) and independent sector within Scotland. Strategic alliances were formed between the research team, policy-makers, health care providers and other stakeholder groups bringing a range of perspectives and influences to bear. Capitalizing on a key partnership with NHS Quality Improvement Scotland (the national standard-setting agency for the NHS in Scotland) research outputs included national evidence-based guidance known as best practice statements and related companion guides for older people. Other outputs were an Internet-based practice development college using a social participatory learning approach, and a conceptual model to promote inclusive practice development on a large scale. A range of partnerships contributed to the success of the project. This chapter examines the development and challenges associated with key partnerships and collaborative processes. The project continues and over time our understanding of partnerships in best practice evolves. Here we reflect on insights gained whilst undertaking a large-scale action research programme in the complex and ever-changing world of health care, and consider whether lessons from the field of nursing can apply elsewhere.

The chapter commences with background information and an overview of the project. We focus on one of the project products, the practice development model, before discussing issues and processes related to partnerships and the involvement of stakeholders. Later we consider other outputs, namely, the Internet-based college and the models used to develop care guidance and consumer resources. We conclude by sharing lessons learned which may be helpful to others planning similar large-scale involvement projects.

Background to the demonstration project

Despite the current emphasis on nurses providing evidence-based care, there is debate about how this can be achieved. Considerable effort has been expended on systematically developing care guidance using hierarchies of evidence (for example, see Scottish Intercollegiate Guidelines Network [SIGN] National Clinical Guidelines, www.sign.ac.uk, or National Institute for Health and Clinical Excellence [NICE] Clinical Guidelines, www.nice.org.uk). The assumption is that guidelines developed from a systematic review of scientific evidence are more robust than those based on other knowledge, including consensus and expert opinion. This fails to acknowledge that scientific evidence goes through some very human filters during the guideline construction process (Malterud 2001; Raine et al. 2004). In addition, the exclusion of professional craft knowledge (Rycroft-Malone et al. 2004) means that professionals must translate guidelines to fit both their beliefs about practice and the context in which they work. By actively involving practitioners in 'guideline production' we aimed to overcome this problem.

At the outset, the scope for developing nursing practice in Scotland was unclear with considerable variability in available resources. Many nurses working with older people were geographically and/or professionally remote from peers who wanted to champion better care. Furthermore, ways of involving older people using their expertise to enhance care experiences were underdeveloped. Against this background our project aimed to design a national approach to promote and disseminate best practice in partnership with both service providers and users. Given the emerging critique of evidence-based guidelines, the GNDP sought to overcome existing limitations and develop a nursing-focused model for the process of care guidance construction.

An overview of the Scottish demonstration project

In identifying the challenges that the project faced (Table 3.1) we recognized that solutions would need to be agreed by all stakeholders. We would also

Table 3.1 Challenges and solutions

Challenge	Solution
To understand and describe best practice from the professional and older person's perspective	Best practice statements and companion care guidance
To motivate and empower practitioners to deliver best practice	Agreed values reconciliation and explication Social participatory learning in a CoP
To create resources and mechanisms to support the achievement of best practice across the range of practice environments	Virtual college Demonstration sites

have to address theoretical, methodological and logistical concerns, whilst satisfying policy-makers and future strategists that the solutions identified had demonstrable impact, were affordable, and worthy of possible mainstreaming. We did not want the products of our endeavours to sit on library shelves; we wanted them to be used in practice and to influence policy. This required that we worked collaboratively with multiple stakeholders and a number of agencies; hence the attraction of action research.

We used an involvement methodology (longitudinal, multi-site, action research) to collaborate with nurses, older people and other key stakeholders to identify, test and refine solutions. The solution which emerged has been called the Caledonian Model.

The Caledonian model

The emergent Caledonian framework (Figure 3.1) offers a template for a national approach to practice development connecting national care guidance directly with practice.

A special type of group, known as a community of practice (CoP) (Wenger 2003), collaborates to draft evidence-based guidance in the form of a best practice statement. This includes science, practice know-how and older people's experiences of and preferences for care. The draft guidance is tested in a local demonstration site such as a hospital ward or care home to ensure it is achievable and to prepare implementation resources for others providing care. A virtual college is used to enable the two groups to work together to share experiences, develop skills and understanding, and find solutions to enable evidence-based practice. Once the care guidance is in its final form, and following external consultation, it is published and disseminated by the national

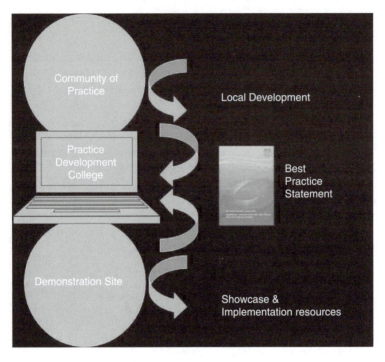

Figure 3.1 Overview of the Caledonian framework.

agency, NHS Quality Improvement Scotland (NHSQIS), becoming a resource for the wider community involved in the health care of older people. The virtual practice development (PD) college, its members, and the demonstration site act as resources for others seeking to implement the best practice statement. This multifaceted framework has emerged through alliances with stakeholder groups and a shared determination to enable best practice to be more than rhetoric.

Figure 3.2 captures the dynamic way in which the Caledonian model utilizes the scholarship of practice and enquiry and blends elements of both technical and emancipatory approaches to practice development. This, coupled with the active involvement of older people, combines integration, learning and application to achieving evidence-based practice. The energy these processes create fuels progress towards sharing understandings, and our experience over five years reveals the importance of meaningful partnerships between practitioners, older people, academics and policy-makers (Tolson et al. 2006). Having described the principles upon which the project is based we consider selected components in more detail.

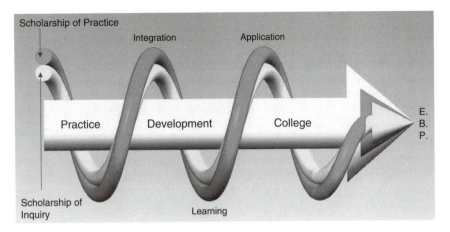

Figure 3.2 Representation of the practice development model (reproduced with permission. Tolson, D., Schofield, I., Booth, J., Kelly, T.B. and James, L. (2006) Constructing a new approach to developing evidence based practice with nurses and older people, *World Views on Evidence Based Nursing*, 3(2): 62–72).

Designing the project

As typifies much action research, details were initially vague but matured over time. Our involvement methodology was influenced by several theoretical perspectives. The enhancement approach, which encourages practitioners to use theory and values to advance practice, was selected for its focus on practitioner empowerment (Holter and Schwartz-Barcott 1993). Realistic evaluation provided a formative evaluation framework identifying and reinforcing what was working well in support of our quest for continual improvement (Pawson and Tilley 1997). We also drew on other accounts of practice development, helping us to unpack the complex relationships between context, evidence and facilitation (Clarke and Wilcockson 2002; McCormack et al. 2004). We approached others, including potential funders, with only a 'rough sketch' of our ideas, requiring a 'leap of faith' and commitment on their behalf.

Involving practitioners

An initial group of 36 nurses, working in a range of roles, mainly from the NHS in Scotland volunteered to join the project. Very quickly it became apparent that we were collaborating in a way that reflected the essential elements of a CoP (Wenger 2003). Members of a CoP are mutually engaged on a joint enterprise and, in the process, develop a shared repertoire of resources that are available to all group members. As we progressed strategies were adopted to nurture features of a true CoP (Henri and Pudelko 2003).

Team-building strategies fostered a sense of togetherness and promoted bonding between group members, either during preliminary days held at the university, or online using the computer. In order to help participants remember details of each other, they prepared brief notes explaining their jobs and practice interests, augmented by photographs that provided an *aide-mémoire* when they were unsure who they were meeting online. In doing this many individuals included comments reflecting their beliefs about practice. For example, one nurse working in an acute hospital ward noted, 'I believe passionately that older people must be well informed and deserve choice'. Another from a care home stated that she had introduced person-centred documentation. By sharing such views and experiences the need for an explicit and agreed value base was identified. This represented a milestone in becoming a CoP, with a shared philosophy, rather than a network of individuals with a common interest.

The inaugural CoP (core group for short) shaped and tested approaches supporting large-scale practice development, and began to agree the value base which should underpin advances in caring (Kelly et al. 2005a; Tolson et al. 2005). Over time the project expanded beyond the capacity of a single group and 11 further communities were formed, as shown in Table 3.2. Each new community had an explicit purpose relevant to the longitudinal study and

Table 3.2 Overview of the 11 Communities of Practices involved in the demonstration project

CoP	Membership	Purpose	Lifetime
1 Core Group	36 NHS and Care Home Registered Nurses	Pioneer working methods and practice development model and advance practice locally	2001–04
2 Demonstration Site 1 Care – NHS Community Hospital	All nursing staff, membership of multidisciplinary team and housekeepers	Field test Nutrition best practice statement (BPS) and working methods	2001–03
3 Care Home Group	30 Care Home Registered Nurses	Refine working methods and advance practice locally	2002–05
4 Demonstration Site Care Home	All staff	Field test Depression BPS and development of implementation resources and practice audit	2002–04

5	Demonstration Sites 3 and 4 – Care Home and NHS Rehabilitation Ward	All Staff in Care Home. Nursing and assistant house physician (AHP) teams in NHS	Field test Physical Activity BPS and development of implementation resources and practice audit. Test twin demonstration site model	2003–05
6	Demonstration Sites 5 and 6 – Care Home and NHS Acute Ward	All Staff in Care Home. Nursing and AHP teams in NHS	Field test Oral Health BPS and develop implementation resources and practice audit. Test twin demonstration site model	2003–05
7	Involvement Group	21 older people and carers	Expand involvement of users in virtual college and develop companion resources for older people	2003–05
8	Work-based learning modules Group	18 registered nurses	Pilot uni/multi-disciplinary degree level module variants of PD experience	2003–04
9	Communication Group	23 registered nurses	Develop Hearing Disability BPS and test compressed facilitation PD model	2004–06
10	Demonstration Sites 7 and 8 – NHS Primary Care Setting and Day Hospital	All nursing and AHP	Field test Hearing Disability BPS and development of implementation resources and practice audit	2004–06
11	Impact Group	22 registered nurses	Evaluation practice impact of Caledonian PD Model	2005– ongoing

refining the practice development model. Each also had points of connection to existing groups, to encourage a continuous process of reflection and critical peer feedback.

A particular challenge was giving practitioner groups time to test and refine approaches and grow the confidence and clarity in their methods and procedures to enable them meaningfully to involve older people. Compounding this challenge was the recognition that our increasing reliance on the Internet-based college could potentially restrict access for the users we were determined to involve, namely, older people.

Developing a shared value base

The original core group recognized that practitioners are reluctant to implement evidence-based guidance which does not reflect their beliefs about practice or relate to older people's preferences. Therefore it was essential that all involved in the project shared a common set of values that were explicit and accessible to all.

Influenced by Pawson and Tilley's (1997: 164–9) interpretation of 'realistic evaluation interview methods' the value base was developed through a series of group interviews, both online and in real time. Based on group discussion, the facilitator drafted emerging descriptions of gerontological nursing and its underpinning value base. Participants took the emerging description back to practice asking colleagues for critical comment. Older people commented on the penultimate draft. A further five months of work was required to achieve a description of gerontological nursing and principles underpinning practice (Kelly et al. 2005a). These are revisited by each new CoP to ensure relevance. Current versions are displayed on the website to encourage external comment and criticism (www.geronurse.com). The initial definition of gerontological nursing was agreed in 2004 and remains unchanged:

> Gerontological nursing is a relationship centred approach that promotes healthy ageing and the achievement of well being in the older person and their carers, enabling them to adapt to the older person's health and life changes and to face ongoing life challenges.

The principles of gerontological nursing are most often practised within areas dedicated to the care of older people, however, they can be applied across all adult settings. The underlying principles also remain unchanged since 2004:

- Commitment to relationship-centred care.
- Commitment to negotiating care decisions.
- Promoting dignity and respect.
- Maximizing potential.
- Commitment to an enabling environment.
- Establishing equity of access.
- Commitment to developing innovative practice.
- Consistency of vision.
- Commitment to teamworking.
- The value of reciprocity.

These principles are continually used to inform and shape all project-related work including the best practice statements (BPSs) and approaches to facilitation and collaborative working within the Internet-based college. Central to these values is the concept of working with older people.

Involving older people

An extension to the ongoing GNDP was designed to remedy the lack of user participation in the development of the BPS, as well as to demonstrate how older people can use interactive computer technology to facilitate their own learning community. Although we minimally included older service users by asking people their views and inviting comment from national organizations representing older people, we were acutely aware that the end beneficiaries of the processes (older people themselves) did not have an opportunity to be involved in shaping best practice. We acknowledged that we were using a consumer model of participation, and that we had aspirations to move towards an empowerment model, where people participate by contributing their particular knowledge and skills (Barnes and Walker 1996). Policy developments within Scotland in the areas of inclusion and public use of interactive technology provided impetus for European and government support for the project (National Audit Office 2003). Health and social care policy is committed to the inclusion of patients' voices in quality improvement efforts and in setting standards for care. Furthermore, policy dictates that patients are empowered to take a proactive role in service development (NHS Scotland 2003). So whilst the BPS empowered staff to provide the highest standards of care, we had yet to provide the information in formats that would similarly empower the public.

This phase of the project explored ways to increase service user input into health care practice standards whilst enhancing access to information technology for older people. Specifically we wanted to promote opportunities for older people and formal carers to participate and learn within their own virtual learning community, centred on the same virtual college as the practitioners, and to develop accessible user guides based on existing BPS concerning the prevention and detection of depression and nutrition for frail older people.

Therefore we recruited 21 older people via adverts in the local press followed by a snowballing technique. We intended to involve a mix of older people and carers, including care home residents, but the latter proved difficult for a variety of factors. Twenty-one participants enrolled and 17 remained throughout the life of the project. The average age of the 13 women and 8 men was 68.8 with a range from 56 to 94. Twelve of the participants had never used a computer before, and the rest had extremely limited knowledge of computing. Preparation for involvement entailed the age appropriate adaptation of IT equipment and training, and we deliberately recruited a mature computer professional who was skilled in adult education to lead this aspect of the project. It was anticipated that the older participants would work collaboratively to develop accessible 'lay' BPS resources and that they would interact with and influence nurses working with older people in ongoing nursing CoPs.

We aimed to foster a proactive partnership by enabling participants to develop their IT knowledge and skills, so that they could take a confident role within the project. Personal computers were customized with appropriate adaptive equipment to reflect any functional limitations participants might have, and given on long-term loan to all participants residing in their own home.

The virtual practice development college was adapted to make it more accessible for participants with sensory or mobility difficulties. Participants worked with computing professionals to alter colour, text and images in the process of developing their own online learning community. Some participants took exception to the smiling older woman that we had used on much of our centre promotional material. This remained an unresolved issue because opinion was equally split. Nevertheless it did remind us of the need to consider the issue of how older people are represented, for future projects.

Information technology training, on a one-to-one and small-group basis, was designed to develop the general skills relevant to using interactive computer technology, such as sending an email and using the Internet, and those specific to the virtual college, such as using the interactive discussion forums. Participants received a minimum of a monthly visit from the lead computing professional, to provide additional training, help troubleshoot any computer-related difficulties, and assist people to access the virtual college. We were mindful of the need for continued technical support and confidence boosting, so feedback gathered at these visits was used to further adapt either the virtual college or supporting technology to increase accessibility.

The training began with basic computing skills such as keyboard skills, editing text, understanding file structures. However, older people wished to do things that interested them such as sending and receiving emails to family members or visiting websites of interest. Therefore, the training became customized to individual interests and project goals. Principles of adult education suggest that education and training should start with the needs, experiences and interests of adult learners (Merriam and Caffarella 1991). Our participants quickly pointed this out to us and one participant in particular was critical of our initial approach. When the training approach was changed he suggested it was simply common sense and we should have known better. Consequently, most participants quickly learned ICT skills, interacting with the project, as well as family and friends, across the globe. This had several benefits. For example, one participant began to interact more with her granddaughter using computers, and saw the benefits of computing for her granddaughter's education. She purchased another computer for her granddaughter and learned how to build a home network. Over the course of the project, her computing skills surpassed some members of the research team.

One participant with the greatest amount of disability presented a particular challenge in terms of maximizing her level of participation. This participant was homebound and required a great deal of care and support to remain in her own home. She received more training and support than any other participant but was never able independently to use the computer. She required someone to sit with her and manipulate the keyboard and mouse for her. One potential solution was the provision of a web cam so that she could verbalize her contribution, but she chose not to use it.

How to facilitate the work was a particular challenge. For example, should we begin by suggesting that participants look at the BPS and try to 'translate' the professional content into lay language? We posted the two BPSs and invited comment but little was forthcoming and so we started anew with just the care topics. We encouraged people to talk in the forums about their own or family and friends' care experiences. We posted a vignette of an older person at risk of depression in the virtual college and asked participants to post articles from newspapers to stimulate comment. Many of the articles chosen and participants' comments were scathing of the health and caring services, but examples of poor care were used to capture what was important to them and expressed as positive statements within the consumer guidance.

Group processes theory was used to analyse the participants' online interactions (Shulman 1999; Kelly et al. 2006). These fell into two main categories: working on socio-emotional tasks, and the social dynamics of mutual aid. The former are social niceties that grease everyday interaction, such as from the participant who regularly posted a thought for the day and commented on his local weather. The latter is that which gives groups their helping power, like sharing information, giving and asking for support, and individual problem-solving. It was anticipated that once the participants had achieved confidence in using the discussion forums that they would work with the nursing CoPs already established through the ongoing GNDP. This was mooted with the concurrent nursing CoPs and rejected, as the nurses felt that outsiders might inhibit their discussion. A solution would have been to have had a separate joint forum but lack of time prevented this from happening.

Eight people participated regularly in the online discussion forum and others contributed occasionally online and in two face-to-face social gatherings organized by participants and held in a local community centre. Two participants contributed very little to the project, with one person benefiting from the PC to enhance his business and the other viewing the visits from the project team as a social opportunity. A small group of participants expressed a wish to illustrate and produce the final care guidance documents and this they did following further training and independent facilitator support. This work was led by a participant whose spouse had died in the year she joined the project. She was understandably low in mood at the beginning and being part of the project seemed to help her re-engage. Participants demonstrated more positive attitudes to computers and increased knowledge and skill in computer use.

Involving other stakeholders

Much of this chapter has focused on involving registered nurses and older people, so we now turn our attention to the many others who worked with us. The potential stakeholders who might have been involved were considerable, and we attempted to strike a balance between being inclusive and strategic while keeping the numbers manageable, and allowing people to contribute their expertise without becoming overburdened by our demands. Several mechanisms, ranging from local implementation groups to an overarching high-level advisory group, were used.

The high-level advisory group comprised 20 members, representing five national agencies and three organizations representing older people (Help the Aged Scotland, Age Concern Scotland, Better Government for Older People). Directors of nursing from both the NHS and regulated care sector contributed, as did a number of expert practitioners and academics. Representatives were also included from the Royal College of Nursing and the British Society of Geriatric Medicine. Project funders also contributed as appropriate. The consensus was not to include a representative from each CoP at this forum, although this decision was periodically debated. Efforts were made to encourage users to feed into the advisory group by requests on the virtual college. We accept the criticism that this was a somewhat tokenistic gesture and was judged to be a resounding failure!

The advisory group met two to three times per year and commented on periodic progress reports. This group was chaired by the lead researcher (Tolson) and clerked by an experienced administrator. The remit of this group was to offer strategic direction and vision for each cycle of the work, and to appraise the team of relevant developments. Committee agenda and minutes were posted in the virtual college.

At a more operational level a project management group was convened, including senior project staff, research assistants, practitioners, administrators and managers from demonstration sites, which met monthly. The group adopted a rotational system in chairing and minuting the meeting. This assisted the team to see project management issues from a variety of perspectives, but was met with mixed responses, including trepidation from novices to committee work. Over time, it became easier to recognize the boundaries and limits of devolved leadership, and this rotational strategy seemed to work well.

Local implementation groups were assembled by the practice teams and often included nurses, health care assistants, allied health professionals, doctors, patients and family members, volunteers, housekeepers and porters. These groups were encouraged to invite someone from the project team and most often they identified the person who was acting as their practice development facilitator. Two groups invited the lead researcher to attend periodically but this was not the norm.

The conduit linking these various groups was the virtual college where meeting records could be archived once any sensitive content had been removed.

Prior to finalizing each best practice statement, NHS Quality Improvement Scotland, undertook an external consultation exercise. This targeted specific groups and known experts in the UK. Feedback was also invited on the penultimate draft via the public website. In this way the process was as inclusive and responsive as possible and on several occasions international stakeholders participated.

Practice development college

The prototype PD college used freely available software and was based on a building metaphor with easily identifiable rooms (Buggy et al. 2004). This system became unstable owing to increasing demands and the college was transferred onto a managed learning environment platform called Blackboard. The college is password protected and entered via a public website, www.geronuse.com. The website contains project information and completed resources. The PD college provides a safe place for members to collaborate, learn, report progress and discuss development challenges and share solutions. The design of the Internet-based PD college has been influenced by the CoP members and is periodically reviewed in light of user feedback.

The core group worked alongside computing professionals to prepare their own set of user specifications. These included accessibility, password protection, a help desk and the use of familiar terms to help them find their way in the college. Privacy and security of records and archived conversations were important to all, and the option to lock rooms, to secure files and to choose whether or not to use automatic recording were requested. Although initially hesitant of their technical knowledge, participants were soon able to contribute. The use of the building metaphor was helpful as practitioners could use familiar language, and have fun. One humorous suggestion was to have a toilet to flush away bad ideas. The computing professionals worked closely with the practitioners to shape the college and all went well initially. However, as usage increased and work in progress accumulated, the practitioners found it increasingly hard to find their way around. Consequently, the number of rooms was reduced and the building simplified. At this point the system failed and we migrated into Blackboard. Efforts to fully involve the three communities of practice using the college proved too time-consuming and, to avoid prolonged closure, project staff took the decision to shape the new college themselves. Feedback and comments were encouraged from all users and staff, and action taken accordingly. For example, online discussions became unwieldy and in response to members' comments, discussion forums focusing on task-related work were separated from broad discussion and support issues.

User statistics determined patterns of use, which fluctuated. Overall the pattern of time spent working both independently and collaboratively increased over time and the balance of individual and group activities was directly related to the stage of the practitioner's project-related learning.

The PD college seeks to provide a transformational learning experience, using a variety of facilitation strategies (see Figure 3.3) (Tolson et al. 2006). Learning can be facilitated exclusively online or using a blended approach. All our participant communities preferred the blended model with on average one hour per week online and periodic real-time study days (maximum of six per year).

Members of each community share the journey focusing on 'seeing possibilities for improvement' and finding solutions to local implementation

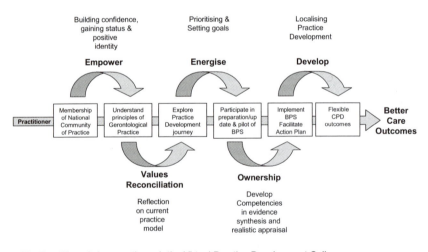

The Practitioner's journey through the Virtual Practice Development College

© Glasgow Caledonian University

Figure 3.3 Transformational learning journey (reproduced with permission. Tolson, D., Schofield, I., Booth, J., Kelly, T.B. and James, L. (2006) Constructing a new approach to developing evidence based practice with nurses and older people, *World View on Evidence Based Nursing*, 3(2): 62–72).

challenges. On average it takes each practitioner 18 months to complete their first journey and demonstrate better care locally. This involves cascading learning through their teams, implementing revised local policies and practices in line with an NHSQIS Best Practice Statement. Subsequent effort to develop practice locally is swifter and less reliant on college-based facilitation. Accessible implementation resources and periodic external facilitation speed up local achievements.

The practitioner journey enabled the CoP to satisfy its learning goal, with one measure of success of the learning journey being group behaviour indicative of CoP behaviour.

A CoP is defined by Lave and Wenger (1991) as a group of practitioners who jointly hold a socially constructed view of the meaning of their subject knowledge as well as what it takes to be an expert in the field. As a CoP is defined as a group, positive group dynamics should characterize an effectively working CoP. Consequently, the group dynamics of the original CoP were studied through analysis of online sessions occurring over years 2–3. Clear evidence of group development was found and mutual aid flourished (Kelly et al. 2005b). Supporting each other, shared problem-solving and group cohesion were particularly strong, demonstrating that the online groups were functioning as a CoP (Wenger 2003). Through group membership, practitioners worked together as they engaged in transformational learning. The social participatory learning framework appeared popular, with several stating that they did not realize they were learning but were aware that their knowledge had increased!

Partnerships in developing the BPS

To date five BPS have been developed and published by the national quality improvement agency for Scotland (NMPDU 2002; NHSQIS 2004, 2005a, 2005b, 2005c). Different methods were used to choose the topic of each statement. Initially there was no clear view of the subject or shape of the care guidance to be developed, but we wanted to use a constructivist methodology. Nutrition for frail older people was the initial focus, being agreed as an important topic in the community that was also in line with political imperatives. The second and third topics largely derived from the community members' concerns, and focused on preventing depression and improving oral health. Promoting physical activity amongst older people is a key health policy in Scotland, and was agreed as an area for guideline development following an approach to the national agency for health promotion. The fifth BPS on communicating with older people with hearing disability was agreed by the project team and strategic partners (NHSQIS). Removing practitioners' choice in this way resulted in a less satisfactory experience for them, despite successful completion of the BPS, confirming the benefits of the participatory methodology.

Older people themselves chose the BPS around which to develop the companion user guides. They were asked to review the two published BPS (nutrition and preventing depression) and select one to focus on, sharing their thoughts online through their learning community. The reviews posted showed equal concern for both topics and a reluctance to choose only one. Therefore a user guide for each BPS was constructed.

The framework for BPS construction emerged during the initial BPS development process, reflecting the participatory basis of the demonstration project (Booth et al. in press). Evidence sources were identified through real-time and virtual debate, consulting with colleagues and older people in their own practice areas. These included national audits and committee reports, published and unpublished care guidance and protocols, sources describing both user and practitioner experience and know-how, in addition to the traditional research evidence. Evidence was then reviewed and summarized by a subject specialist recruited to the CoP to lead the review. Subsequently, participants identified the messages for practice from the summary and graded each piece of supporting evidence according to a modified SIGN system (Scottish Intercollegiate Guidelines Network, www.sign.ac.uk). Unlike the SIGN system, our approach included qualitative and experiential evidence for and from practice. The resulting evidence matrix underpinned the first draft of the best practice statement.

Initial versions of the BPS were refined by community members in two ways: first, the values base was applied, to ensure that the draft statement reflected their agreed principles; second, the draft BPS was tested for achievability and relevance in the demonstration site. These dynamic processes took place through the medium of the virtual college. This enabled the CoP members, demonstration site staff and expert adviser to access each other and collaborate in the virtual environment, overcoming difficulties with real-time meetings of such groups. On agreement of the final draft of the BPS, national consultation was undertaken to identify any further opportunities to improve the statement before publication and national dissemination.

Lessons learned

There are few examples of longitudinal, multi-site action research in the literature. At the beginning we recognized that working with a distributed pool of practitioners and multiple contexts of care would provide many challenges, especially geography and scale of the work. Time spent by the principal researcher in building relationships with everyone involved paid dividends, as did the allocation of a principal alternate action researcher (known as the practice development facilitator) to support each group on a day-to-day basis. As the work expanded there was a need to strike a balance between the influence of the principal researcher in promoting project cohesion whilst letting communities grow in their own distinctive way. The consensus view was to strive for the former and this required a number of communication strategies to promote a sense of togetherness. We would recommend that careful attention is paid to this issue by others embarking on similar programmes.

The merits of investing in strategic partnerships speak for themselves and positioned us well in terms of turning some of the project outputs (best practice statements, companion guides) into national resources for users. These partnerships were also central to our success in attracting major research funding from a number of sources.

From the outset we sought to work collaboratively with practitioners and older people. With hindsight, beginning with the practitioner CoP and not a mixed community including older people was regrettable. At the time the vagueness of ideas and the conditions of early grants dictated this stance. We can only speculate on the possible outcomes had we started differently and recognize that our partnership with older people remains at an immature stage.

Conclusion

The experience of using the involvement methodology has been enlightening and has moved us closer to the goal of meaningful research partnerships. Undoubtedly we have much to learn, and admit at times to stumbling over issues which might look obvious to an outsider. The things we stumbled over were often resolvable and related to technical hiccups or making assumptions that we all shared a common language, or repertoire, to use the terms of the CoP literature. Our work has gone some way to achieving partnerships in describing and demonstrating best nursing practice. The characteristics of the various stakeholder partnerships that we achieved were qualitatively different, whether such diversity in partnership working is essential or limiting is yet to be determined.

4 Changing the culture within care homes for older people

Sue Davies, Lewis Atkinson,
Barry Aveyard, Una Martin,
Scott McCaffrey, Ann Powell

This chapter describes the implementation and evaluation of an action group within a nursing home for older people with dementia. The action group formed part of a wider research project, in which researchers worked with staff, residents and relatives over a three-year period, on a series of initiatives aimed at improving experiences of living and working within the home. The action group co-opted representatives of external agencies, and instituted a number of important changes. We describe the processes involved in establishing the action group and identify the impact of the group on the experiences of the different stakeholders. At various points in the text the authors add their personal reflections on this process.

The importance of culture within care homes

The past decade has witnessed growing recognition of the importance of 'culture' within care homes for older people (Help the Aged and the National Care Homes Research and Development Forum 2006). According to Schein (1985), culture consists of shared values, beliefs and assumptions that guide the behaviour of individuals and groups in organizations, whereas Kitwood defines culture as 'a settled patterned way of giving meaning to human existence in the world, and of giving structure to action within it' (Kitwood, cited in Ronch 2004: 64).

Culture is important within care homes for the impact it has on the way that people act and behave (Ronch 2004). To create positive experiences we need to ensure that the prevailing 'culture' values older people, their families and staff (Davies 2003). This is unlikely to be realized unless the needs of all stakeholders, including staff members, are taken into account (Davies 2003; Hurtley 2003).

In an earlier project, Sue Davies, one of the authors of this chapter, identified a range of factors that contribute to 'culture' within a care home, including structural and organizational characteristics, values and goals, as well as the nature of relationships between residents, staff and family members (Davies 2001, 2003). Three types of community were identified: the controlled community; the cosmetic community; and the complete community. She suggested that the 'complete community' provides the most positive experiences for older people and promotes 'best care'. The 'complete community' has the following features:

- Enablement, partnership and interdependence are valued.
- Person-centred and relationship-centred care are practised.
- Staff work as an effective team with mutual appreciation and some blurring of roles; relatives are integral members of the team.
- There are close links with the local community.

As culture is important we need to consider how we might change the culture of care within a care home to create the most appropriate type of community. Partnership-working potentially generates solutions that individuals or groups alone cannot produce, with the contribution of service users now being well established. In care homes for example, a number of initiatives involving older people and their relatives in developing services have been reported (Raynes 1998; Rantz et al. 1999; Reed et al. 1999). However, a limitation of many such projects is that whilst residents and relatives may identify areas for development, responsibility for enhancing these usually rests with the staff. The potential for shared ownership of solutions, as well as problems, may therefore not be fully realized. The action group we describe presents an alternative model involving staff, residents, their relatives and academic researchers as equal partners. Our broad aim was to create opportunities for everyone to contribute to developing the home as an 'enriched' environment in which to live, work and learn. Using action research, the partnership has enabled us to work together to prioritize developments that have improved things for residents, relatives and staff.

Reflections 1: In the beginning

After taking up post as manager of the home in October 2000, I was very inter-ested in the concept of practice development and shared this enthusiasm with staff. I particularly wanted to explore the possibility of developing the home as a 'teaching nursing home' and I arranged for staff to visit other practice develop-ment units. In March 2001, I contacted the Professor of Gerontological Nursing at the University of Sheffield to explore possibilities for working together. Two lecturers within the School of Nursing and Midwifery expressed an interest in working with us to develop practice and we were able to secure a small research grant from the University of Sheffield (£2,000) to support the work. A further sum of £3,778 was allocated by the North Trent Workforce Confederation to enable staff members to be released to attend activities associated with the project. These sums of money were invaluable in helping us to get things started.

In the early days, it wasn't always easy to maintain everyone's enthusiasm for what we were trying to do. However, within the action group, we were able to support each other, and we also learned a lot from other nursing homes. We achieved a great deal, although sometimes progress was painfully slow. I was particularly pleased that some relatives seemed to find a renewed sense of pur-pose through their work with the action group. They certainly helped the staff to feel valued. Collaborating with researchers also helped to ensure that the project built upon current research in dementia care. Without the action group, lots of things would never have got off the ground. I certainly learnt a great deal from the experience of joint working with the university, relatives and residents. I also felt very privileged and humbled to be involved in empowering residents and relatives to be able to make a meaningful contribution to, and have some control over, their destinies. The support and encouragement from Sue Davies and Barry Aveyard (senior lecturers) throughout this journey was wonderful. I couldn't have done this on my own.

(Ann Powell, former Manager)

67 Birch Avenue

The project occurred in a nursing home for up to 40 older people with dementia in the North of England. The home was unusual, being managed jointly by an NHS Care Trust and a local Housing Association. The building was purpose-built in 1994 and divided into four bungalows around a central courtyard. Separate dining and sitting rooms within each bungalow provide a homely environment and bedrooms are all single with en-suite facilities. Most residents have advanced dementia and many also have complex physical health needs. The home has a good reputation in the locality and usually has a waiting list of prospective residents. Many of the residents are well supported by family members. The home provides placements for student nurses.

At the outset we identified the following objectives:

- To establish the experiences of residents, relatives and staff about living and working at the home.
- To use up-to-date research to improve the experiences of residents and carers.
- To enable staff, carers, residents and researchers to establish development projects.
- To monitor the processes and conditions necessary to achieve the above objectives.

These initial objectives were identified by the researchers and the then manager of the home, and their relevance was reconsidered whenever new stakeholder groups became involved.

From the outset, the project was underpinned by the notions of relationship-centred care and the Senses Framework (Nolan et al. 2002), as we wanted to see if applying these theoretical ideas would help to improve experiences within care homes. The phrase 'relationship-centred care' emphasizes 'the importance of the interaction between people as the foundation of any therapeutic or teaching activity' (Tresolini and the Pew Fetzer Taskforce 1994: 11). Nolan et al. (2006) have applied this concept to work with older people and argue that care staff need help to identify ways of interacting with older people and their families that best support relationships (Nolan et al. 2006), using the Senses Framework. The Senses Framework is built upon many years of research in a range of care environments (Nolan 1997; Davies et al. 1999; Nolan et al. 2001, 2002) and suggests that the best care for older people involves the creation of a set of senses or experiences for those older people, for family caregivers and for staff working with them. These are:

- a *sense of security* – of feeling safe and receiving or delivering competent and sensitive care
- a *sense of continuity* – the recognition of biography, using the past to contextualize the present
- a *sense of belonging* – opportunities to form meaningful relationships or feel part of a team
- a *sense of purpose* – opportunities to engage in purposeful activities or to have a clear set of goals to aspire to

- a *sense of achievement* – achieving meaningful or valued goals and feeling satisfied with one's efforts
- a *sense of significance* – to feel that you matter, and that you are valued as a person (Nolan et al. 2002).

Through linking the experiences of older people, their families and staff, the Senses Framework also has the potential to promote understanding of the experiences of others, with resulting improvements in communication and partnership working. Our project used the Senses Framework and relationship-centred care as the basis for improving experiences within care homes.

The 'research'

The project used a broadly constructivist framework (Rodwell 1998) in an attempt to create joint accounts or 'co-constructions' capturing shared views of what was happening. We gathered several types of information throughout the project, including:

- observations by the researchers and informal interviews with residents, relatives and staff
- questionnaires to staff and relatives about their views on care
- staff 'away days' to discuss feedback from the questionnaires and generate ideas for development work
- preparation of a 'needs and priorities' report and feedback to all groups
- a working group to take ideas forward (Support 67 Action Group)
- developing an educational programme for all staff to which relatives were also invited.

The Support 67 Action Group is the main mechanism driving the project. It includes relatives, representatives of staff groups (domestic staff as well as nursing care staff), the manager and deputy manager, research facilitators and senior managers from both the NHS Care Trust/Housing Association that jointly manage the home.

The action group met monthly with members being responsible for leading the initiatives identified within the needs and priorities report. New issues and ideas are raised and guest speakers invited, thereby creating links with external agencies, both statutory and voluntary. The group evolved its own way of working, only establishing ground rules and terms of reference when participants had met several times and felt comfortable together (Table 4.1). Details of this early work are reported elsewhere (Davies et al. 2002; Davies 2003).

Table 4.1   Support 67 Action Group terms of reference

Group membership is open to all relatives and friends of residents of 67 Birch Avenue, all members of staff and managers/key stakeholders within relevant agencies. Group funds are held in an account with the Chapeltown branch of xxxx Bank. A nominated treasurer and three signatories will manage this account.

The purpose of the group is to:

- Provide a forum for relatives, staff and key stakeholders to meet on a regular basis.
- Work together to develop care and services at 67 Birch Avenue in ways that will enhance the experiences of residents, their relatives, staff and students.
- Ensure that developments are based on up-to-date research evidence.
- Raise funds to support these developments.
- Liaise with appropriate managers within Sheffield Care Trust and South Yorkshire Housing Association and other agencies to ensure that developments comply with relevant local and national policies.
- To advise other relevant groups about the needs of older people with dementia.

November 2004

Reflections 2: Evolution, not revolution

I wasn't there when Support 67 was born and I missed its early days. But I was there as it grew and matured. I became the manager at 67 Birch Avenue in January of 2004 and I was excited, if a little bit apprehensive, about this group of enthusiastic relatives and staff that met to discuss progress within the home and plan for the future. I soon found that this valuable resource was not something to be wary of, but helped ensure that the home where they had placed their loved ones was openly accountable to them and involved them in planning for the future and working towards improving services. Relatives also had a relaxed atmosphere in which they could get to know each other, the manager and other professionals better. Over time, the group has evolved and relatives now take the lead in chairing the meeting and managing funds. The manager is no longer the central player in the group, but part of a team that works towards improving the service delivered. This team also looks at ways of enhancing the quality of life within the home by improving the environment and working towards making Birch Avenue a better place to live.

As a manager of a nursing home, I may be expected to initiate practices for the improvement of the home. However, too often, the people who are directly affected by change have little input into what those changes should be and how best to implement them. Support 67 helps to redress this and encourages joint working between management, housekeeping, catering, ancillary and nursing staff to promote quality, person centred care.

(Scott McCaffrey, Registered Manager)

Evaluation

After about a year, we gathered more information using interviews and an away day, to consider our progress. Semi-structured interviews were under-taken with 18 staff members and seven relatives, specifically exploring their experiences of the action group and how they would like it to develop in the future. These were tape-recorded and transcribed.

Residents had been involved in many of the project activities, and a few residents had briefly attended meetings of the action group, but we could not interview residents about their experiences due to high levels of cognitive frailty. However, informal conversations with residents suggested that most found the activities resulting from the action group enjoyable.

Away day

The away day, attended by six relatives, eight staff members and two managers, in addition to two facilitators, addressed the following questions:

- What have we achieved?
- Is the Senses Framework useful in understanding what we have achieved?
- What could we have done differently?
- Where should we go from here?

Participants explored these questions in small mixed groups and came together for feedback that was tape-recorded and transcribed.

This information was analysed to capture participants' experiences of the project, and barriers and facilitators to the change process (see Aveyard and Davies 2006).

Experiences of the project

Four main themes captured both relatives' and staff's experiences of being involved in the project. The themes were:

- creating a shared understanding
- learning to value each other
- becoming a powerful voice
- moving forward.

(See Table 4.2.)

The results of the evaluation are described more fully in Aveyard and

Table 4.2   Themes within interviews with relatives and staff

---

Creating a shared understanding
The action group improved communication between relatives and staff. By spending more time together, they felt this had developed a greater understanding of each other's needs and consequently relationships had improved.

Learning to value each other
The project provided opportunities for staff and relatives to recognize and show appreciation for each other's contribution to life within the home. Feedback during group sessions reinforced to staff that relatives feel they 'do a good job' and provide highly skilled care. Staff were also able to show how much they valued the continuing contribution of relatives.

Becoming a powerful voice
As individual projects developed, staff and relatives found that by working together they had developed into a powerful force for change. A number of participants felt that they were able to exert more influence and promote change by working together.

Moving forward
This comprised three main areas:
• The action group had channelled people's enthusiasm for change, identifying both immediate and longer-term goals.
• The group had helped some families to resolve their own situation, for example in coming to terms with their feelings about placing their relative into long-term care.
• The project was advancing understanding about partnership working in long-term care settings through publications and conference presentations.

Davies (2006). Here we focus on identifying the effects of the project for the various stakeholders. This proved to be a particularly challenging component.

Interpreting the evaluation

In attempting to 'tease out' the impact of the project we made use of the modified authenticity criteria (Nolan et al. 2003a), described in the introduction to this book, which suggests that the success of an initiative can be considered in terms of five criteria: equal access; enhanced awareness of self; enhanced awareness of others; encouraging action; and enabling action. We used the information gathered during the interviews and the away day to explore whether these criteria had been achieved.

Equal access

We made every effort to ensure that everyone had the opportunity to express their views and contribute to developments. The interviews suggest that, for staff and relatives, this was largely achieved. However, ensuring that the views of the residents were represented was challenging. They were always welcome at meetings, and attended periodically, but their cognitive frailty made

Reflections 3:   Filling the void

My husband Ernest first went into care just over five years ago. While it was a relief to hand over the responsibility, it left a huge gap in my life which simply visiting him did not fill. I was fully aware that I still had a say in his care now that he was living at Birch Avenue, however, I was unsure how to channel this and, I suppose like anyone in the same position, I felt somewhat helpless.

Then Ann Powell, the residential manager of Birch Avenue at that time, came up with the innovative idea of setting up a group comprised of residents, relatives, management and staff to work in partnership. She approached Professor Mike Nolan of Sheffield University to seek his guidance, and in August 2002 the group was born. The university came on board in the persons of Sue Davies and Barry Aveyard, research fellows at the university, and the rest is history!

In addition to the usual fund-raising to benefit the residents of Birch Avenue, we have a real voice on behalf of our loved ones and relevant issues are openly discussed within our meetings. Because of the diversity of our membership, that is, residents who are able, relatives, management and staff, democratic decisions have been made to the mutual benefit of all concerned. We also have regular attendance by South Yorkshire Housing Association (who own the home) and managers from Sheffield Care Trust (who provide the staff for the home).

The group also provides a forum to which members can bring their joys and concerns and we have a twice yearly evening meeting for relatives when we get together for a nice social evening, usually with a speaker or some other form of interest. Quite a few friendships have been formed within our group and we are always there for each other. This is particularly important because it can be very isolating when someone you love suffers from this dreadful disease.

All in all, Support 67 is all things to all people; a support group, a fund-raising body, and a decision-making forum. I think I can speak for everyone when I say how much it means to me, and I think it speaks for itself that so many of our members continue to attend our meetings after they have sadly lost their loved ones. There is a real spirit of fellowship within the group, and Birch Avenue and those who live or work there are our first priority.

(Una Martin, founding member, Support 67 Action Group and wife of Ernest, a resident)

sustained participation difficult. We depended largely on staff and relatives to voice the concerns and experiences of residents.

Further into the project, attendance of relatives fell and one of the relatives suggested that the 'formal' nature of the group may be an issue. We had tried to keep the meetings as informal and friendly as possible, nonetheless, the terminology used, with reference to 'minutes' and a 'chairperson', could be offputting for anyone unfamiliar with such activities. We therefore re-labelled future meetings as 'coffee mornings' and dedicated the first half-hour to general socializing, before settling to the 'business' part of the meeting. This resulted in an immediate improvement in attendance, not only on the part of relatives, but also staff.

Clearly, great thought must be given to creating an environment where everyone feels able to participate, whilst acknowledging that people may also choose not to: 'I was a bit wary of the sort of feeling that we want to make a nice support group which people will be expected to join. Have it by all means for those who want it, but it's the level of expectation and almost starting to be cross with people who don't come and I don't think that's a way forward at all' (relative, interview no. 6).

Some relatives felt that attending the group was not appropriate for them: 'A lot of people that went, it were mainly – the wife's ill and they were elderly themselves and they need that support, they need that group, more so than what I do. But I like to keep involved with my mum' (relative, interview no. 2).

For others, attending meetings with researchers from 'the university' could be threatening: 'I think people are frightened of what they might be coming into, whether they'll show themselves up, what might be expected of them' (staff member, interview no. 1).

There were also practical constraints. Staff worked 12-hour shifts followed by several days off, so the potential for getting everyone together was limited, with no ideal time which allowed everyone to take part. Consequently, some staff felt that they had 'missed out':

> I suppose maybe they [the researchers] could have got in more to talk to people. Like I say, I'm not criticizing. I don't know how much time you have spent coming in but to be honest with you I don't think I've ever been on duty when there's been a meeting going off or anything where I could talk to anybody. I know there's been plenty of ques-tionnaires and letters and things, I've always read, but it's not the same as speaking to people is it.
>
> (Staff member, interview no. 5)

Residents living in smaller units also meant that staff needed to supervise residents, further limiting their availability. Disseminating information about the project proved challenging, we soon discovered that written minutes were not an effective way of ensuring that everyone remained informed about developments. Personal contact with members of the action group emerged as the best way to share information but this was time-consuming. As things progressed, notes of meetings were summarized into posters, with key projects and decisions presented as 'flash points' (Figure 4.1). This proved an effective way of communicating with the wider care home community.

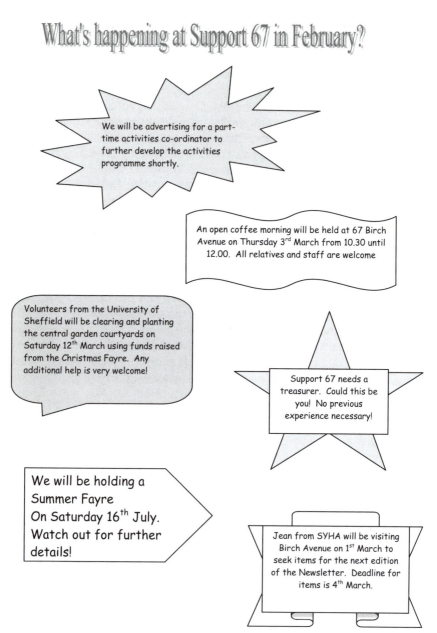

Figure 4.1 Feedback poster.

Enhanced awareness

The project had enabled everyone involved to appreciate each other's viewpoints and experiences, as illustrated in the following exchange which took place between a staff nurse and a relative at the away day:

> *Relative*: Sometimes, visiting can be difficult and if I can take him and shave him and do his hair and make him smell nice, that makes visiting a lot easier, because I'm doing something for him and also it's helping me, because sometimes an hour's visit can seem like 12 hours.
>
> *Staff member*: But there's no reason why you shouldn't be involved and I think the staff appreciate that, that, you know, you've cared for him before us. There's nothing that we're doing for him that you haven't already done, so if you want to continue with that role, I can't see why there is any reason that you shouldn't, and it gives you a purpose.

There was also evidence that staff members felt that they had learned from each other, both within the Support 67 meetings and the education sessions established as part of the wider project:

> Especially like with the auxiliaries, if they see qualified and auxiliaries all in together all learning together and saying oh I didn't know that. Like we're split up into little groups you know to answer questions, and you think you've got them all and then it might be just something like xxx that comes up and you thought of that one.
>
> (Staff member, interview no. 11)

However, the extent to which it was possible for everyone to develop such insights was limited by a number of factors. In particular, creating time for all staff within the home to participate was a continual challenge.

One possible effect of not being able fully to involve all staff members was a lack of understanding about the motivation of some of the relative participants, and a failure fully to appreciate their particular perspective:

> I think relatives have been on a par with staff more, they've felt like they could open up to the staff more which I think is a good thing. Because, like I said earlier, this is their family home. But I do think that there have been issues regarding relatives taking over a little bit. Feeling as though, not realizing that we're here to do a job in a sense and you've got to take a stand and think that they're trying to help here because you can lose touch of the fact that

they're trying to help and just think they're getting a bit on your nerves.

(Staff member, interview no. 10)

This quote illustrates the ongoing challenge of ensuring that all participants have the opportunity to share any concerns. Fortunately, notes of meetings provided many examples of delicate issues that had been discussed, with views expressed on both sides, without causing friction. One example was the issue of relatives visiting during mealtimes. Staff found it difficult to make visitors feel welcome during mealtimes, feeling that it was potentially embarrassing for residents who needed a lot of assistance to eat if other residents' relatives were present. The relative members of the group explained how they appreciated the opportunity to visit at mealtimes, both to share a meal occasionally and sometimes to assist their relative. After much debate the group put together some guidelines which were circulated for comment, and an issue with the potential for conflict was discussed and resolved.

Reflections 4: Finding new meaning

Since my wife entered Birch Avenue in April 2005 and is now receiving the expert kind of care that should be available to all in her situation today, I have found myself also being looked after by the staff in the home. On my regular visits the amount of 'tender loving care' given to me and others like me is amazing. On top of this we have the action group (Support 67) of managers, staff and relatives, with residents if they are able. This group is a strength and fellowship so much needed when families are facing the ultimatums of life. I am very privileged to be part of it because it has filled what could have been a very sad and depressing time of my life with fulfilment and long-term hope – I say this because several of the members have already lost their loved one and have stayed as members of the action group. The close love and fellowship we share also manifests itself in our efforts to achieve things to improve the care and support for the residents – in 2007 we will have developed a sensory garden offering a safe and beautiful haven for all in the home. Such can be the results from good cooperation and working, and I know this will only increase in the coming years.

(Lewis Atkinson, Chair, Support 67 and husband of Connie,
resident at 67 Birch Avenue)

Encouraging action

This refers to the extent to which action is stimulated and facilitated by the (research) process. In other words, is there a catalyst for change as a result of new insights and awareness? The wealth of ideas produced during the project can be seen as a catalyst for change, and the interviews indicated that such ideas would have been unlikely to have emerged without the project:

> From what I can see that [the project] has been a force for good and a force for change, a force for doing what I think we need to do. Looking at what's happening and looking at what needs to be done and finding a practical way of achieving it, but not just from one person's perspective but from staff's perspective, client's perspective, carer's perspective and partnerships . . . especially with the uni coming in it's pushed people a little bit hasn't it, they just need that little bit of shove you know 'go on, do it, have a go'. If you fail it doesn't matter, you've had a go.
>
> (Staff member, interview no. 7)

Relatives were also aware how the group had identified priorities for action: 'I think it has helped, it's helped to meet people as well you see, know different people. If no one came there'd be no incentive. It might not go as far as we want it to go but at least you know what is needed' (relative, interview no. 4).

Enabling action

The final criterion, enabling action, relates to whether stakeholders and participants are empowered to act. The ultimate test is therefore whether real change actually occurs. In spite of the numerous ideas that emerged during the project, there was undoubted frustration at how long things took to change. This partly reflected the organizational arrangements, whereby two separate bodies shared managerial and administrative responsibilities. Limited funding to support many of the suggested developments was also acutely felt: 'I think we're more aware of things although things are perhaps going a little slowly. But they're bound to go slow because things that are being mentioned require what is at the bottom line, money that is very hard to get. You see we throw millions away but needy people don't get it these days' (relative, interview no. 3).

The architecture was also a barrier to some developments, particularly the lack of a large communal area, limiting the potential for shared events. This was identified as an early priority and was finally realized shortly after the final interviews when two dining rooms were converted into a larger communal room with dividing doors. Notwithstanding such delays, considerable progress was made in relation to all of the initial priorities identified by the group (Table 4.3).

Table 4.3 Achievements of the Support 67 Action Group

- Activities programme
- Relatives support group
- Booklet for new residents and relatives
- Fund-raising
- Uniforms for staff
- Education programme
- Skills profile for qualified staff
- PAT dog 'Missie'
- Garden project
- Building modifications project

Reflections 5: Handing it over

Working as part of the action group has for me, as a nurse and an inexperienced researcher, been one of the most powerful experiences of my nursing career. Seeing the partnership develop has been an incredible experience: there is no doubt that staff and relatives have had to take risks and learn to trust each other and see each other's point of view. Through doing this they have achieved so much.

At times it has been frustrating. Things can be very slow to change and what seems like a common-sense decision or initiative can seem to take an age to come to fruition. For me I need to step back a little now. I still see the group as playing its part in developing the home, and it seems at times to be becoming a fund-raising group. However, it is not my role to decide how the group is run: I am a member who wants to stay involved and will advise on practice and research when asked. The group though does now seem very strong and set to flourish for a long time.

(Barry Aveyard, Lecturer in Nursing)

Shared experiences of culture change within care homes

In preparing this chapter, we became aware of several initiatives attempting to change the culture within care homes using collaborative approaches. In reading their reports, we realized that we shared a number of common experiences. Scalzi (2006) for example describe the barriers and enablers to changing the organizational culture in three nursing homes on the east coast of the USA. Barriers included exclusion of nurses from culture-change activities, perceived corporate emphasis on regulatory compliance and the 'bottom line', and high turnover of administrators and caregivers. Enablers included a critical mass of 'change champions', shared values and goals, resident/family participation, and empowerment at the facility level. Similarly, Robinson and Rosher (2006) describe their experiences of attempting to promote a resident-centred environment within a large nursing home in the US Mid-West. Their suggestions resonate with many of our own experiences and, in Table 4.4, we reflect on their recommendations and the extent to which these were achieved within our own project. This also provides more of a flavour of project activities.

Table 4.4 Recommendations for infusing culture change

Recommendations (Robinson and Rosher 2006)	Our experiences at 67 Birch Avenue
Begin by developing a vision. The vision must be shared and endorsed by all, from corporate executives to front-line staff	This was achieved through the away days, and the educational programme, when staff developed a collage reflecting what they wanted to achieve within the home. This was made into posters that were displayed around the home. With hindsight we should have included family members in these activities. Later, residents, staff and family members were involved in the preliminary phase of a related research project in which they were invited to share what was most important to them about living and working in the care home. These comments were fed back to members of the group
Commit to an organizational decision-making change that empowers those closest to the residents, the front-line staff	The Support 67 Action Group was the main mechanism for achieving change. We felt it was essential that family members were involved in this group, as well as staff. The action group was represented on other decision-making bodies within the Trust
Provide education on organizational restructuring for administration and team building for staff. Early in the education process, identify front-line staff who can lead the teams. Provide additional training for the team leaders and allow them time within their job description to lead the way	With hindsight, more efforts should have been made to engage the qualified nursing staff as leaders. We did not get the qualified staff on board early enough and consequently, struggled to engage them fully in developments *Continued*

Table 4.4 continued.

Recommendations (Robinson and Rosher 2006)	Our experiences at 67 Birch Avenue
Provide intensive education to staff, residents, families, and volunteers on culture change. Anticipate that there likely will be staff turnover for various reasons. Before beginning, develop a programme for orientation of new staff and ongoing education of all staff	Our initial education programme was successful but largely attended by staff. Talks at relative support groups were useful. For the future, we would recommend more shared training sessions and additional content within staff induction programmes. The booklet for new residents and their families was one attempt to share the philosophy of the new culture with newcomers
Because culture change occurs slowly, early in the education process, select a simple pioneer practice that can be implemented easily. Make the change and emphasize the positive outcomes with all staff. They will be able to believe that change will truly come to their nursing home	We began with selecting three changes that would improve experiences – one each for staff, residents and relatives. We probably tried to do too many things at once and progress initially seemed slow. However, within the first year, we had secured funding for occupational therapy input (residents), established the relatives support group (relatives) and persuaded the Housing Association to purchase uniforms for staff (staff)
If major barriers are encountered that threaten the culture change journey, stop and focus on maintaining the vision and preserving the changes that have been made, while dealing with the pressing issues. Focus on the major purpose of culture change: to improve the quality of life for the residents. Do not give up!	A major review of the service provided at 67 Birch Avenue by the NHS Trust managing the home two years into the project, acted as a distraction from the work of the action group as staff became preoccupied with other issues. However, ultimately, the review process was helpful to the work of the group by recognizing and acknowledging its role as an important decision-making body within the home

Source: after Robinson and Rosher 2006

Conclusion

Changing the culture within care homes requires recognition of the complex and multidimensional nature of life and work in these settings (Dewar 2006). A review of literature on quality of life in care homes carried out for the charity Help the Aged (Help the Aged and the National Care Homes Research and

Reflections 6: Moving on, letting go

For me, Support 67 was like a dream come true. I had spent several years (while undertaking a PhD) interviewing relatives about their experiences of helping a loved one move into a nursing home, and hearing about the guilt and sadness, and loss of control that many relatives experienced at this time. I became convinced that the notion of care homes as 'communities', where everyone has an important contribution to make, offered the most likely way of transforming experiences, but didn't really know where to start to make this a reality. The opportunity to work closely with the community at Birch Avenue was a chance to learn about the process of achieving change in ways that would benefit everyone.

The next three years provided some of the most rewarding (and the most demanding) experiences of my career. Particular memories include:

- the challenge of persuading staff of the value of taking time out to attend an away day when they were most worried about leaving the home short-staffed
- the looks on their faces when we fed back some of the very positive comments from family members in response to our questionnaire
- senior managers' enthusiasm for engaging with relatives and staff, and their willingness to try to make things happen
- twelve volunteer university students arriving on a chilly March day to clear gardens and plant spring flowers
- the tenth anniversary celebrations in December 2004, lots of 'grumbling' in advance, but everyone pulling together in the end, a brass band playing Christmas carols on an unseasonably warm December day, children dancing in front of delighted residents wrapped up in blankets in their wheelchairs
- the wonderful welcome I received whenever I walked through the door.

In 2005 I moved to the USA and my direct involvement at the home came to an end. For some time I had been concerned that if we (university staff) withdrew, then the group would grind to a halt. This has been far from the case. The Support 67 Action Group is now an established part of the culture of the home and goes from strength to strength. Relatives and staff support each other and achieve far more together than they could independently. It can be done. It can happen anywhere with the right ingredients – good leadership and a committed group of individuals.

(Sue Davies, Visiting Reader in Gerontological Nursing)

Development Forum 2006), concluded that homes should work to develop cultures that support relationship-centred care. The review also suggested that the interdependence of staff, residents and family members is crucial to the success of a home, and that any attempt to promote a positive culture within the care home setting needs to nurture these important relationships.

Within this chapter, we have described an initiative to develop a collaborative model of partnership working involving staff, residents and family members within a care home for older people with dementia. Our experience demonstrates the importance of effective leadership, involving all stakeholders and the availability of expert advice in achieving a positive care home community. The role of 'champions', people who are committed to the change, and have the energy to see it through, is also clear. However, access to sufficient resources, particularly in terms of staff time, is also essential.

5 'A changing life': co-constructing a personal theory of awareness and adjustment to the onset of Alzheimer's disease

John Keady, Sion Williams, John Hughes-Roberts, Pat and Mo Quinn

Introduction

In this chapter we provide an account of an emerging qualitative research approach that engages people living with long-term conditions as co-discoverers and co-researchers in the theoretical construction of their own lived experience. This approach, termed 'Co-Constructed Inquiry' (CCI) (Keady and Williams 2005; Williams and Keady 2005), has evolved since 2003 in partnership with people with dementia, their families and JH-R, a clinical nurse specialist within a memory clinic in North Wales – and co-author on this chapter. Along with two other families and one person with dementia living alone, the two remaining co-authors (MQ, a person with Alzheimer's disease, and PQ, her husband) have been instrumental in helping to identify, test and refine CCI and the language used to communicate its underlying properties and methods.

Co-Constructed Inquiry comprises three sequential acts, namely: Building the Set; Performing the Production; and Bringing down the Curtain, with each act divided into different stages, scenes and parts. The opening act of 'Building the Set' involves working 'behind the scenes' to establish the study, seek funding, negotiate and identify the theatre of study (that is, its substantive area) and research script (its aims and objectives), obtain ethical permission, cast the actors (that is, principal investigators for the co-construction, in this study MQ, PQ and JH-R), liaise with supporting cast members (that is, the clinical area of JH-R, the consultant psychiatrist and MQ's extended family) and ensure that all contributors are aware of their role within the production. The theory-building process of CCI is conducted in its second act, 'Performing the Production', and is embedded within personal narrative and individual life-course, allowing the actors to co-construct a theoretical model of lived experience. This is performed, first, through the production of a 'life-story script' and second, by abstracting a 'personal theory' from the narrative account. With permission and/or collaboration of other actors, selected personal theories undertaken in the same theatre of study can be compared and contrasted in order to produce one 'collective theory' of the experience; a process that is outside the scope of this chapter. The third act of a CCI, 'Bringing down the Curtain', is about exit and dissemination strategies by the actors and cast members taking part in the research process.

We describe each of these acts, paying particular attention to the development of MQ's 'life-story script' and her co-constructed 'personal theory' which explains (in MQ's words, using her autobiographical narrative) her early awareness of, and adjustment to, her Alzheimer's disease (the theatre of study for the research script). The chapter concludes with a discussion about the implications of MQ's personal theory for practice. However, to set an appropriate context, we briefly rehearse approaches to understanding early awareness in dementia.

Early awareness in dementia

The concept of awareness in dementia is not new. In a translation of Dr Alois Alzheimer's original case notes on Auguste D's admission into the Frankfurt am Maine insane asylum in Germany in November 1901, he wrote:

> **Writing:** When she has to write Mrs Auguste D, she writes 'Mrs' and we must repeat the other words because she forgets them. The patient is not able to progress in writing and repeats, *I have lost myself* [our emphasis].
>
> **Reading:** She seems not to understand what she reads. She stresses the words in an unusual way. Suddenly she says twins. *I know Mr Twin* [our emphasis]. She repeats the word twin during the whole interview.
>
> (Maurer et al. 1997: 1548)

Auguste D was 51 at the time and she died in the asylum on the 8 April 1906 aged 56. Whilst these medical notes are only snippets of Auguste D's life, they nevertheless tell an important story. For example, and as our italics under the 'writing' sub-heading illustrate, she struggled to absorb altered meanings of self into her new identity. Furthermore, Auguste D's identification of 'Mr Twin' during a reading test is important as it informs contemporary practitioners that cognitive and neuropsychological assessments are only meaningful if they demonstrate an appreciation of a person's life biography, comprising a shared understanding/discourse of life events (see also Keady and Bender 1998). Failure of biographical awareness results in assessments that are superficial in nature, objectifying subjective life events. Maurer et al.'s (1997) work also emphasized that Alzheimer's disease (as it was to be called following the post-mortem study of Auguste D's brain (Alzheimer 1907)) is a condition of both middle and older age; an issue not lost on MQ and PQ and their family. Accordingly, recent discourses about service provision for younger people with dementia within older person services (DoH 2001b, 2005) must be challenged as a threat to positive person work, social inclusion and self identity. One hundred years on, much work remains to be done.

The early 1990s saw a call to re-orientate the dementia care literature away from an (over)emphasis on 'caregiver burden' to the involvement of people with dementia in understanding their own 'illness and its course' (Cotrell and Schulz 1993: 205), and the academic and practice community has responded enthusiastically, especially concerning early awareness and adjustment (for a review see Clare et al. 2006). As Harris and Keady (2006: 6) recently identified, the experience of dementia is an evolving dynamic that embraces the whole person, raising areas of 'ethical, social-psychological and neurological significance'. Crucially, recent years have seen people living with dementia articulating their own needs and campaigning for changes at macro and micro levels of political and health/social care systems (see the work of the global Dementia Advocacy and Support Network International at www.dasninternational.org, accessed 18 December 2006, or nationally the Scottish Dementia Working Group at www.alzscot.org, accessed 18 December 2006). Such involvement was exemplified by Gloria Sterin (2002) who, before her untimely death in 2006, wrote with heartfelt passion about her detest of the word 'dementia' and the need to be seen as a person who can cope with the disease, albeit within an altered perception and understanding of time.

Increasingly, people with dementia caution against a uni-dimensional view of their life, highlighting that their life is lived within the context of a relationship (Nolan et al. 2006), with the complex dependency and interdependency that results. The study of families in dementia care is an important and emerging area, to which we will return. However, first we will briefly outline the main elements of CCI.

Co-Constructed Inquiry: an overview

Our aim in developing CCI was to answer the challenge set by Charmaz (2000: 510) for a revisionist approach to grounded theory that covered the 'mutual creation of knowledge by the viewer and viewed {that} aims towards interpretive understanding of subject's meaning'.

In her extensive writings in the field of chronic illness (Charmaz 1990, 1991, 1995, 2000), Charmaz (2000) argued that the traditional approach to generating grounded theory using constant comparison and theoretical sampling (Glaser and Strauss 1967; Glaser 1978) took an objectivist standpoint that limited the contribution of the participant to confirming/disproving the researcher's derived theory/theoretical codes. Accordingly, Charmaz (2000) questioned the 'fit and work' (Glaser and Strauss 1967) and generalizability of all (previously) reported objectivist grounded theory models. She argued that the role of the researcher in grounded theory is not to bring objectivity to the theoretical process, but, instead, to forge personal relationships enabling 'the viewer and the viewed' to shape meanings in their encounter allowing for the mutual creation of knowledge. Consequently, reality arises from interactive processes and their 'temporal, cultural and structural contexts' (Charmaz 2000: 524), a position that questioned the philosophical foundations of traditional grounded theory research.

Instead, Charmaz (2000) applied the principles of constructivism (namely, stakeholder involvement, partnership working, relationship formation, biography and narrative work) to the mid-range theory-building properties of grounded theory (Glaser and Strauss 1967; Glaser 1978) the result being 'constructivist grounded theory'. Whilst strongly contested by Glaser (2002), constructivist grounded theory brings a co-researcher model to the practice of grounded theory research, building, over time, shared perspectives and in-depth testing of subjective meanings and interpretations. Simply put, constructivist grounded theory concerns how participant(s) construct the realities of their lives using their symbols and language, with the role of the (co)-researcher being to help identify, construct and agree shared meaning in the substantive area of enquiry.

Our interpretation of Charmaz's (2000) position holds that constructivist grounded theory is about generating evidence from a biographical perspective, whereby the 'real expert' is not the researcher with his/her knowledge and skills, but the person living with the condition under exploration. Successful constructivist grounded theory requires a set of biographical and relationship-centred keys that help to unlock and document this experience in a facilitative and partnership-orientated way. Accordingly, constant comparative analysis, which is so important in traditional grounded theory study (Glaser and Strauss 1967; Glaser 1978), becomes subordinate to the individual participant's meanings and how this narrative is embedded – and constructed – within their own life-course. Charmaz (2000: 524) described this shared journey as a search for 'conditional statements' that do not generate the 'generalizable truths' comprising traditional grounded theory, but rather 'generic concepts' that may (or may not) be applicable to other – arguably similar – substantive fields.

Whilst we broadly agree with Charmaz (2000, 2006), she neither spelt out how to conduct a constructivist grounded theory study nor how to mutually create knowledge, leaving a significant vacuum limiting empirical application; an observation recently reached by Mills et al. (2006). Co-Constructed Inquiry is intended as a way forward, and its theoretical underpinnings are a blend of the:

- values of Glaser's (1978) approach to generating grounded theory
- principles of constructivist grounded theory (Charmaz 2000)
- longitudinal application (and exchange) of autobiographical narrative (Gubrium 1993; Roberts 2002; Keady et al. in press)
- engagement of practitioner-research methods (Reed and Proctor 1995).

By working in partnership with people with dementia and all the authors named at the head of this chapter, we also developed and tested 'guided auto-biography' (Keady et al. in press) as a method of producing a 'life-story script' in order to gain in-depth biographical knowledge so that meanings and perceptions of living with a long-term condition are reflective of a person's active life-course.

Co-Constructed Inquiry is also embedded within a practitioner-research approach (Reed and Proctor 1995), primarily to keep the evolving methodology consistent with the lives of people living with long-term conditions, acknowledging that this journey is likely to evoke a variety of emotional responses, including upset and depression. People living with a long-term condition (and their family, however constructed) have a 'right' to experience emotional and psychological 'lows', and an adequate cooperative method of enquiry has to be responsive to such emotions, however prolonged their duration. Moreover, adopting a practitioner-research approach (Reed and Proctor 1995) helped to: legitimize enduring 'helping' relationships in long-term conditions; provided the opportunity for co-constructing the life-story script and personal theory; built on the theoretical sensitivity of practitioners (Glaser 1978); and provided the context for conditional statements/generic concepts (Charmaz 2000) to emerge and be tested.

Co-Constructed Inquiry embraces precepts identified by Charmaz (2000) focused on a series of embedded values (see Table 5.1) that also provide criteria to underpin the research process. These criteria are applied to each of the three acts of CCI, namely:

- Building the Set
- Performing the Production
- Bringing down the Curtain.

The language and analytical framework of CCI was developed collaboratively with people living with long-term conditions ensuring that the process of

Table 5.1 CCI: embedded values

Values	CCI denotation
Relationship	Requires prolonged and sustained engagement
Trust	Requires the creation of a shared and mutually respectful relationship
Self-awareness	Based on biographical work focused on past-present narratives
Neutrality	To find a safe place to engage in CCI for both/all actors, making opportunities available for joint working
Equity	Equal access to research props for both/all actors in order to facilitate co-construction
Ethical safeguards	Practitioner-researcher demonstrates a sensitivity towards being with vulnerable groups
Creativity	Ability to conceptualize lived experience, be open and reflexive to change
Supervision	Preparation, support, mentoring and 'directing' of all actors

co-construction is meaningful and relevant. Consequently, CCI uses theatrical and dramaturgical metaphors to illustrate its features and theory-building properties. Hence, in Performing the Production and the co-construction of the personal theory, the life-story script is interrogated for 'centre-stage' storylines and their components using a 'what, how, when' framework, with the results placed on a storyboard ready for additional interrogation. In CCI, the contents of the storyboard become the visual prompts for the mutual creation and abstraction of personal theory, providing transparent theory-building process.

We elaborate upon these processes actively involving MQ and PQ, after describing the three acts of CCI.

Act 1: Building the Set

The first act in generating a CCI involves 'Building the Set', a 'hands-on' 'directing' phase where the foundations of a CCI are laid within the local setting and available resources. To date, this initial 'directing' task has done done by JK and SW who assembled and built the set by, for example:

- negotiating the theatre of study and research script with stakeholders
- securing study funding
- negotiating with the clinical area over specialist practitioner release (members of the clinical area become part of the supporting cast, especially the direct clinical manager(s) of the specialist practitioner)
- seeking ethical permission to conduct the study
- gaining and securing administrative support to facilitate the work of co-researchers

- casting the actors to perform the CCI – initially focusing on the specialist practitioner(s) – and then casting (rather than sampling) people living with the long-term condition
- being available to provide ongoing supervision/direction to the actors
- leading an educational programme for all recruited actors so that their part in the production is understood.

What is vital in auditioning the cast is securing an understanding about what is required and establishing that the person living with the long-term condition especially, has an aptitude towards reflexivity and creativity in the presentation of their condition, and fully accepts their diagnosis at the time of their casting. Whilst coping and adjustment may fluctuate over the period of their involvement in the CCI (hence the, specialist, practitioner-research approach described previously), the casting involves both the practitioner and potential participants asking:

- Is this for me?
- Am I comfortable with opening up my life?
- What am I hoping to achieve by taking part?
- Do I think creatively and imaginatively?

The participative nature of CCI mandates an educational programme for all involved and agreement about the embedded values underpinning the work (see Table 5.1). This establishes expectations and agreements about how to 'run' the performance, with the directors providing the necessary 'props' to facilitate co-construction, for example, ensuring the availability of digital voice recorder, tapes, ideas books and so on.

Act 2: Performing the Production

This second act is, in essence, the theory-building process of CCI and is longitudinal in design. Constructive relationships and searching for 'conditional statements' (Charmaz 2000) from individual biography are core conditions, as is a language and actions that are understandable to people with long-term conditions (and practitioners) who may have limited knowledge of the research act.

Performing the Production involves three discrete but interrelated sequential parts, the first two (definitely) involving the person with the long-term condition and the practitioner-researcher in the production of a:

- life-story script
- personal theory
- collective theory.

We will now develop each of these elements.

Life-story script

Engaging people with long-term conditions, such as MQ (and her husband PQ) in generating a personal theory requires the production of a life-story script, comprising a combination of 'guided autobiography' (Keady et al. in press) and Gubrium's (1993) life-story interview (see Table 5.2) particularly question 8, 'chaptering your life') which provide the methodological framework for script production.

Integral to CCI is that stories are exchanged between actors to identify points of connection and create the conditions for trust, awareness and sharing to emerge, as illustrated in Figure 5.1.

Here, MQ chaptered her life around the following seven headings: an introduction to my life; childhood; working life; raising a family; retirement; my illness; and moving on. We will return to these headings later, but they took 16 months to generate (January 2004–May 2005). However, MQ also interviewed JH-R using the same life-story schedule and JH-R chaptered his life story around four headings: childhood; working life; personal life; and present day. As JH-R reported at the time of this exchange:

> The initial fear of losing control soon passes and as the interview develops the experience can become quite enjoyable, therapeutic

Table 5.2 The life-story interview

Topics to cover:

Life in general

1 Everyone has a life story. Tell me about your life in about 20 minutes or so if you can. Begin wherever you like and include whatever you wish.
2 What were the most important turning points in your life?
3 Tell me about the happiest moments in your life.
4 What about the saddest points.
5 Who have been the most important people in your life?
6 Who are you closest to now?
7 What does your life look like from where you are at now?
8 If you had the opportunity to write the story of your life, what would the chapters be about? (Probe about the last chapter.)

Self
How would you describe yourself when you were younger?
How would you describe yourself now?
Have you changed much over the years? How?
What is your philosophy of life? Overall, what is the meaning of life to you?

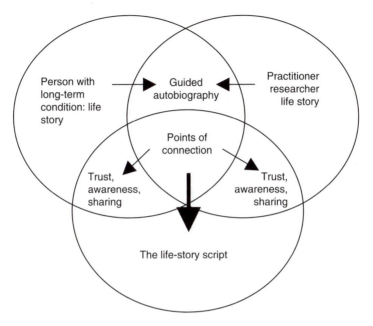

Figure 5.1 Generating a life-story script.

even . . . nurses are used to asking the questions and listening to people. To have someone who is interested in you and prepared to listen to your story can be a rewarding experience.

Once the chapter headings have been agreed, 'fleshing out' occurs based on relational values with space for 'improvising', by adding to, or reinterpreting the life-story script throughout its production. This continues until the person with the long-term condition is satisfied with the completeness of their script and that it is ready for being 'signed off', an act that signals the start of the production of personal theory within a CCI design.

Personal theory

The co-construction of personal theory from the 'signed off' life-story script follows the following sequence:

- Read through the chapters on the life-story script and agree meanings.
- Search for the 'centre-stage' storylines relating to the theatre of study, by jointly plotting words, phrases, life maps and diagrams that highlight important explanatory lines.

- Place these centre-stage storylines and their supporting words and properties on a storyboard, ensuring that the storyboard is open to continual negotiation and entry (improvising).
- Order and rank entries on the storyboard, by applying a 'what, how, when' framework, that is *what* is the centre-stage storyline(s), *how* is this storyline(s) supported by other entries and *when* is the centre-stage storyline exhausted. Effectively the storyboard is the coding frame allowing for theoretical abstraction and linkage of key concepts.
- Link the centre-stage storylines together through a plot capturing the main ideas and representation of experience.
- Finalize and agree that the personal theory is an accurate and true representation/integration of the person's experience of the theatre of study.

The production of a personal theory constitutes the first exit point from CCI. To date, we have found this can take anything up to two years to complete, with opportunities for (such as in the production of this chapter, for instance) additional dissemination and personal theory refinement. Actors may also take part in the final part of theory production, namely, the generation of a 'collective theory'.

Collective theory

The final part of 'Performing the Production' involves the generation of a collective theory capturing theoretical stories across a number of cases in the same theatre of study. This collective theory can be generated together with the actors in the study, or by the initial directors in liaison with the practitioner-(co)researcher and then 'fed back' to the original actors for agreement.

Act 3: Bringing down the Curtain

The final act of a CCI represents a closure of the (co)research encounter and the continuation (where necessary) of practitioner involvement in the life of the person living with the long-term condition, and their family. Bringing down the Curtain also involves dissemination of personal theory, although reflecting embedded values of CCI this is conducted in partnership with the actors; as the personal theory is a shared and reciprocal production, and is not the property of the practitioner-(co)researcher, or the directors of the study.

Applying the principles

Our primary aims were twofold. First, to explore transitions through the early diagnosis of dementia and further understand a person's ways of coping and adapting to their condition and life experiences – this constituted the 'theatre of study' and the 'research script'. Second, to document change over time thereby developing and testing the theoretical framework for a constructivist grounded theory (Charmaz 2000) – an act that became CCI. Using a practitioner-research approach (Reed and Procter 1995), data collection was integrated into routine home visits by the specialist memory clinic nurse (JH-R) with the person with early dementia and their close family member, as appropriate.

Commencing in November 2003, six people with an early diagnosis of dementia (and five of their family members) were recruited into the study; one of the study participants lived alone. Participants had received an early diagnosis of dementia through the Conwy and Denbighshire memory clinic and agreed to home visits by JH-R. Recruitment into the study was invited at the 'monitoring phase' of the memory clinic, that is, at the three-month follow-up visit for those people with dementia that the responsible medical officer assessed as being 'well adjusted' to the diagnosis and able to give informed consent. Informed consent was further assessed by exploring the person's:

- awareness of the procedure they had been through
- adjustment and level of acceptance of their memory loss
- level of competence and ability to give informed consent to a procedure
- retained verbal fluency and level of concentration.

Contact with the five families and one person with dementia was a minimum of one visit per month by JH-R, with the biographical data (later termed a life-story script) gathered through a 'chaptered' life-story interview (Gubrium 1993). Each interview was tape-recorded and transcribed (with consent) and returned to the person with dementia for verification and assimilated into a life-story script. Interviews to develop the life-story script ranged between one and two hours, with an average visit of 1 hour 30 minutes. For the data-set as a whole, there have been 85 practitioner-research contacts, 45 of those facilitating documented research contact. Research contacts relating solely to MQ and PQ are displayed in Table 5.3, and this information also includes the results of the Mini-mental State Examination (MMSE) (Folstein et al. 1975) and the Geriatric Depression Scale (GDS).

To aid understanding of the right-hand columns in Table 5.3, the MMSE (Folstein et al. 1975) comprises a series of questions each scoring one point if

Table 5.3 MQ and PQ: practitioner-research contacts over study duration

Visit number	Date of interview	Activity	MMSE score (MQ)	GDS score (MQ)
1	10/10/03	Semi-structured interview with MQ and PQ – Introductory visit	24	7
2	19/01/04	Second semi-structured interview building on key points of first interview with MQ	30	
3	29/04/04	Life history with MQ and PQ		
4	24/05/04	Life history with MQ – using Gubrium's (1993) interview schedule		
5	30/06/04	Life history with PQ (told my *personal* story)		
6	18/08/04	Development of chapter 1 – an introduction to my life	28	2
7	24/09/04	Development of chapter 2 – childhood (MQ & PQ)		
8	12/11/04	Development of chapter 3 – working life		
9	2/12/04	Development of chapter 4 – raising my family		
10	21/01/05	Development of chapter 5 – retirement		
11	25/02/05	Development of chapter 6 – my illness	25	0
12	22/04/05	Development of chapter 7 – moving on		
13	6/05/05	Signed off life-story script (MQ and PQ)		
14	10/06/05	Exploration and discussion of first Personal Theory Diagram – Draft Version 1 (MQ and PQ)		
15	08/07/05	Visit became Clinical Visit (MQ and PQ)		
16	22/08/05	Exploration and discussion on Personal Theory Diagram – Draft Version 2 (MQ and PQ)		3
17	3/10/05	Exploration and discussion on Personal Theory Diagram – Draft Version 3 (MQ and PQ)		
18	07/11/05	Clinical Visit (MQ and PQ)		
19	28/11/05	Discussion – Version 3 – MQ's Personal Theory diagram	23	3

20	29/03/06	Follow on visit		
21	08/06/06	Final Visit: Personal Theory agreed and 'signed off'		
Score average			25	3

Note: MQ diagnosed with Alzheimer's disease January 2003; Date of birth: 2 April 1938.

answered correctly. The questions measure the person's levels of orientation, memory, attention and calculation, language skills and writing and drawing abilities. A maximum score of 30 points is possible. Whilst the screening and diagnostic properties of the MMSE are open to question (White et al. 2002), people with Alzheimer's disease generally score 26 points or less (Alzheimer's Society 2002). At the commencement of the study, Mo's MMSE score was 24 and at the end she was scoring 23, with an average of 25 for the duration of the study. This highlights MQ's 'high' level of performance and retained abilities over the time of her participation. In contrast, the GDS is designed to measure depression in older people (Yesavage et al. 1983). In this study the '15-item' version was deployed (Shiekh and Yesavage 1986). Each of the 15 questions has a 'yes/no' response, with the scoring dependent upon the answer given. The 15-item version has cut-off score of 6/7; above this score suggests the presence of a depressive illness. As can be seen, at the start of the study MQ's GDS score was 7 and at the end her score was 3 with an average score of 3 for the duration of the study.

The method of process consent was adopted at each clinical/research contact to ensure willingness to participate and understanding of the aims of the project (Dewing 2002). JH-R also kept detailed theoretical memos during each encounter and received regular supervision on both his clinical contact and ongoing data analysis by both JK and SW. Permission to conduct the research study was provided by the appropriate local research ethics committee in North Wales.

We will now provide brief extracts from parts of MQ's life-story script, the extracts are in italics and sometimes segregated by dotted lines in order to denote their different placement in text under the same chapter heading.

MQ: My life-story script

Chapter 1: An introduction to my life

I was born and raised in Liverpool; I was the youngest of seven children, two boys and five girls. It was a very close-knit family and I had a happy childhood. When I was born I had paralysis of my arm and I spent a lot of time in hospital. There were a lot of things I couldn't do such as playing out and playing ball games. When I was ten I went to Myrtle Street Hospital and had a big operation on my arm. I was in hospital for quite a long time, lying on my back with my arm strapped up. I had a happy upbringing, my dad was lovely and my mother was the ruler of the house. My Dad was a docker and a carter before that. He was a nice man, a gentleman.

Chapter 2: Childhood

At five years of age I went to school at St Alexander, a Catholic school, I met Pat there. I stayed there until I left school at the age of fifteen years. I don't remember my brother because he was killed in the Second World War and is buried in Crete, but I got on well with my sisters. My eldest sister took me everywhere; she didn't get married till late on in life so everyone used to think I was hers. She used to take me into Liverpool and we'd go to those Fullers cafes and have tea and cakes and different things, and to the pictures – she taught me a lot really.

Chapter 3: Working life

When I was 15 I went to work in a tobacco factory, my sisters worked there so it was just a follow on. I could have gone to work in an office but my Mum said 'no'. I went to a Catholic school and the Sister who was in charge, Sister Theresa, used to pick certain girls out and we used to learn typing, a bit of office work and that, and I had a job in an office but Mum wouldn't let me go, she said 'Oh no, you're no better than your other sisters'. She was a lovely Mum but very strict about certain things. I worked there for years and years, until we had our first son, I worked until I was about six months pregnant.

I worked in Jacob's, the biscuit factory for a while, just part time, and then I worked in the kitchens in the Masonic for quite a few years. We then moved to North Wales and I worked on the school meals for Clwyd County Council. I worked in a secondary school in Rhyl.

Chapter 4: Raising a family

I got married to Pat in 1958 and we have five children, the biggest surprise was when we had the twins. I've got seven grandchildren. Dave is our oldest child, he is an electrical engineer for a local electricity company. After Dave we had the twins, Debbie and Mike. Mike joined the army, Debbie is a nurse. Two-and-a-half years later after the twins we had another daughter, Gill. She trained to be a printer and then started working in the retail trade where she has enjoyed considerable success. Steve's the youngest; he got his

degree in chemistry. He goes all over the world advising companies on differ-
ent techniques and things but then they wanted him to take over responsibil-
ity for a laboratory in Germany, which was supposed to be for three years,
but he's just started his fourth year now.

I enjoyed bringing up my children, some people say it's hard work but I
enjoyed them, I've always liked children.

Chapter 5: My illness

I was diagnosed with Alzheimer's disease in January 2003; I was 65 years
of age. I first became aware something was wrong when my husband made
arrangements to do things, he would tell me, but I would deny any knowledge
of the arrangements, even though it was written on the calendar. I would say
'Why didn't you tell me sooner?' We had no idea this was the start of the
illness, not at this time – we had a series of disagreements – things were said
that should not have been said. This lasted about two to three years. It then
became more frequent. We had known each other since we were children.
We were never like this. At first I thought it was my age. Then my husband
decided to speak to my GP [general practitioner]. He began to think it was
Alzheimer's disease. We were beginning to associate the symptoms with my
sisters who have Alzheimer's disease.

Initially, I went to the surgery by myself. I forgot to tell my GP about
my problems. In the end my husband insisted on coming with me. From
then on things moved forward quickly. We saw the CPN, who arranged an
appointment with the specialist.

My earliest awareness of the condition started with me feeling terrible, I
didn't like my husband going out without me. I blew up. I was ashamed of
my behaviour. I could of hurt him. I was never like that. I loved my children
and grandchildren – they used to ask me to babysit – I just couldn't do it any
more. I was really nasty with them. I felt trapped in the house. You feel it
building up in your stomach. Your mouth goes dry. It's an awful feeling, you
feel like exploding.

I was frightened of being alone and something happening to me. I was also
afraid of something happening to my husband. Who would look after me if
he became ill?

Chapter 6: Moving on

I enjoy my life. I don't sit and think of the future much. Pat's marvellous with me and I very much appreciate all the help we get from the ACE club. I don't worry about the future at all I just take each day as it comes and I enjoy my life. I sleep a lot!

I'm still very interested in clothes, things like that, shopping, and Pat encourages me to go round the shops. And I still like to do my housework, Pat helps me a lot but I still like to do the dishes and tidy around.

If I knew someone who had just been diagnosed I'd tell them to be open about it and don't hide away. You're still your normal self, you're still a person and you can still do things. I think some people delve too much into the future but I just take it one day at a time. I'm not trying to avoid the issue but I think just live today and be happy, it's no good worrying about the future.

My personal theory

In developing MQ's personal theory, the first part of the process was to search for and agree the 'centre-stage' storylines and plot these on a storyboard. This was done by MQ, PQ and JH-R over a one-year period (6 June 2005–8 June 2006 – see Table 5.3). From these entries, it became apparent that 'control' and 'balance' were important and meaningful words and experiences for MQ and PQ as they continued to adapt and adjust to the onset of MQ's Alzheimer's disease. For MQ especially, a loss of control and the subsequent impact that this had on the balance of her life were important features: 'the most important' as she put it. As MQ stated, the fact that she had brought up five children and continued to work was testimony to the love and structure that she had previously integrated into her life. A loss of balance in MQ's life as a result of the (undiagnosed) onset of Alzheimer's disease was, initially, met with an overriding sense of worry and fear.

By carefully plotting and linking these words and phrases using the 'what, how, when' framework, a picture began to emerge that MQ, PQ and JH-R forged into a diagram that explained MQ's experience of living with Alzheimer's disease. After a number of refinements, the final (as at June 2006) personal theory emerged and this is shown in Figure 5.2.

MQ's personal theory plots, in her words, the experience of living with Alzheimer's disease. The early (undiagnosed) signs of dementia are captured in

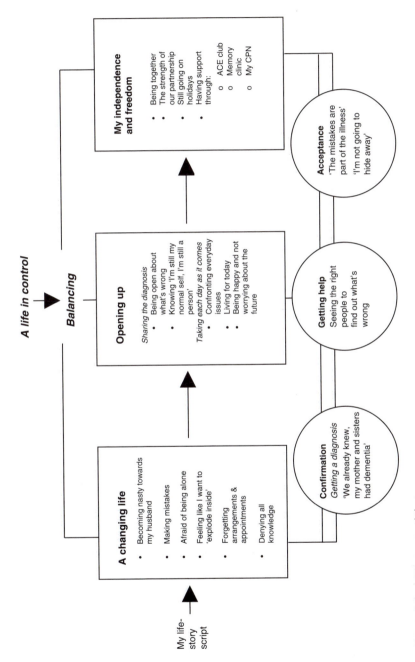

Figure 5.2 MQ's personal theory.

the box headed 'A changing life', which represented a shift in the dynamics of MQ's and PQ's relationship (as the brief extract under MQ's chapter 4 'Raising a family' reveals) and the emotional reaction of MQ to this initial awareness was to lose balance in her life, it was in danger of becoming 'out of control' until confirmation of the diagnosis was made. The movement 'back into control' was drawn from MQ's own family history and knowledge that her sisters and mother had been diagnosed early in life with Alzheimer's disease. Whilst traumatic, familial exposure to Alzheimer's disease and PQ's and the GP's knowledge of such events helped to reaffirm relationships between MQ and PQ and provide new understandings.

The other boxes in Figure 5.2 are self-explanatory, but the meaning of the ACE club in the box headed 'My independence and freedom' needs explanation. The ACE club is a day club for younger people with dementia that meet regularly for social outings and are based in Rhyl, North Wales – the club enables people with dementia to live life to the full by promoting positive life choices (for a review of the philosophy of the ACE club see, Davies-Quarrell 2005).

For MQ it is significant that the shape of the personal theory looks like a motor vehicle as it symbolizes her continual desire to 'move on' (as reflected in the title of her current chapter in her life-story script). The 'engine' for momentum is provided through her (ongoing) life-story script and the importance of confirmation (of the diagnosis), getting help (to live with the condition) and acceptance of the mistakes that reflect life with Alzheimer's disease and the need to confront and overcome them. This movement is diagrammed by the three circular 'wheels' at the foot of the personal theory which provide the ongoing propulsion to MQ and PQ to live their life 'day by day'.

Discussion

Long-term conditions cannot be understood as a series of changes in functional status but, instead, need to be seen in the context of each person's 'concerns and commitments', therefore posing the question 'but how do clinicians ascertain the touchstones of meaning for clients within chronic illness?' (Ironside et al. 2003: 180). As the development of CCI demonstrates, we would suggest that it is through prolonged and sustained engagement with a narrative account of people's lives that the practitioner will be best able to understand the 'touchstones of meaning' for people with dementia and their families. Furthermore, a narrative process and research relationship needs to be underpinned by shared values and language (Zgola 1999) if the ideals of a constructivist grounded theory are to be met (Charmaz 2000). In MQ's personal theory the box headings (A changing life; Opening up; My independence and freedom) and her transcending needs for 'a life in control' and a sense of 'balance' (see Figure 5.2) provide a meaningful discourse from which to plan supportive interventions. Currently this centres on maintaining MQ's relationship with her husband ('being together', as stated in the third box) and holding on to her independence and freedom for as long as is possible. Importantly, the life-story script constitutes a 'living document' as MQ continues on her journey through Alzheimer's disease in partnership with those close to her, and others yet to enter her life.

As noted by McAdams and Janis (2004), a narrative configures an individual's understanding of self and the construction of identity has a degree of purpose and unity. The weaving of the 'synchronic' and 'diachronic' elements of identity into a temporal dimension presents a construction of self that can be understood separately as occurring in the past, but also synthesized into the present into a temporally organized whole (McAdams and Janis 2004). As illustrated by MQ and PQ this provides a powerful platform for understanding the complexity and relatedness of responses to Alzheimer's disease and how adjustment is constructed. In the MQ's case, making mistakes and balancing her formative experiences capture her early 'illness' (MQ's description), placing affective responses within a relational context. Both making mistakes and balancing occur primarily in relationship with others, mapping out the broader canvas of the early experience of Alzheimer's disease. It would be interesting to see if these conditional statements/generic concepts have meaning to others living through a similar situation and form dimensions of a collective theory in CCI.

As Gubrium and Holstein (1997) argue, human beings 'theorize as we talk'; however, the use of an approach such as CCI with people with dementia may present particular challenges. Whilst we acknowledged issues regarding cognitive impairment and consent in CCI, we also affirmed the importance of people's active involvement as co-researchers. The adoption of process consent (Dewing 2002) required to 'getting to know the person' in order to re-establish consent at each clinical visit – and as Table 5.3 illustrated, two of the visits were conducted as practice visits when it was clear that MQ required clinical help, not the demands of a research relationship. This highlights the importance of relationship-building that is embedded in constructivist approaches (Charmaz 2000). Indeed, Whitlatch et al. (2005) argue that it is possible to maintain the involvement of people, even with significant cognitive impairment. This is a study that remains to be conducted and it is important to note that the life-story script does not need to be compiled in words alone – communication is deeper and more dynamic than this (Killick and Allan 2001) – and it is up to the research community in partnership with stakeholder groups to conjure imaginative, informative and inclusive research designs.

Conclusion

To date the actions and language of CCI have proven to be understandable to participants, helping to make accessible some of the potentially complex analytical and coding procedures used in traditional qualitative research methods. Whilst our use of theatrical and dramaturgical metaphors is by no means unique (see, for example, Bowers 1988; Mienczakowski 1995; McCall 2000; Schneider 2005), we have found that people with dementia and their families (and other participants living with other long-term conditions) intuitively grasp and apply their meaning when engaging in co-construction and the mutual generation of knowledge. Notwithstanding the refinements that still need to be made, we hope that our experience in developing CCI is seen as a positive step along the road to genuinely participative knowledge-making.

Acknowledgements

This research was funded by a grant from the North Wales Research Committee.

All participants in the CCI programme.

6 Innovative approaches to living with dementia: an Australian case study

Tina Koch, Jonathan Crichton

Introduction

This chapter describes an ongoing interdisciplinary research study[1] with community dwelling people living with dementia. The study took as its starting point Meininger's (2005) work, which provides a basis for using a life-story approach to advance the quality of care. Meininger was motivated towards narrative through his work as a chaplain in institutions and group homes for people with intellectual disabilities, where one of his roles was to bring together an account of a person's life for the funeral service. He asked family and friends to talk with him about aspects of that person's life. It was his responsibility to merge stories and to create a eulogy. The eulogy, he observed, gave those attending new insights into the dead person's life and likes hitherto unknown. 'They often told me that listening to the story changed their view of the person who had died' (Meininger 2005: 106). In the effort to compensate for the diminished authorship of many institutionalized people, Meininger began to gather stories with and from those surrounding the person whilst still living. His argument is not to wait for death before revealing stories about a person's life.

Building on Meininger's insights, it is our aim to extend storytelling practices with people living with dementia both to perpetuate self-identity, and as a mode of participatory research. Therefore, we are developing a research framework within which to investigate and enhance the nexus between the identities of community dwelling people living with dementia, their social networks, and their communication with others.

Such biographical approaches, utilizing photos, personal documents and memories, have been used with people with dementia in nursing homes (Clarke et al. 2003), but have not yet been adopted with people residing in the community and their support networks. In our current study, we generate stories with community-dwelling people living with dementia, and their significant others, including health care providers. Working with participants, we merge their stories into one narrative. The narrative, a composite of stories generated, is written so that it can accompany the person through life and into particular health or social care settings. This narrative can assist in the presentation of self-identity, and help to personalize care and sensitize those involved towards new understandings in future interactions and advance planning.

One important aim is to address the problem that current diagnosis and treatment of dementia neglects the changing identities of the person, and their particular biographical, historical and relational contexts. Whilst some aspects of identity like age, gender or ethnicity are 'frozen', others reflecting personal qualities are fluid, being 'constructed' during interactions. Hence, identity is a dynamic and evolving process from ongoing interactions between the individual and more or less negotiable aspects of her social environment. This matters because those living with dementia are, by virtue of their condition, often unable to maintain a coherent account of their own identities, which become progressively dependent on how others perceive and interact with them. Identity as an interactional accomplishment highlights the narrative or discursive properties of communication with people with dementia, and identifies several 'external' influences on the preservation of self or personhood (Nussbaum 1991; Kitwood and Bredin 1992; Mills and Coleman 1994; Ramanathan-Abbott 1994; Golander and Raz 1996). Such research looks beyond the internal (that is, neuropathological and neuropsychological) focus and addresses the equally important role of external, or social psychological, factors in maintaining personhood (Kitwood 1990). It emphasizes how interpersonal interactions significantly impact on the person with dementia's sense of well-being, as self-identity is constituted by and through social interaction (Mead 1934; Hadden and Lester 1978; Coupland et al. 1993; Shotter 1993).

Longitudinal research is required to explore storytelling approaches more fully, both to resolve methodological issues, and to explore how these approaches can be introduced into practice, and integrated into the culture and management of care. Here we explore the methodological issues storytelling raises, particularly how to conceptualize research and represent the changing identity of those living with dementia. Accordingly, we have trialled a research framework where the life of a person with dementia has been '(re)storied' into a narrative. Family and caregivers, both formal and informal, may use this narrative to 'see the person' (Clarke et al. 2003). It is intended that the narrative, as findings, can accompany the person and later, as dementia advances, through particular care settings and/or the health care system. The person's narrative, as a document, provides a resource as the person's memory is challenged and decision-making capacity is reduced.

Literature review: dementia and identity

As biomedical research continues to seek a cure for dementia, psychological perspectives based on personhood and promoting a new paradigm of dementia care have emerged (Kitwood 1997). Kitwood (1997: 8) defines personhood as 'a standing or status that is bestowed upon one human being, by others, in the context of relationships and human being. It implies recognition, respect and trust'. Consequently, personhood in dementia is socially embedded and gaining knowledge of the person's life and experiences of dementia can enhance their quality of life, by maintaining personhood in the face of failing mental powers (Kitwood and Bredin 1992). These authors developed dementia care mapping (DCM) as an attempt to evaluate care from the person's point of view. We embrace the principle that the person's life experience, unique personality, and network of relationships should be valued. However, DCM involves an observational method of personal interactions between the person and their carers, and does not actively involve the person with dementia. Kitwood's approach therefore differs from ours as we actively engage the person with dementia, their significant others and carers in the telling of stories.

The need for research to include people with dementia is becoming well established. Cowdell (2006) reviewed 22 current studies that actively engaged older people with dementia in research 'with' rather than 'on' them. She concluded that researchers had given thought to ensuring that their work was ethical, meaningful and preserved the personhood of individuals.

The literature suggests that how others interact with the person with dementia can have significant impact on the individual's sense of self (Small et al. 1998). The development of positive relationships between the person with dementia and carers is central, and may be achieved through understanding the person's life and identity (Epp 2003). Clare (2003), working with people with early dementia, concluded that awareness and adapting to dementia are closely associated with individual styles of coping. Exploring previous coping styles through listening and analysing stories may further our understandings in this area. Sabat and Harre (1992) found that self-identity remains intact long after the loss of cognitive function, and that the loss of personae can be prevented if the caregiver and others do not position the person with dementia as helpless and confused. For us, this reinforces the need to acknowledge the person living with dementia as a participant, both in their own right and in the research process.

Golander and Raz (1996) recognize that identity is perpetuated, co-constructed and reconstructed through interactions in nursing homes. They give an example of this where a carer labels a 'demented' male resident as a medical doctor, reinforcing this with a small briefcase with papers and a stethoscope. It was claimed that the new 'occupational' identity filled the resident with new life. His behaviour changed completely. He documented cases on the paper provided and 'used the stethoscope to check other residents' (Golander and Raz 1996: 281). Of course a critical case can be made for endowment of positive images, whilst this resident's behaviour may be changed from wandering aimlessly to listening to the breathing of other residents; it can also be viewed as normative control. Nevertheless, it does demonstrate a key aspect of our approach: that identity is dependent on and can continue to be shaped through interaction with others.

Using a self-identity questionnaire with 104 older people with dementia in Washington nursing homes and adult day-care centres, social psychologists Cohen-Mansfield et al. (2006) found that these data could be utilized to shape role identity. The next goal of their research is to investigate the different ways in which knowledge of self-identity could be used to improve care. Although our data generation comprises storytelling with community-dwelling participant groups, as opposed to employing structured questions, the next phase of our work is to explore the way in which the self-identity narrative can be utilized within a person's current and future life. We therefore share Cohen-Mansfield et al.'s interest in exploring how such identity work (Vittoria 1998) can proceed.

A key focus of identity for the person living with dementia is situating dementia within one's own life. In an integrative literature review and meta-analysis of 28 qualitative studies of living with early dementia, Steeman et al. (2006: 723) concluded 'Living with dementia is described from the stage a person discovers the memory impairment, through the stage of being diagnosed with dementia, to that of the person's attempts to integrate impairment into everyday life.' Early on the person uses self-protecting and self-adjusting strategies to deal with threats to security, autonomy and being a meaningful member of society. People with dementia struggle to hold on to their identity; simultaneously they try to adjust to the changes dementia produces. Fitting dementia into one's life is a cyclical and continuous process. The diagnosis may threaten the person's sense of existence, 'resulting in fear of losing the ability to retain their personal identity in the future' (Steeman et al. 2006: 5). Frustration, uncertainty and fear are experienced as memory loss makes integration of strategies into everyday life difficult. Proactive care involves both the individual and the family as active participants so that adjustment to living with dementia can occur collaboratively. Researchers such as ourselves need to acknowledge that we are, as interactants, implicated in this collaborative process of adjustment.

Our theoretical orientation is to self-identity in dementia (Sabat and Harre 1992; Golander and Raz 1996; Kitwood 1997; Mills 1997; Harris and Sterin 1999; Sabat and Collins 1999; Cohen-Mansfield et al. 2000; Pearce et al. 2002; Clare 2003; Holst and Hallberg 2003), and our central thesis is that attention to identity is significant for the well-being and the quality of care of people with dementia (Cohen-Mansfield et al. 2000; Epp 2003; Leeson et al. 2004; Payne and Seymore 2004). Using this perspective, we seek a research framework enabling proactive care through identity work and the support of an 'authored' story to accompany people with dementia in encounters with health care professionals. This approach may reveal the 'person behind the patient' (Clarke et al. 2003); one who can be acknowledged and valued. More importantly, such identity work may support Barnett's (2000) proposed 'rementia' with, he suggests, people with dementia experience learning despite cognitively degenerative neurologic impairment and continuing to make life-affecting decisions when provided with responsive support and services.

Literature review: storytelling

> [S]tories are all we have. It is all we have to fight illness and death. We don't have anything if we don't have stories . . . A story told one way may cure . . . told another way it could injure.
>
> (King 2003)

We view storytelling as a vehicle for human encounter and communication. A story emerges through the pull and push between the person's telling and the world in which the story is told (Garro and Mattingly 2000). When listening to the stories people tell, we acknowledge speaking is not only the narration, but also a medium in which self-identity is created, negotiated, confirmed and shared. Storytelling and claiming and/or reclaiming self-identity is part of narration work (Kleinman 1988; Gergen 1991; Kelly and Field 1996; Nettleton and Watson 1998; Brody 2003), and offers insights on the way in which self-identity shifts. However, in their historical account of the self since Mead (1934), Holstein and Gubrium (2000: 13) caution that:

> The self has fallen on hard times. After decades of attention to self awareness, self improvement and self esteem, an embattled self cascades from all quarters. Some claim that self indulgence is society's downfall, with the narcissistic individual undermining community. At the same time, warning that we must nurture, sustain, and safeguard the self are giving way to a new, playfully dismissive signal that all therapeutic efforts are ultimately futile . . . Still, there are echoes of renewal, even glimpses of a new ending. Increasingly we are hearing that our lives are storied . . . not only is there a story of the self, but it's been said that the self is narratively constructed . . .

Holstein and Gubrium (2000) intimate that renewal is possible, through telling a story, but only if we are prepared to think about the self as a valued social construction that is continually reproduced, moment by moment, through the concerted efforts of individuals in their daily lives. 'The tensions afflicting contemporary experience can be avoided if we can sense the self visible as a project of everyday life' (Holstein and Gubrium 2000: 13), so that a 'self that remains empirically grounded . . . a social construction that we assemble, live out as we take up or resist the varied demands of everyday life' (Holstein and Gubrium 2000: 10). This emphasis contrasts with the notion of personhood advanced by Kitwood (1997: 8) as 'a standing or status that is bestowed upon one human being, by others, in the context of relationships and human being'. We align ourselves with Holstein and Gubrium's (2000) view of the self as an ongoing, *in vivo* project of co-construction, created and sustained through interaction 'between' people.

The study of narrative is interdisciplinary. Storytelling, Reissman (1993: 1) succinctly argues, is 'what we do with our research materials and what inform-ants do with us'. People construct past events and actions in personal stories to claim identities and construct lives:

> How individuals recount their histories, what they emphasis and omit, their stance as protagonists or victims, the relationship the story establishes between teller and audience, all shape what indi-viduals can claim of their own lives. Personal stories are not merely a way of telling someone (or oneself) about one's life; they are the means by which identities may be fashioned.
>
> (Rosenwald and Ochberg 1992: 1)

The story metaphor emphasizes that we create order, construct texts in par-ticular contexts. We ask why a story is told in this way. What is included and excluded in the story is dependent on human agency. Stories are not accounts describing the real world 'out there'; rather they are constructed, creatively authored, rhetorical and replete with assumptions, and interpretive (Reissman 1993: 5).

The notion that the self is not something we 'are' in some reified sense but involves an active ongoing (re)construction of self is appealing, because 're-making' oneself in everyday life is intuitively plausible. Not only are stories products of language, which shapes and permits differing versions to be told, they become crucial to our social interactions, as Bruner (2002: 9) proposes:

> A self is probably the most impressive work of art we ever produce, surely the most intricate. For we create not just one self making story but many of them, the job is to get them all into one identity and to get them lined up over time. For it is not just who and what we are that we want to get straight but who and what we might have

been, given the constraints that memory and culture impose on us, constraints of which we are often unaware.

Further, making the 'self' entices us to 'keep the two manageable together, past and possible, in an endless dialectic, how my life has always been and should rightly remain and how things might have been or might still be' (Bruner 2002: 10). For Bruner there is no 'one' essential self that just sits there ready to be portrayed in words. Rather, we constantly construct and reconstruct our selves depending on our situation, with the guidance of our memories of the past and hopes and fears of the future. It is through narrative that we create and re-create self-identity, that self is a product of our telling. It is fluid.

This notion of a story being malleable, with self-identity taking slightly different shapes based our experiences of living in a social world, is both appealing and empirically credible. If we can envisage a life story as emergent and adaptive, keeping in mind that not everyone wants, or is able, to revise or re-story their life, we may be able to observe the shifts in self-identity. However, if the story continually adapts to new situations, allowing us to make transitions into new stages of our lives, what happens when we cannot make these adaptations within a changing world? If we lack the capacity to render stories about ourselves, what happens to identity? This highlights the situation of the person living with dementia and others in their immediate circle.

What happens to storytelling when the person is diagnosed with dementia? In dementia's early stages a person may want to story their life, and talk about self-identity, if only to leave a record for later. The story may become more viscous as their storytelling capacity is reduced. Increasingly, the person with dementia begins to rely on others to voice, and eventually unilaterally to construct, not only their past and present life story but also their future wishes and desires. These prospective chapters of their story are especially salient: a record of wishes and desires may assist with advanced planning, preparing for a time when a person's decision-making capacity becomes seriously compromised.

Laura's narrative: one case study

Here we draw on one case study, the story of Laura. The boundaries for the case are interviews with (1) Laura, a community-dwelling person with a medical diagnosis of Alzheimer's disease (second stage), (2) her social/institutional environment, and (3) her social network. Her social network included the person herself and all those in regular contact with her: her husband, daughter, son, local medical practitioner, respite carer and hairdresser. The study was guided by the following interrelated questions:

- What social network develops around the person with dementia and how does this evolve?
- How is the identity of the person with dementia perceived by the person herself and by other participants in her social network?
- How do these perceptions shape, and how are they shaped by, language and communication within interactions in the network?

Following approval from the university's Ethics Committee, a newsletter was distributed in the workplace and university explaining the study and asking for volunteers. We were approached by Ellen, whose mother, Laura, lives with dementia, who felt the study would be mutually interesting and useful. Ellen asked her mother, several members of her family, friends and the GP, and when they agreed to participate, and had consented both verbally and in writing, we commenced with storytelling. In order to characterize and track the evolution of the social network, each network participant was interviewed about the person's past, present and future interactions and identities. Observations of the settings in which the person interacts with others in their social network constitute the second data source. Both authors attended the interviews and reflections about each interview were shared and documented immediately afterwards. Reflexive researcher journal accounts comprise the third data-set. Storytelling took place over six months. Stories were transcribed verbatim, and analysed using a storyline protocol established for Participatory Action Research (Koch and Kralik 2006).

The narrative

The narrative is a composite of seven stories. Its size (6500 words) prevents sharing the full narrative here. It has been woven together from seven interviews with Laura, Ron (her husband and full-time carer), Ellen (her daughter), James (her son), Myrtle (a friend and occasional respite home 'sitter'), Marjorie (her hairdresser), and her GP. The authors were the interviewers. In the first meeting Laura, Ron, Tina and Jonathan (researchers and authors) sat around the dining-room table in her home in Henley Beach, a seaside suburb in Adelaide. She was comfortable in her chair and smiling. In talking with us she often looked at Ron, seeking help to find answers. She appeared frustrated by her loss of memory, as is shown in her one-line sentence response to our questions about her life.

- Oh yes, I forget that story, what was that? My mind's not too good now.
- Can't remember on the spur of the moment.
- Oh yes. See . . . I forget.

- I don't remember anything about that.
- I'm 80 . . . What am I? 84?
- I forget. I've hit 84 now I don't remember too much.
- I don't remember that.
- No, I can't remember.

When we met we did not know the best way to engage with Laura, which questions to ask to prompt a longer story. So we asked Ron to take the lead. Ron acted as her memory guide, a role in which he was clearly comfortable; he prompted her with care and understanding. It would be hard to imagine how a life can be storied without those caring prompts. At an emotional level, she seemed to understand the significance of their shared memories, commenting that 'we laughed about it, didn't we'.

When given the last word, Laura said 'I'd like to stay here, I wouldn't want to go from here.' It was clear that what matters is that Laura can stay at home with Ron; their lives are intertwined. And for Ron, her husband, the last words were 'Well I've made up my mind that I'd like to stay here as long as I possibly can and look after Laura.' Notwithstanding this attachment to each other and to their home, the impact on the family of 'sudden' dementia can be devastating. Marjorie, in talking about Ron, revealed that caring for Laura is 'an enormous responsibility, absolutely huge'. We also gradually came to understand a little more about the contours of Laura's identity as a person who has been 'a very strong woman' and, in subsequent interviews, her son said it was important to share that 'she was always a very caring person'. Those around Laura use past tense to describe her identity but at the same time they emphasize that, despite her memory loss, Laura's responses are consistent with previous behaviour, and her unique coping mechanisms. An example is given by her son, when he said 'How are you today Mum?' and she responds as always, 'Oh, not too bad, struggling along.' As the stories unfold Laura's identity is simultaneously revealed and constructed through our interactions. We come to understand that Laura is 'a very caring person, a very likeable person', and referring to her sense of humour 'she has a funny way'. Her sense of caring and of humour is invariably cast in the present tense: a poignant grammatical marker for the continuing strength of her relations with others and of their current role in maintaining her identity.

Laura has a close circle of family, with whom she gets on extremely well. They have a substantial input in looking after her. Taking his care role very seriously, Ron has worked out a comprehensive routine which includes the way in which Laura can be settled at night to avoid wandering around the house. It is acknowledged by the son that a good routine is paramount to his mother's day-to-day management.

Talking with Laura is central to our study, and learning how to talk with her is also crucial. Building a relationship with someone after dementia has taken hold is possible. As Myrtle says 'what matters is that they are treating her in a way that is respectful of her intelligence, her would-be intelligence'. In the effort to sustain conversation, Myrtle uses long-term memory prompts to enable Laura to come forth about things she liked many years ago. What is known about the person with dementia facilitates 'making' conversation by drawing on shared knowledge of mutual significance. In addition, a sense of humour helps towards restoring relationships and repairing the inevitable miscommunications.

In our effort to summarize the richness of the stories, we conceive them as stories told for, about, and potentially with Laura. We believe that the collective narrative provides 're'-authorship of her life. It gives some shape to her personhood, even if she is not able to articulate it herself. Family and friends may find that the story contributes to the preservation of her identity as her memory fades.

We envisage that this narrative can accompany Laura through the health care system, or into residential care. It will assist those who provide care to acknowledge the person behind the dementia. Most importantly, this story will describe what matters to Laura in her current situation. This narrative describes, and is co-constructed, through her current care environment, the routine that sustains her, and the person network that surrounds her.

Conceiving the narrative

The storytelling approach is premised on careful and respectful listening. It begins with 'Tell me your story'. Stories are sought from the person with dementia, the person's family or close intimates, perhaps carers or friends and members of health care team. Social contexts are important because what they reveal about the identities of the participants; the religious, ethnic, gender and other contexts in which a person lives her life contribute to her own and others' sense of who she is. Describing the context is part of the narrative. Participants are those who surround the person with dementia. In this study we combine these stories into a narrative to be 'used' as an identity document to accompany the person with dementia in everyday life, present and future. The narrative has a life beyond the study to instruct, and to make ready a means for dealing with uncertain outcomes of plans and anticipations.

The meaning of the narrative is itself not fixed: it will evolve, to be read and reread differently in the future, by different readers, with different interests in and understandings of Laura. It is in this sense, as language, that the narrative is a focus of interaction between its authors and readers, part of the ongoing project of co-constructing Laura's identity. Whilst acknowledging the role of individuals in authoring their own identities, there are both theoretical and practical reasons for conceptualizing identity as accomplished through interaction with others. Earlier we argued that the account rendered may become a frozen narrative, however, there is a possibility that identities can shift even when the person with dementia is no longer able to contribute through storytelling. Surr (2006) suggests that self in people with dementia is a 'complex interplay . . . including personal relationships, the social context and opportunities for and abilities to tell stories'. Although Surr's research participants were nursing-home residents, and dementia had advanced, she argued that preservation of the self could be assisted if care staff were aware of the person's social and biographical contexts. Social interactions are primarily conducted in, and constituted by, participants' use of the linguistic options available to them within the language system, what Trappes-Lomax (2004: 146) has termed the 'instrumentalities' of interaction. Moreover, how participants' employ and interpret these linguistic resources in interaction, how they communicate, shapes and is shaped by how the perceived purpose of the interaction, and its relevance to its broader social/institutional context(s), including participants' perceptions of their own and each other's identities and relationship(s) (Candlin 1997; Crichton 2003). For those living with dementia, interactions are distributed across the social and institutional contexts through which the person moves, typically in different locations, for different purposes and involving participants, such as family members, friends and medical and health workers, with different perceptions of, and in different and evolving relations to, the person with dementia and to each other, all of which are expressed in their own distinct language.

In conceptualizing the diversity of interactions and the relationships between them, we draw on the notion of 'social network' developed by Milroy and Gordon (2003) in their research into covariance between patterns of interaction and language change. The value of this construct is that, as opposed to identifying contexts of interaction by reference to particular social/institutional contexts (for example, the family, medical centre or nursing home), social networks are referenced to the lives of particular individuals. In this sense, social networks are not 'socio-centric' but 'ego-centric' (Milroy and Gordon 2003: 119), focusing on how the identities of individuals with dementia develop within their particular social worlds. Using Milroy's (1987) framework, networks may vary depending on whether they are 'dense/loose' and 'open/closed', and whether ties between individuals within the networks are 'strong/weak' and 'multiplex/single'; factors which provide a means of characterizing the range and evolution of networks for people living with dementia.

King's (2003) reminder that 'a story told one way may cure . . . told another way it could injure' is paramount. This is a timely caution that researching with people in storytelling approaches requires, above all, ethical awareness and sensitivity. Disclosures contributing to the person's self-identity will emerge, and not all revelations will be appreciated. Inevitably, contradictory stories about the same person emerge, but we believe that story-tellers are not deliberately attempting to mislead us. Rather, interpretations vary as people develop impressions based on aspects of that person's life with which they are familiar, highlighting the interactive nature of the narrative. As Brody (2003: 110) argues, there are many ways of seeing and telling the story:

> The goal is not to achieve consensus or to 'fix' the problem but rather to heighten awareness of the nature, source, and reasons for moral disagreements that have given rise to conflict, to provide a safe forum for the full hearing of the arguments on all sides of the dilemma and to offer a range of normative perspectives of the dilemma . . . and together to consider the best way of moving forward.

Inevitably, there are parts of the story participants simply do not know, and often the words tell us more about the person giving the story than the person to whom the narrative relates. This problem highlights the fact that stories can attest to different identities, and raises the methodological problem of how to conceptualize, acknowledge and manage the 'ownership' of different stories within the research and in the creation of the narrative. To address this prob-lem, we conceive the narrative as co-constructed at every point through the collaboration of all participants in the study. An iterative analytical process has been created to identify potentially disparate stories, highlight points of agreement and disagreement that emerge and weave together the stories into a narrative for further consultation and discussion. The risk that we face as researchers in failing to address the ownership issue is that it may appear that we have appropriated the voices of participants in the narrative below. This is simultaneously an ethical and methodological matter, in which we risk compromising the authenticity of participants' voices and the credibility of the study.

Knowing what information to gather, how to gather it, and how to inter-pret it are all essential parts of the skill and art of storytelling research. Listen-ing can sharpen our attunement to perspectives as they are constructed; it alerts us to which voices are given authority, which storylines are considered relevant, and which possible resolutions are given consideration. There are storytelling skills that help in our work when reading transcripts. Consider-ations when listening and reading a particular story include asking questions about the storyteller: from what perspective is the story told and what does this perspective leave out? When all stories are gathered it is prudent to ask about the way in which differences between stories can be reconciled, and to examine the narrative for emerging patterns from the accumulated details, repetitions, images and metaphors. How is language deployed here? To what ends? What is unique and what is shared? What is recurrent? What is included and excluded? Precisely because the narrative is meant to accompany the person with dementia into the future, it needs to be written with the aware-ness of audience and this will influence choices of diction, syntax, image and metaphor. Such choices are not incidental; they constitute the story, and therefore the identity of the person for and about whom the story is told. At the same time, if the narrative is not engaging, its audience will disregard it. So it is important to include multiple voices, in the language associated with them, and draw attention to interpersonal relational and emphatic capacities. Most importantly, for the narrative to be 'used' in practice, it needs not only to be engaging but to be accessible for a wide readership.

Our participative world view guiding this storytelling approach means sharing of power through continual invitation of all participants to read the narrative, commenting, revising, concluding and validating it through a col-lective hearing. We call on collaborative enquiry to guide the way in which stories are told or retold, and we constantly consult, change and adapt a narra-tive according to the desires of its owners. Following the participative process, interviews, observations and analysis with feedback cycles continue until a narrative is developed. The next stage is that this narrative will reside with the care plan in the person's home and provide authorship of the person's identity. The written 'life' story is expected to inform care.

Conclusion

Through facilitating storytelling, in collaboration with all people who sur-round Laura, we have developed a narrative. This does not pose or threaten common-sense notions of living with dementia, rather it confirms the ordin-ary. Laura contributed a little to this narrative but we could sense the import-ance to her of her emotionally safe social network. We suggest that the way in which the family and others within the network are able to make sense of Laura's dementia, and continue to shape her identity, is through what we have termed 'curation', a process that we argue is central to the question of what happens to self-identity when someone lives with dementia.

Our interest in the notion of curation emerged through gathering stories with everyone significant in Laura's life. We consistently observed that, when telling their stories, the teller works to render the best possible storied account. Indeed, there appears to be a heavy responsibility attached to storying anoth-er's life. There is a presence of 'care'. This appears to be an ethical imperative. What is driving the stories is not a lifestyle choice, a biomedical history or functional/cognitive appearance, but a network coming together with concern – to 'curate' the self-identity of the person living with dementia. Understand-ing the significance and implications of curation for care provides the interest for our ongoing enquiry. It appears that curating is a social role which arises from an active concern for the other. It combines action, realized primarily in language, with a desire to support the identity of the other, with curation possibly collectively reproduced through interactions in social networks. Ron, for example, appears to play back his wife's self-identity, not just telling her story for the interviewers, but to and for her, a re-rendering and reconfirmation of her identity.

However, self-identity is fragile as it can only be preserved by members of a social network, with curation being linked to a support network. It comes into existence and it is sustained on, by and through the interactions of the people in the network. It is the notion of collective care which we understand to be central to curation. In this process, curation involves telling stories not merely 'about' Laura, but simultaneously 'for' her, and potentially 'with' her when she is co-present. In the latter situation, our study suggests that the selections and interpretations of the teller are cued by and referenced to their understanding of the responses of the person living with dementia, a process which combines telling 'about', 'for' and 'with' in a reproduction and reconfirmation of the self-identity of the person living with dementia.

Based on this case study, we suggest that 'curation' is a necessary condition for the maintenance of the self-identity of people living with dementia. Curation is therefore significant for care because an understanding of the continuing self-identity of any person is necessary for communication with them *as* a person, that is, as an individual with his or her own, coherently connected, past, present and future life. Such communication contributes to the well-being of the person living with dementia and, in turn, of their support network, and is essential for the acknowledgement and promotion of self-identity within person-centred care.

Consistent with this understanding of curation, we focus on the continuing identity of the person living with dementia, and the collective ownership of the emergent narrative are recognized. In eliciting stories we are not focusing exclusively on the person's past at the expense of their present. We include the present and how Laura and significant others understand things now in seeking a coherent picture, which can be carried forward into future care referenced both to the understandings of the support network and to future audiences who may be involved in care. This is our responsibility as researchers who, as participants, are also members of the network and therefore involved in curation. This requires researchers to attend to, and reflexively monitor, the emergent story in the light of their own emergent understanding. At the same time, researchers are implicated in and no less responsible than other network members for actively producing and reproducing the present identity both 'with' and 'for' the person with dementia. It is current and active. It is ethical, it involves care, it involves networks and it involves an inextricable link between interaction, self-perception and perceptions of others.

Meanwhile, we recognize that the identity of the person with dementia is only understandable within the network that supports them. This raises a further obligation on researchers to attend to the future identity of the person, and how the narrative foreshadows and effects future interactions in care, because unless there is some kind of carry-over of that identity, that network knowledge, into future care, then it is not only going to be lost but it is going to be displaced, along with the ongoing project of identity co-construction through storytelling which we have termed curation. We write about the theoretical notion of curation elsewhere (Crichton and Koch forthcoming).

The narrative developed through this study has helped us understand Laura and, most importantly, it reminds us and future carers and the family what is important for communication and encounters today. Laura has recently moved into a care facility. Her family have provided her narrative to the staff. Our next step is to evaluate this narrative in the institutional contexts of care and observe its practical effects. The study is ongoing.

Note

1. This research has been funded by a Divisional Research Performance Grant from the University of South Australia.

7 Looking in a fairground mirror: reflections on partnerships in learning disability research

Alex McClimens, Gordon Grant,
Paul Ramcharan

Introduction and scope

This chapter offers some reflections about emergent partnerships between academic and service user researchers. Context is important here because the service users in question are people labelled as having a learning disability, whilst the authors are not. However, we are not suggesting that we have neither any disabilities nor learning difficulties; we encountered difficulties learning as the path we trod was unpredictable, with trial and error typifying our experience.

Our account is also partisan, being the product of our own constructions. Though we have striven to access and represent what our service user research colleagues experienced along the way, we present a patently one-sided view of partnership work. We make no apologies for this. A concern for honesty rather than accuracy has guided us. This is how it felt, if perhaps not precisely how it was. Here we are making just one interpretation of a reality available. Any knowledge claims are therefore partial, contestable and possibly conflicted, hence the one-sided view.

The struggles academics have understanding and responding to theoretical formulations often pose problems in implementation. Experience in enabling participation or emancipation through research (Ramcharan et al. 2004; Walmsley 2004) both starts and falls with the relationships that develop with new research colleagues, whether disabled or not. This chapter reflects on the opportunities and challenges of building such relations.

We begin by wrestling with issues about science and power relations in research, and how one of us became involved with a group of individuals labelled as having learning disabilities. When they became interested in pursuing research of their own, funding issues arose, as did questions about regulation, control and accountability. When the remaining authors of this chapter became involved a different set of dynamics came into play that shaped the course of our partnership work. The chapter charts that course and the factors that shaped its direction. We conclude by offering some reflections about partnership work and knowledge construction when academics and service users work together on a research project.

A bit of history

In the eighteenth century Antoine Lavoisier (1743–94) and Joseph Priestley (1733–1804) were in dispute over a previously unknown gaseous by-product they discovered independently when heating red calx (mercury oxide) under laboratory conditions. They were initially at a loss to explain its appearance. Priestley saw no value in further work and dismissed the gas as 'dephlogisti-cated air' or phlogiston. Lavoisier persevered and eventually established the scientific law of the conservation of matter. He named the new gas 'oxygen'.

By experimentation and observation such early pioneers could resolve knowledge claims fairly readily and with some authority. The composition of light, for example, the boiling point of water and the distance between astro-nomical objects can all be accurately measured. Even taking variables into account, such as temperature or altitude, the scientific method can accom-modate such diversity by expanding the frame of reference with an appeal to the rule *ceteris paribus*, that is, other things being equal. By such means the natural sciences occupy a place of unparalleled expertise. Even the word itself 'science' is a Latin word for knowledge.

But what if other things are not equal? What if the knowledge claims are disputed and cannot be resolved by established methods? What if the methods themselves are in dispute? What happens when the process and practice of research addresses an area or a population that seems at odds with standard academic or scientific practice? Or indeed if people simply choose their actions and reactions whether they are predictable or not; whether based on scientific 'fact' or not; whether intentioned or not: social acts in their many forms are *real in their consequences*.

Our self-consciously reflexive account examines the issues of power and knowledge production arising when the research process is undertaken by a mixed group of individuals variously labelled with 'learning disability' and academic/professional qualifications. This chapter is not 'scientific' in the sense portrayed by Lavoisier and Priestley, being based on emergent research that was neither intentionally positivist nor post-positivist. The people involved wished to undertake research that was exploratory and interpretive, using group and participatory methods which, when done rigorously, are equally 'scientific' (Lincoln and Guba 2000). What follows considers the difficulties and dilemmas experienced when academics and people labelled as having learning disability attempted to work together as research partners.

The account is deliberately personal as events are described, reflected upon and discussed subjectively, consciously avoiding the calculating gloss of objective analysis. Shields and Walsh (2006) advocate a similar standpoint when they use the metaphor of the car crash to illustrate imbalances in the authority of explanatory accounts. The survivors of the fictional car crash have a personal story to tell but their narrative is subsumed within the 'official' version of events sought by law enforcement and insurance agencies. The 'user/survivor' perspective has, they argue 'the potential to observe emergent realities' (Shields and Walsh 2006: 195). So fasten your seatbelts. This could be a bumpy ride.

The Burton Street Project
(www.burtonstreet.org.uk, accessed December 2006)

Service user involvement in health and social care research is not new but engaging individuals labelled with learning disability in the process is sufficiently fresh to attract some critical attention. Here we examine what happens when qualitative social scientific research, wearing its Marxist influence on its sleeve, unashamedly subjective and value-laden, and with its participatory hat tilted at a rakish angle on its user-involved head, collides with bureaucracy, administrators and cross-institutional financial arrangements. The setting is real but some names have been changed to protect the innocent.

The Burton Street project began as a grass-roots community education initiative in the Hillsborough area of Sheffield in the 1990s. Using an old school building as a base, the business expanded rapidly to include some day-care provision for individuals labelled with learning disability. The project has subsequently been re-envisaged as a community college offering accredited and non-accredited courses for adults labelled with a variety of learning difficulties and associated conditions.

In summer 2004 my (AMC) interest in life history and narrative brought me into contact with some of the people who attended Burton Street. There I met colleagues from the local Trust's psychological service who worked with some of the service users. In ensuing discussions the psychologists were asked what else they did and 'research' was part of the answer. The service users were keen to know what this meant. From these chance remarks the research interest group emerged.

In responding to users' interests and addressing their concerns, we hoped to avoid the pitfalls presented by oppressive power relations that frequently characterize such joint ventures. The users wanted to be actively involved, rather than being coerced or co-opted, but in what precisely? In moving from involvement *as process* to involvement *as product* we had to ensure an understanding of how the process worked. We therefore devised a ten-week curriculum to introduce what we perceived to be core research methods. For, as Walmsley (2004) observes, people with learning disabilities need to know *how* to do research.

Consequently we covered ethics, single case study design, basic statistics, the broad differences between qualitative and quantitative approaches, interviews, participant observation, simple survey techniques, questionnaires and consent issues. After ten weeks the same interested group of students remained, but now with some rudimentary knowledge of how to undertake research. The next stage was to put such knowledge to use.

Despite the increased participation of people labelled with learning disability in research (Walmsley 2001) the process nevertheless throws up particular challenges, especially the process that underpins participation (Greenwood et al. 1993). Indeed, process is all, as we would soon discover.

We meet weekly, but without a defined project the group made do by making guest appearances. Two of them might, for example, talk to a group of medical students on treating people with learning disabilities as people first and symptoms second. Others might make a conference presentation. Gradually the group built a local reputation. From the outside things must have looked good. But even in these early 'successes' had we, the academic/professionals, unwittingly transposed our own scientific values? The implication is that research can only be properly undertaken when the researchers have been inculcated into the rituals. Is this really what user involvement is about? From this perspective the professionalization of user involvement in research is ideological. The process is 'normalized' until it reflects the professional model by which the alternative is made mainstream, indeed does the selection of methodology simply professionalize the research process and further marginalize would be users (Ellis 2000)?

Sh£w me the m£ney!

To maintain momentum we successfully applied for a small grant providing start-up funds and meeting maintenance costs. But this seed funding came with strings attached: it was university money designed to support local, credible, applied research; it had to be sufficiently scientific to produce publishable findings; it was to improve the university's Research Assessment Exercise (RAE) profile; and it needed to be spent quickly. At this point another of us (GG) became involved. Devolved research funds were at his disposal, providing four conditions were met: (1) there was a written research proposal, (2) there was an infrastructure in place to support the group, (3) the money was used in an accountable way, and (4) that deliverables were produced. He attended meetings of the Burton Street Group to explain these ground rules, which were formalized in writing.

Whilst initially a cause for celebration, it later turned into a bureaucratic nightmare for the group, particularly for the group member acting as financial secretary. For reasons beyond the control of the immediate partners, the transfer of funds from the university to the centre took months. Negotiations were fraught. We had all been freely donating our time but now that the Trust insisted that colleagues from psychology who were supporting the group be paid at a rate equivalent to private practice. This effectively put them well beyond the scope of the budget. They continued on a voluntary basis. The students were not allowed to earn more than £5 a week for fear of compromising their benefit arrangements.

Two weeks after the money was transferred from the university the finance system at the centre changed. We wanted to pay people on the day, perhaps a week in arrears, thereby linking attendance and payment, and mirroring the 'real' world. The 'system' thought otherwise. Eventually, some five weeks later, we obtained the funds. One of us (AMC) had to sign to secure the money's release, on behalf of the intended recipients, who were deemed unable by the financiers to perform this function themselves. I had to literally dole out a bunch of fivers to what was by now a queue of very excited individuals, who might never had so much cash in hand before. I remember thinking that I had approximately £50 of my own in my jeans and thought so little of it. People ran from the office clutching the cash. I called after them, 'Put it in your pocket at least!'

I closed my eyes and imagined the headlines in the local paper.

Woman with learning disabilities mugged in street

DI Bloggs has told this to our reporter. 'The woman has been robbed of a sum of money, believed to be approximately £35, all in used fivers, which she had been given by a university lecturer. Naturally we are keen to interview this person . . .'

A research career would be over before it had properly begun.

Participation

Where does the Burton Street Project sit in relation to prevailing thinking about user involvement in research? Taking Chappell's (2000) distillation of the criteria for emancipatory research based on the contributions of writers like Zarb, Morris and Oliver, there are two boxes that can be ticked: (1) it provided an opportunity for people with disabilities to be researchers themselves and (2) it enabled people to adopt a reflexive stance in relation to their work. Two further qualifying criteria – (3) being commissioned by democratic organizations of disabled people and (4) having an accountability to democratic organizations of disabled people – appear to put the project outside the emancipatory model. Evidence for a fifth qualifying criterion, improving the lives of disabled people, was yet to be produced. The project, therefore, sat more comfortably within what could be termed a participatory research model, if only by being labelled as not emancipatory.

Space precludes consideration of the range of ideologies constituting participatory research practice and how these are expressed in terms of methodologies. However, the project required: academic and user researchers to work together; to make this work, a supportive infrastructure and training was needed for user researchers; external funding was necessary, but this created a complex accountability framework; and engaging in work together was becoming messy, protracted and with no clear outcomes in sight, yet. Further exploration of the minutiae of working together explains why progress was so unpredictable.

Picture this

With the goal of conducting research interviews, and also to keep a record of our progress, we bought a camcorder. Two of the students from the group volunteered to make the purchase. They had two options. They could either get cash from the account and buy the equipment over the counter, much as any 'normal' person might do, or they could make the purchase by prior arrangement, ordering from a limited range of retailers. This was, of course, the preferred option for ease of administration.

We eventually got an over-the-counter DVD/camcorder. Being a new toy it was something that everyone wanted to play with. Then we got a request from colleagues at the centre asking if they could 'borrow' the camera, to which the group, being understandably protective of its new purchase, said 'no'. It was locked away in a cupboard with the rest of our paraphernalia.

We could describe the pantomime quality of some of the exchanges we had with administrative staff but you would find these hard to believe. There was a Kafkaesque air about things. The key had to reside in the office. The office was, naturally enough, open only during office hours. Most of our meetings were conducted 'after hours'. We had to sign for the key. Some of our colleagues could not sign their name. Such details are merely inconvenient and are fairly easily circumvented. However, it became increasingly evident in our dealings with various parties that the legitimacy of our enterprise was founded on professional/academic status rather than on the efforts of our learning disabled partners.

For example, when we arranged conference attendance or a teaching session we would supply contact details. These would always include the names and addresses of the group members involved. Correspondence, however, was invariably addressed to one of the academic/professionals. We had to share this communication with our colleagues, some of whom had a mobile phone, none of whom had email, and all of whom relied to varying degrees on others to help organize their lives. Sometimes messages were not passed on. People forgot meetings and appointments were missed, cancelled, postponed or rearranged. Bookings that had been arranged in advance failed to materialize on the day. Frustration mounted.

Our weekly group meetings were always conducted face-to-face in one of the rooms available to us. For those attending the centre this meant alterations to homeward travel plans and rearrangement with families and/or carers, and for others negotiation with employers, families, and a renegotiation of child-care arrangements. Everyone had to cater for holidays and one-off circumstances. Occasionally these competing demands conspired against attendance by any of the professional/academics, so there was no meeting and no progress. Delays inevitably occurred and the knock-on effect accumulated. Whilst our colleagues were keen to take on various levels of responsibility it was soon clear that their good intentions did not stretch to self-regulation or organizational duties.

These examples indicate that whilst those involved in the project were prepared to work in an inclusive manner this was not necessarily reciprocated or even recognized by those operating outside the immediate environment. The many small routine wrangles became energy sapping. Delegation became a matter of hope more than expectation. And that is before we arrive at weightier, more esoteric, but equally pressing concerns.

Knowledge construction

> Foucault argues that what counts as true knowledge is ostensibly defined by the individual, but what is permitted to count is defined by discourse. What is spoken, and who may speak, are issues of power.
>
> (Parker 1989: 61)

One of the main reasons for undertaking research is to discover new knowledge. How this knowledge is arrived at is determined largely by methodological issues, epistemological concerns over the construction of knowledge and ontological concerns over what there is to know. These in turn are governed by the social and scientific location of the research, the political climate and the values that drive the researcher(s). If all of these are not shared then user involvement can come unstuck.

The opening lines of *The German Ideology* and the later declaration that 'the ideas of the ruling class are in every epoch the ruling ideas' (Marx and Engels 1947: 39) are relevant here. Any subsequent variant of ideology, it seems, must be able to accommodate this apparent contradiction; that in exposing the 'true' nature of social practice ideology reveals itself to be no more than another layer of make-believe. Our attempts at research were at all times controlled by the academic/professionals amongst us. To pretend otherwise would be to wilfully misrepresent events. But we were occasionally guilty of closing our eyes and pretending that as academics and professionals we were not the ruling class. We very much wanted to believe that there was a shared ethos.

Our weekly meetings, for example, were determinedly democratic. We experimented with procedures because we wanted group members to share some control. To prevent a babble of voices we adopted the rule of the pen for a while. Whoever held the pen could speak. We used tape recorders to gather people's opinions and we made sure that everyone had the opportunity to speak because having each voice heard was important to the group. All of this was mightily time-consuming. The meetings turned into meetings about meetings. Business was carried over, process came to dominate, and any focus on a product became irrelevant.

So what then are the implications for the knowledge produced in such circumstances? Did we have to take so long to discover that user involvement, if done properly, is difficult and time-consuming? User involvement is not a product; neither is it entirely processual, it is a way of thinking. Butler (2002) offers an analogy with art that may be useful here. He describes museums and galleries as 'legitimizing' the status of their collections through displays and exhibitions. Scholarly books and journals can perform the same function. By operating careful selection criteria, editorial policy will either publish or reject work according to its perceived harmony with current thinking. And current thinking is that 'user involvement' is a good thing.

So how are people labelled with learning disability situated within the production of research? Their involvement can only be premised on presence or participation; ornament or function. In either case the 'ruling ideas' are clearly the property of the 'ruling class' of academics. Hence, as Curran et al. (1982: 26) point out, 'ideology becomes the route through which struggle is obliterated rather than the site of struggle'.

Voice and ventriloquism

Acknowledging that our university funding was in some sense buying a product from us provided a motivating factor to maintain interest and focus to our collective work. Primarily the group wanted to be involved to make a difference and to be heard. In answer to the specific question of what they wanted to say in the proposed article responses were as follows:

- 'What we are all about . . .'
- 'Why are we taking part . . .'
- 'We should put pictures in article . . .'
- 'What we've learnt from being in the group . . .'
- 'Want people to read an article with our name on it . . .'
- 'Want people to know who we are, want people to know what we can do . . .'
- 'Want people to know what we got out of it . . .'
- 'We would like them to like it . . .'
- 'Want to tell them a story about what we do here . . .'
- 'Want people to know where we are . . .'
- 'Want it to be interesting . . .'
- 'Tell them about our lives . . .'

With this clear desire to have their say we wanted to avoid acting as puppeteers and pulling strings or putting words in the mouths of our colleagues. This was crucial to our own beliefs about the nature of collaboration. The involvement experienced by the individuals in this instance was benign in terms of the influence exerted by us, the professional/academics involved. Their reflections on the experience continue to be positive. This has not always been the case.

The 'involvement' in research as experienced by Paul Hunt (1981), for example, was oppressive and demeaning. Hunt critiqued his own involvement as the subject of research in 'Settling accounts with the parasite people', criticizing the research, the researchers, their methodology and the findings. He highlighted how, far from instigating change that might benefit their 'subjects', the researchers remained content with report writing, even when their report contained bleak descriptions of care.

Beresford (2005) summarizes this position in more general terms when he says that:

> The starting point for many service users' view of research is as part of a structure of discrimination and oppression; an activity which is both intrusive and disempowering in its own right and which serves the damaging and oppressive purposes of a service system over which they can exert little or no influence or control.

Clearly, sympathetic methodologies have to be adopted that can simultaneously illuminate the research topic and treat the respondents fairly. The qualitative research paradigm and, more particularly, the participatory approach is sensitive to the needs of under-represented groups. Understanding is privileged over explanation and this is often achieved by giving prominence to the accounts of respondents. Bernard (2000: 167) suggests that the participatory process 'holds hope for the marginalized; it gives voice to those who are usually silenced'. This chimes with our own efforts. In this detail the aims of research and the value of user involvement in policy and practice may harmonize.

And yet there is a corollary. All interpretations of user involvement in research in part acknowledge that individuals and groups make a unique contribution to knowledge construction by virtue of their identity and social location. But simply to allow oppressed groups and individuals a platform is no guarantee of redress. Potts (1998: 27) puts it this way; 'the authenticity of individual "voices" cannot be as effective in securing political change as a social theory based on collective experience'.

Ouch! (or pain is what the patient says hurts)

So is research merely social commentary or can it affect social change, and does this polarize involvement around 'users and losers' (Hubbard 2004)? The drive towards inclusion suggests a belief that change can occur, premised on the assumption that the inside knowledge of individuals will be more relevant. As far back as Mead and Malinowski the search for the 'authentic native voice' has led researchers to walk for many a month in someone else's moccasins.

In searching for the insider perspective the ethnographer seeks local or native knowledge, believing that expertise accompanies first-hand accounts. The assumption here is that any such account is superior to one achieved using standardized approaches. Health care practitioners, too, tacitly share this perspective. So, for example, pain is what the patient says hurts rather than that defined by objective measurement. And both ethnographers and health care practitioners keep good theoretical company, supported in their beliefs by Wittgenstein and Foucault. Wittgenstein asserts that the meaning of a word is defined by its use in the language. Foucault suggests that true knowledge is the property of the individual.

The overwhelming impression is that self-report forms a sound basis, on clinical and theoretical grounds, for knowledge construction. Research has followed this lead in its recent insistence on user involvement. Hence addressing policy-making concerns by asking consumers what they want has been given more prominence by politically active disability organizations (Union of Physically Impaired Against Segregation [UPIAS], Disabled Peoples' International [DPI], People First) who remain strident in canvassing for inclusion.

It was largely through the efforts of the Chicago School that sociology developed an interest in minority and under-represented social groupings, and the interests of individuals who have a learning disability fit neatly into that tradition. This relationship though has two distinct drawbacks: a power differential and a reliance on 'expert' testimony. Our efforts at Burton Street displayed both.

The power relations within research partnerships, particularly those involving lay and academic/professional collaborators, are invariably skewed in favour of the latter. Funding sources and allied qualifying criteria naturally channel this towards the academic/professional, prohibiting an emancipatory position (Goodley and Moore 2000). However, funders are now routinely anticipating an element of user involvement somewhere in the proposal. Again, this can be interpreted as enlightened or just another case of ideology in action.

The 'expert' testimony too is contestable. Individuals labelled with learning disability are assumed somehow to have unique insight into their condition, despite the fact that for many, the label, for all its stigmatizing qualities, is an irrelevance in their daily existence.

There's no such thing as a free lunch

Our objective to produce an article caused some initial misgivings but fitted in well with the ambitions of the group, being exactly what group members said they wanted to do. In our conversations we passed the tape recorder round and let everyone have a say. What follows is therefore a composite response to the question, 'What is research?'

> Research is about asking questions, talking to different people, interviewing them, getting information, putting it on a database and writing it up. Everyone can help with the writing up. But we might need some money to help buy equipment. We want to put it in a magazine so people can read it.
>
> We work as a team, listening to each other, all pulling together. We've never been to research before. Some of us were sceptical at first. The idea was put to us and we liked the sound of it. It's our idea, our themes, our questions to put to other groups.
>
> In a way it's a good thing to get information from other groups. It's like expanding our ways to theirs and working together is good because it means group and inclusiveness. What we're doing is good, working as a team to let people see what we are doing and to gain knowledge.

The professional academics in the group went into literature review mode and brought back articles to read to the group. We looked at work by WFSA/Tarleton (2005); Ham et al. (2004); Townson et al. (2004) since they were all accounts of collaborative working undertaken by groups similar to our own. 'See!', we said. 'It's that easy!' Except, of course, it was not and is not.

The article emerged, eventually (Abell et al. 2007). How it arrived is a story for another day.

Interviews and service evaluation

The management of the project asked us to undertake a survey of user attitudes to the services they received. This was part of an overall strategy for change involving new building work and a reconfiguration of working practice for staff and service users alike. With this promise pending we took the opportunity to revisit the lessons previously learned around interviews and interviewing. We spent a lot of time practising interview skills. We discussed open and closed questions, prompts, confidentiality, ethics, disclosure of sensitive information and interview etiquette. The group took the microphones and ran with them.

We soon got the opportunity to practise these skills for real when the users and staff at a local day centre agreed that we could visit and try out new interview techniques.

One of the group, here referred to as 'P' interviewed a member of staff who will be identified as 'G'. It went something like this:

P: Now we're talking to G. How long have you been working here, G?
G: I've worked here five and a half years . . .
P: Do you like it here?
G: I love it, it's fantastic . . . it's one of the best places I've worked.
P: How much do you get paid?
G: (falters) . . . well . . . in the range of . . . say . . . £15K . . .
P: Oh my God! We should come and work here!

There are clearly issues concerning sensitivity here but there's no mistaking the enthusiasm. With the interviews recorded we (the professional/academics) transcribed the tapes and shared some initial analysis with the group, looking for common themes and any contradictions or anomalies. This went well and the feeling that perhaps we might be engaged with something worthwhile was fleetingly apparent.

After a delay of around six months we eventually got permission to interview anyone who attended as a service user. In preparation we revised our understanding of our goals, the practicalities of taping, and ethics of consent. We produced information sheets. We arranged access. In late 2006 the first interview was conducted by Burton Street researchers and the process continues at the time of writing. We anticipate completing our evaluation in the summer of 2007. Of the 14 original members of the research interest group only a core of four or five remain.

Conclusion: reflections in a fairground mirror

Why the fairground mirror? Well because fairground mirrors usually give an intentionally distorted reflection. This account is distorted in that it is only one-sided, being our perspectives, but we have aimed nevertheless to be faithful to our own experience. For the complete picture to emerge, the perspectives of service user researchers themselves unfettered by academic interpretation must be added.

Looking back, what did we learn from this experience? First, some not so surprising things. Preparing the group for research led to an unavoidable emphasis on learning and group work, shaped by an appeal to shared decision-making. It was an intensive and time-consuming process for everyone, to the point where attention to process almost became *the* product. Securing university funding, whilst a catalyst, directed the project down a participatory rather than an emancipatory path, wresting key elements of control from the group, though there was little sign from group members that they were looking to achieve emancipation for themselves or for their peers through the research process.

Regarding working together there are some rather more interesting things to note. Taking ideas from, and extending thinking about, constructions of partnership – the Senses Framework – applied to family carers and their relations with services (Nolan et al. 2003b), it could be said with some confidence that for group members three of the six senses were self-evidently in place: the sense of *security* coming from feeling safe in relationships, the sense of *belonging* in feeling part of things, and the sense of *purpose* from having personally valued goals and in engaging in shared and meaningful activity. Despite the travails of securing funding and the trial and error characterizing early development work, group members stuck together, made individual and collective contributions, and continue to work together in publishing from their experiences, albeit in reduced numbers. This demonstrates a surprising degree of commitment and resilience when conventional returns (monetary reward, promotion) were absent.

Evidence for the three remaining senses, the sense of *continuity* from experiencing links and consistency over time, the sense of *achievement* from making progress towards desired goals and the sense of *significance* derived from feeling that you matter, was mixed as well as more limited. The group began as 12 individuals but is now a core of four or five. Reasons for the reduced numbers mirror domestic and lifestyle changes, as much as waning interest in the project, but have affected continuity of membership. The group's obsession with process meant that the sense of achievement associated with realizing project goals was deferred for a long time, and the publication schedules of journals meant waiting in a queue like everyone else who had papers accepted and awaiting publication. This left a void that was difficult to fill. Although initially buoyed by the recognition and status associated with securing research funding, this soon faded, so the sense of significance experienced by the group was also difficult to maintain. To these senses we might add a seventh, the sense of *empowerment*. Did group members feel empowered and liberated through what they had experienced? We would offer an equivocal response. Yes, they felt liberated in engaging in something that they valued, that set them apart in some respects from their peers; they felt proud; but no, they made little impact on the rather oppressive forces of research production, nor have they (yet) freed themselves from positions of relative disadvantage within the community. This raises a final but important issue that deserves further discussion, namely, claims for knowledge construction and the benefits that arose from this project.

The interviews undertaken by the group, commissioned by the project management, though cast as a piece of service evaluation, are generating robust findings that are considered by the commissioners to be 'fit for purpose'. Consequently such knowledge addresses local need. And perhaps this is good enough. The results will inform management policy and practice, with benefits for the individuals and groups using the service. We wait to see whether intellectual disability as impairment will render higher-level abstraction and theorizing associated with data analysis less amenable to practice, as some have suggested (Kiernan 1999; Walmsley 2004). 'Doing research' involves a multiplicity of tasks, some making more intellectual demands than others, and expecting people with intellectual disabilities to be involved in all stages of research may not be practicable; indeed, it may even be unethical if it places unreasonable demands upon some individuals. Involving people with learning disabilities in all stages of research is, we feel, a comfortable delusion that does not necessarily serve the public interest. There is an added onus of responsibility on those engaged in collaborative research to be transparent about who is taking responsibility for what, about exactly what service user and academic researchers are contributing to the enterprise, and the ethicality of each stage of the enterprise.

Having written this chapter from the perspective of academic researchers in a collaborative research enterprise, we restrict our final comments to what we think academic researchers can best contribute and what they ought to trade in working collaboratively with people with learning disabilities.

We could discern elements of each of the three roles (and more) that Stoecker (1999) identifies for academics in participatory research. He talks of the researcher as *initiator*, as *consultant* and as *collaborator*. Though the idea for research was initiated by the group, there were many occasions when the initiative had to be taken by an academic researcher. We acted in consultant or advisory roles at times, but premised most of our work on a collaborative model where we did our best not to 'take over'. The trouble with this stance is that, as Stoecker (1999: 345) asserts:

> Community members are not used to the 'talk' world of academics, and they are often sceptical of it. And real collaboration takes a lot of time – for meetings, for accountability processes, for working through the inevitable conflicts – that may be in especially short supply for community group members.

Collaboration was our working ideal, because we considered it to be more empowering to group members, though it was not necessarily the most efficient way forward. Under the guise of collaboration we found ourselves troubleshooting (sorting out personal money and transport problems), organizing (designing research training), educating (running research training workshops), co-authoring (drafting letters and publications). These were necessary and important roles for us to fulfil given that the group was not self-regulating. We should not, therefore, have been so surprised by the way activity expanded, affecting time horizons and attendances.

Rodgers (1999) talks of trying to get it right, suggesting a struggle with the process. There is no shortage of similar commentary and the growing literature suggests a genuine movement towards democratic forms of knowledge construction. But, and there is a but here, including individuals with learning disabilities in the research process poses unique challenges about consent, understanding and purpose that potentially undermines the whole project. Collaboration suggests a partnership and, providing we are honest enough to concede that the partnership will be an unequal one, then perhaps the struggle can and should continue.

However, the struggle engages with an unrepresentative population. For even if individuals with learning disabilities are able to contribute to the process (and this can be challenged) it is evident that articulate, talkative subjects make up the bulk of this cohort. This perpetuates the structural inadequacies of university-led research as a response to social inequity, exposing the ideological dilemma at the core of user involvement: inclusion for some means exclusion for others. For truly collaborative research to ensue, more effort must be made to include those individuals who are less able to communicate. This may well present insurmountable methodological difficulties.

In conclusion we must concede that, while the principle of user involvement is sound, the practice is not always smooth. Our experiences suggest that the inclusion of individuals with learning disabilities in the research process poses the unique challenges noted above that may yet undermine the whole project. Does this mean user involvement does not work? Not necessarily. But, for those of us working in the learning disability arena, future research needs to respond to issues around the binaries of consent and coercion, process and product, and the understanding of methods and purposes as demonstrated by people with learning disabilities.

So what should academic researchers be prepared for when entering the collaborative research arena with service user researchers labelled as having learning disabilities?

- Resistance, inertia, disinterest: *we* know that research can change the world, the world just doesn't know it yet.
- Misrepresentation, mistrust: prophets are often without honour in their own country; research is no different.
- Chronic fatigue syndrome: two years to write a paper? *Two years!*

And what should academics be prepared to trade?

- Power, authority, expertise: people might salute your presence in the faculty building, but you are not in the faculty building now.
- Integrity: if you want to cook omelettes you have to break the eggs.
- Fame, fortune, family: keep a photograph of your loved ones nearby; it may be the only time you see them!

8 Doing user research: narratives of mental health service user researchers

Graham Shields, Ray Wainwright, Gordon Grant

Introduction

In this chapter we write about experiences of engaging in user-led mental health research. Two of us (GS and RW) speak as mental health service user researchers and one of us (GG) as an academic researcher. It will become clear later why we distinguish between which of us is speaking, but we wish to say from the start that this account is one that we have all agreed.

As noted in the opening chapter, user involvement in research has not emerged by accident as a significant subject for debate and scrutiny. Policy in the UK has been driving the design and governance of health and social care services towards a model where there is more transparent accountability to the public and recognition of service user experience and knowledge as part of the modernizing agenda (DoH 2001c, 2006). This has been a formidable agenda for change, not least because it has required a fundamental re-valuing of traditional sources of knowledge and power (professional and bureaucratic) in the shift towards a culture that embraces the service user (or patient) and family, as expert in their own right. These ideas are not particularly new; some writers having been promulgating them, based on good evidence, for over a decade (Nolan et al. 1996).

Timescales associated with these changes can therefore be quite protracted. Since issues of power and authority are so integral to organizational and professional cultures it is not surprising that steps towards democratization and empowerment should become so drawn out. The structures and cultures within which research is embedded are little different, but this now means that the rules by which universities and research funding bodies govern research become important, alongside those in health and social care services, in understanding how the inclusive research agenda is played out.

The commitment shown by government to this inclusive research agenda expressed through INVOLVE (2004) has been important in establishing the legitimacy and credibility of this enterprise. In recent years there has been a growing volume of mental health research in the UK that is now not only user focused (Simpson and House 2002) but also user led (Thornicroft et al. 2002; Trivedi and Wykes 2002; User Focus Monitoring Group 2005). Guidelines for good practice in mental health research have been published (UK Mental Health Research Network 2005), emphasizing principles deemed essential to good collaboration when academic or professional researchers and service users are working together. These include:

- clarity and transparency – about respective roles and responsibilities
- respect – for each other's views
- diversity – when seeking to build research capacity among local service users
- flexibility – in determining working arrangements, so to optimize service user involvement
- accessibility – of information and working materials.

Mental health service users have reportedly made it clear that being included in all stages of research is their top priority, even outstripping their priorities for research themes and topics (Thornicroft et al. 2002). Wykes (2003) has argued that user involvement can make a difference to clinical research by improving and refining research questions, changing outcome measures and adapting methodologies – based on sharing user experiences. There is also some evidence to suggest that service users feel able to speak more freely when interviewed by a service user researcher rather than those involved in commissioning or providing services (Faulkner and Layzell 2000; Rose 2001; Allam et al. 2004).

Desirable though inclusive research might be, its implementation can be extremely demanding within mental health services, and unless there are clear aims from the start, as suggested by the first of the UK Mental Health Research Network (MHRN) principles above, relational difficulties can be encountered that impede progress (Shields and Walsh 2006). Service user inclusion in research, therefore, is no easier than inclusion in services or in other life spheres.

Concerns have been expressed that user-focused or user-led research in the NHS does not receive the recognition it deserves when NHS reporting systems fail adequately to capture the experiential dimensions of knowledge gain or the often complex and time-consuming processes that underpin such knowledge gain (Grant et al. 2006). There continue to be challenges then in establishing the credentials of service user involvement in research at this time.

Despite the steady stream of narratives and oral histories, many from the survivor community and family carers, about the experience of mental ill health, recovery and service responses (for example, Hill et al. 1995; Karp 1997, 2000; Rose 2001), there are singularly few accounts from mental health service users about their engagement in research *as researchers*, and what they feel about it. Accounts are often filtered through the lenses of academic and professional researchers.

An exception is the account by Reeve et al. (2002) of a community mental health study in Canada. In the experience of the mental health consumer researchers in this particular study, conditions were created in which different types of gains were made, including the development of research skills, self-confidence and self-esteem, and there were even signs that the experience was aiding recovery for some individuals. These might all be construed as examples of individual capital (cf. McKenzie and Harpham 2005). But additional gains were also reported in terms of trust, teamworking, camaraderie and enhanced feelings of status by association with a team of academic researchers – all of which can be seen as forms of social capital. Interestingly, Allam et al. (2004) come to similar conclusions in summarizing what service user and carer researchers reported following an evaluation study of an assertive outreach service in England.

In both of the above studies, challenges did not go unnoticed. For example, for some people there were difficulties about expressing fears and anxieties. Managing emotions in interview situations was not easy. Maintaining a grip on objectivity, when required, was sometimes difficult, especially when empathy and reaching co-constructions with interviewees were also important. In the Canadian study the point was also made by one consumer researcher that there needs to be a balance between being empowered to take part but having that responsibility without feeling overwhelmed. Individual differences in the capacity of consumer researchers to deal with these issues represent another challenge to be addressed.

If we are to understand and evaluate the products of user-focused and user-led research in mental health services, it is necessary that efforts continue to be made to make transparent the processes involved in implementing such research.

In this chapter, an attempt is made to address this in a particular way. Two narratives follow, each written by researchers who have experience of living with mental illness. Written independently of each other, the narratives are personal reflections about a part of each person's research journey. In the first piece, GS speaks of his engagement, on a part-time basis, as a researcher in a mental health NHS Trust, and of the structural factors within the Trust that shaped his experiences as a user researcher over a period of more than four years. In the second narrative, RW focuses on one particular issue, ethics, when he was forced to face some personal demons in being challenged by the requirements of the interview process within his PhD study. The narratives are presented as uninterrupted discourse so that the reader can obtain a 'feel' for each person's story and make a judgement about what is important, in the manner that might be advocated by the great Studs Terkel. Each narrative is followed by a brief commentary – our own – where we attempt to summarize what we think was important about each narrative in turn. In the concluding discussion we offer further reflections about the structural, ethical and methodological challenges to be faced when service users are actively engaged in research roles.

Graham's narrative: battling with the rules for engagement in research

My schizophrenia began its manifestation in 1989 when I was a student at Lancaster University studying an MSc in Operational Research (OR). At the time I had the intention of applying it to the water industry in which I had worked as an engineer. I found that I was interested in the application of OR to the NHS and my dissertation looked at modelling nurse supply. I was subsequently employed by a Regional Health Authority but it became totally untenable for me to work full time as there was no understanding of my needs or special support offered. Like many educationally qualified users of mental health services, I cannot guarantee health and strength to fit into normal structures of work on a particular day, and for us to be involved in research the question of flexibility has to be addressed. That we cannot work in the usual way does not mean that we are necessarily incapable of performing high-quality research but it may diminish our capability at networking and, importantly, of being able to persuade others that our findings are valid so that alliances can be forged.

In 1999, I became a member of the Beverley Community Health Council (CHC) offering my knowledge of OR, employment in the health service and experience as a user. It became apparent to me that there were many local issues that needed researching, that the CHCs, rather than being abolished, needed to be expanded to provide facilities for professionals and users together to examine issues independently of existing authority structures. Questions that had come to mind included: issues relating to the merger of the ambulance trusts, possibly requiring a simulation model; the lack of provision of drama therapy and its potential effectiveness and the variation in availability of mental health services between Hull and the rest of the East Riding. As a member of the CHC, I asked for resources and this eventually led to me contacting the R&D (research and development) unit of the Humber Mental Health Trust where I was employed one day a week under the excellent 'Positive Assets' scheme of supported employment.

I have worked for the Trust for five years and have been principally involved in the following:

1.   I was set the task of establishing a user-led research panel of users and staff that would have autonomy and a budget to initiate and scrutinize research projects. The job was, perhaps, impossible as we had no clear idea about what research could be undertaken and were uncertain about many factors. We argued at length about our structure and who would make decisions, about what constituted quality and how to decide both how to allocate money and who decided who got it. Power, money and personality clashes dominated our discussions: the politics were insurmountable given our lack of definition and fundamental factors, such as our finances, being at the whim of forces beyond our control. A Trust, if it wants to have quality user research, must have a very solid commitment to it, in terms of facilitation, money, the active seeking of users and time, and it must take into account that users on their own, by virtue of their illnesses, may find conflict and responsibility too much of a burden to be effective decision-makers. The panel met for about two years.

2.   A spin-off from our work was the creation of a small group of users which met to discuss spirituality and mental illness. The group had the hope of producing an anthology of user experiences and beliefs based upon the spiritual model which would be used to inform practitioners of this perspective. We put together an ethics form only to discover that the money which we felt had been promised was no longer available. Trust policy dictated that work undertaken had to be paid for even if users were willing to work unpaid. The whole process of getting approval for access to Trust address lists was so slow and unnecessary that the users lost interest and the project collapsed.

3.   My own personal research has been to develop a computer simulation model in Pascal which models the total numbers of adult inpatients across the Trust and addresses questions of organization and change. I had to collect my own data, which was in a relatively raw manual state, and process it to produce length of stay characteristics and arrival rate patterns. The modelling suggests that owing to the natural fluctuations in total numbers that alternative ways of managing the units, such as having one large unit, could, potentially, save up to 12 per cent of nursing costs if a system of flexible staffing were introduced, that this would not only improve efficiency but improve the level of care in some instances. A unit could be freed to operate as a day hospital, reverting to an inpatient unit when demand required it, with the bulk of the units operating at capacity.

My modelling suggests the viability of using one large unit for all admissions with a rationale for controlled admissions to the other units from this unit. A major difficulty has been my inability to persuade other members of staff of the validity of my arguments which, in part, stems from being a part-time user employee even though I have an expertise.

The particularly good part of my employment experience has been the support and friendship offered to me through Positive Assets which, at times, has been the best therapy and counselling I have received throughout my illness. Through sharing with my support worker, I have been able to communicate with the organization in a way which lessens stress and helps to overcome any lurking paranoia.

As indicated earlier, user research probably requires more independence than can be offered by a Trust, particularly if research outcomes are critical of significant amounts of practice. I do not wish to appear cynical because I believe that those of us who are involved in research can change things and influence people whether we are in the system or outside it. Being involved in an R&D department has had the benefit of not only concrete service user research being undertaken, which has led to several papers being published in peer-reviewed journals and a number of conference presentations, but has also enabled the assertion of the user perspective to managers on a number of committees and steering groups. There is always a risk that such involvement will be tokenistic, a tick-box exercise, and there can be a surprising amount of stigma regarding the credibility of an academically qualified schizophrenic.

Some of my work, particularly the computer simulation, could have been undertaken by a professional researcher without any experience of illness, but I have been able to colour this research with insight I have gleaned, and possible ways of running mental health services became apparent to be tested by the modelling in a way that a more usual researcher would, perhaps, have been unable to do. Whilst it may look like normal OR, it is indeed user research informed by the user perspective.

User researchers, such as myself, could find a user reference group useful to help preserve our unique perspective and to provide opportunities to experiment with ideas and to offer support. Trusts, or whatever body is responsible, need to find ways of publicizing activities amongst users encouraging them to come forward. Red tape often appears to get in the way of access to address lists or makes the possibility work with, or without payment, difficult. Promises are often broken about the availability of resources which frustrate the development of interest and activity.

But service user research activity is worthwhile though perseverance and commitment are needed by all involved.

Commentary

Cast within a temporal perspective, this narrative is told along a storyline that has the familiar beginning, middle and end. At the beginning the narrator tells us of his research and career aspirations and how mental ill health appeared as a form of biographical disruption (Bury 1982). A clear statement is made asserting that mental illness does not necessarily diminish the capacity to engage in high-quality research, but that it may impinge on the stances taken by others towards the credibility or validity of the work that can be done in a research role. In this particular instance fitting into the normal routines of work was not easy so networking in the workplace, a taken-for-granted part of most jobs, was problematic. Immediately we can begin to see how the forging of potentially key alliances in research may present as a serious challenge for mental health service user researchers. This was to prove an undercurrent.

The narrative then shifts its focus to the period when GS took up a part-time research appointment in a local NHS Trust where he was charged with setting up a user and staff research panel to stimulate research projects. In the early days there were some uncertainties about what this required and, as a result, hurtling into this void were clashes about power, money and personalities. The reference to conflict and responsibility being 'too much of a burden to be effective decision-makers' underscores the need to think very carefully about the infrastructures to support user involvement in research, especially in the preparatory stages. There is now overwhelming evidence about this (Reeve et al. 2002; Allam et al. 2004; INVOLVE 2004; Smith et al. 2005).

Subsequently, aspirations about producing a user-based anthology about spirituality and mental health were undermined by system factors – withdrawal of funding and the slow speed of securing Trust approval – resulting in loss of interest by the service user group and the collapse of the project. Another systemic difficulty, though one not widely reported in the literature, was that concerning being a part-time employee in the Trust. For the narrator this seriously affected his integration into the workforce; being around for only one day a week made it difficult to network sufficiently and to influence key decision-makers. The dangers, therefore, of service user research becoming diminished in its capacity by Trust structures were becoming evident.

However, the experience has had a very positive side too. The narrator speaks to the value of support and friendship gained through peers and allies, 'the best therapy and counselling I have received throughout my illness', something also noted by Reeve et al. (2002). Also significant was the key part played by the narrator's support worker who was described as being able to help GS to 'communicate with the organization in a way which lessens stress and helps to overcome any lurking paranoia'. Given the earlier reference by the narrator to difficulties associated with persuading colleagues and decision-makers about the credibility of mental health service user research and experience, this signals the importance of knowing much more about what roles support workers play in this context. Being able to maintain a commitment, with this support, has in the end made it possible to influence service managers in positive ways about the value of taking fuller account of service user experience, and there have been tangible outputs in the form of published papers and conference presentations from the associated research.

The narrative makes tantalizingly brief reference to the issue of the independence of service user research within an NHS Trust. Whilst speaking to the value of being able to influence change from within the organization, he is also aware that being organizationally independent may permit more critical stances to be taken of policy and practice. The extension of networks that allow service users to stake their claims about experience as evidence and to articulate ways of working together to shape and undertake research, through perhaps the UK Mental Health Research Network or the emergent local comprehensive research networks, might be one way forward.

Ray's narrative: interviewing persons diagnosed as mentally ill – the burden of responsibility

I have experienced a severe form of bipolar disorder for many years. During the nadir of my illness I did many things and experienced many thoughts that I wish I could forget. True, time heals and even re-fashions events in a mould of black humour. However, true guilt is not so easily assuaged: in my own eyes I remain diminished by the excesses of my behaviour. Thus, the conflict between intellectual appraisal and the demands of personal responsibility remains unresolved. When my consultant asked me, 'Can you accept that your suicide attempts have been due to your illness?' my reply was considered but almost immediate: 'Intellectually, I can, yes. But as a person, no: my *soul* knows otherwise.'

This conflict is the source of this article. As a researcher wishing to interview persons with experiences of mental illness about how this experience has shaped their identities, I asked myself, 'How would I respond to my own questions?'

My response was unease. Despite all the searching questions of a COREC (Central Organisation of Research Ethics Committee) form followed by vetting by an LREC (Local Research Ethics Committee), which included the protocols for a detailed Participant Information Sheet to ensure fully informed consent, one overarching question remained. How deeply can a researcher invite a respondent to explore their experiences without violating their rights as a person? The ethical duty of one person to acknowledge the humanity of another is a cornerstone of methodology. The terms of my conflict were stark and simple. If I would not be prepared to be interviewed then I had no right to ask it of another person.

An in-depth interview aims to investigate the experiences of the respondent and his or her reflections on those experiences. As such, it is an artifice: a construction designed to realize an ulterior motive. Good interviewing technique is aimed at ensuring a courteous and relaxed atmosphere in which a respondent feels comfortable (for example, Fox et al. 2001: 6–20–22; 8–3). Holstein and Gubrium describe the 'basic model' of interviewing as 'prospecting for the true facts and feelings residing within the respondent' (2004: 143). In this context they quote Louis 'Studs' Terkel as asking 'casual' questions 'the kind you would ask while having a drink with someone; the kind he would ask you . . . In short, it was a conversation' (Terkel 1972: xxv, quoted by Holstein and Gubrium 2004: 143).

However, the truth remains that an interview is an artifice. In this connection, Item 27 of the BSA [British Sociological Association] Statement of Ethical Practice is somewhat daunting: 'In many of its forms social research intrudes into the lives of those studied' (BSA 2002).

Moreover, this statement is more than a simple warning against overzealous or insensitive probing. Rather it is recognition of the constructionist process implicit in *any* social interaction. Holstein and Gubrium (2004: 143) subscribe to the view that an interview is dynamic, a process of construction. Extrapolating this stance leads to the technique termed 'Active Interviewing' in which a respondent is a participant in meaning-making (Holstein and Gubrium 2004: 149–56). However, this distinction appears to rest on a matter of degree. Proctor and Padfield quote several sources in support of the conclusion that 'the account rendered in the interview is, *in part*, . . . a product of the occasion itself' (1998: 133, italics in original). Accordingly, they recommend that 'researchers need to be more *empirically* sensitive to the effect of the interview' (Proctor and Padfield 1998: 134, italics in original). This practice includes an awareness of the degree of reassessment of experiences by a respondent.

Again item 27 of the BSA Statement of Ethical Practice is daunting: 'Even if not harmed, those studied can feel wronged by aspects of the research process. This can be particularly so if they perceive apparent intrusions into their private or personal worlds, or where research gives rise to false hopes, uncalled for self-knowledge or unnecessary anxiety' (BSA 2002). The phrase 'uncalled for self-knowledge' held a peculiar resonance for me. On undertaking a course of CBT (cognitive behaviour therapy) I told the therapist that my greatest fear was that 'the genie would be let out of the bottle'. I was, literally, afraid of what might be revealed of my thought processes. Although I learned many useful devices, it is an unfortunate truth that the overall effect was destabilizing. To learn of and confront a Core Belief does not automatically confer ascendancy over it. Sometimes, and here I readily acknowledge personal weakness, those deep-rooted convictions defy the most carefully calculated of logical challenges.

Items 28 and 29 of the same document served to increase apprehension. Item 28 begins 'members should consider carefully the possibility that the research experience may be a disturbing one'. Item 29 begins 'Special care should be taken where research participants are particularly vulnerable by virtue of factors such as age, disability, *their physical or mental health*' (my italics). In combination with Item 27, the picture painted of an interview by these guidelines is threatening indeed. Noting this, Elliott cites Parr (1998: 94) and Lieblich (1996: 177) as eliciting unanticipated accounts of painful life experiences in the course of interviews (Elliott 2005: 135–6). Yet the author also offers a balancing observation 'It is important, however, not to over-estimate the possibility that qualitative interviews may have a disturbing or negative impact on the interviewee' (Elliott 2005: 137).

By this route the focus returned to the precise nature of informed consent and its implications. As stated earlier, my participant information required approval by a Local Research Ethics Committee. The basis of this was derived from the ethical basis of research as detailed by Foster (2003: 10–11). This can be summarized by three approaches:

1. Goal based: are the goals of the research appropriate?
2. Duty based: the way the research is conducted.
3. Right based: concerning consent and confidentiality.

These approaches should be applied in a complex counter-balance. The intellectual devices of research need to acknowledge the requirements of the individual. Thus, although research may have a desirable goal, its methodology must obey the constraints of morality: for example, a researcher is bound by a moral duty to prevent harm to a research subject wherever possible. The third aspect of ethical approach, consent and confidentiality, is intended to ensure the right of a respondent to self-determination.

In her examination of the ethics of narrative interviewing, Elliott quotes Finch (1984: 50) as expressing grave misgivings concerning the effectiveness of confidentiality (Elliott 2005: 136). However, from a practical point of view, these appear unfounded. It should not be beyond the combined resources of researcher and respondent to ensure that references to names, places, and even personal pursuits can be suitably coded. For instance, regular attendance at a sports centre can be coded as (*Sport*) or even (*Hobby*). Thereafter, the question of confidentiality is much more direct: by knowingly consenting to be interviewed, a respondent agrees to place their confidence in the integrity of the interviewer.

This, in a nutshell, is the entirety of informed consent. By requesting it of another person, a researcher recognizes their right to self-determination.

After reading the participant information sheet, and checking particular aspects if necessary, a person *chooses* whether or not to be interviewed. If they elect to be interviewed, then it is with the understanding that they continue to act with self-determination; to continue participating or withdraw from the research should they wish to do so; to speak of personal experiences knowing that they might cause themselves pain by doing so; and to interact with the researcher as an equal.

To state that this understanding was sufficient to resolve my inner conflict would be simplistic. I remain extremely wary and unsure of myself, burdened with the responsibility of knowing that I could cause another person pain in the pursuit of my own ends. Yet, on reflection, such a burden is a good thing, a reminder of what it is to be aware of a respondent as another human being, a person; and to listen well, to remain aware of the purpose of the interview but also alert to the sensibilities of the respondent. To be relaxed and friendly – within the interactive and constructionist ebb and flow of an in-depth interview there remains a sound basis for the conversationalist approach of Studs Terkel. Accordingly, I believe that the first question of an interview should be a statement of intent by the researcher to regard the respondent as a person. A question that expresses a genuine and human interest: 'How are you?'

Commentary

This narrative, in comparison to the first, focuses largely on one issue – the experience of interviewing. At its heart the narrative raises a fundamentally important question for anyone engaged in interviewing – knowing when you may be testing the limits of the vulnerability of the interviewee and of yourself as interviewer. In this instance, however, the issue is compounded by the perceived vulnerability (mental ill health) of the interviewee, leading to the subsidiary question posed by the narrator: 'How would I respond to my own questions?' or, as he later asks: 'How deeply can a researcher invite a respondent to explore their experiences without violating their rights as a person?'

The double-edged nature of this question was felt even more sharply by the narrator as someone sharing the interviewee's label of having been diagnosed with a mental illness. Despite submitting his research proposal to ethical scrutiny by an LREC, and emerging with a clear signal to proceed, he was still vexed by this question. Even his forays into the research methodology literature did little to assuage the strength of his feelings about the issue. Citing some authoritative texts to strengthen his moral stance about 'active interviewing' only served to reinforce the view that he had to be *empirically sensitive* to the effect of the interview and the inter-subjective nature of the transaction involved.

At this point the narrator admits to his fear of his own self-knowledge emerging in the interview in a manner that might be destabilizing, to the interviewee and himself. Referring back to his own experience of CBT where, by definition, he was being forced to face his own thought processes more deeply, he was concerned about their possible destructive force when the 'genie was let out of the bottle'. This experience had already led him to believe that knowing and confronting a 'core belief' was one thing – managing ascendancy over it was another. Put another way, the intellectual challenge was something that could be anticipated, even calculated, but the emotional challenge was one that carried no guarantee of success. Indeed, there were strong and lurking fears about failure that could have lasting consequences for him, the interviewee and the credibility of his data.

Talking us through the processes of gaining informed consent, the narrator seems to be trying to convince himself that this should be sufficient to resolve his inner conflict. Though in the end he comes to a balanced view, he indicates that he feels 'wary and unsure of myself, burdened with the responsibility of knowing that I could cause another (person) pain in the pursuit of my own ends'. The implication here is largely an ethical one: how can ethical protection be given not only to those that take part as subjects in research, but also to those who may feel vulnerable as researchers even after all the preliminaries like training and ethical clearance have been completed?

Conclusion

In Studs Terkel's view narratives are best left to speak for themselves, uncontaminated by comment and interpretation from others, but we cannot avoid the temptation of offering some further thoughts about the implications of what has been shared so far.

Taken together, the narratives speak to quite different issues. This in itself is interesting given the exposure of the two narrators to mental health service user research over a period of years. It serves as a reminder that individual variations in experience of user research still matter at this stage in our understanding.

The first narrative speaks largely to *structural impediments* to service user research within an NHS Trust, especially:

- dealing with the management of uncertainty in the early stages of establishing the scope of a user and staff research panel
- the part-time nature of the enterprise and the imposition on effective networking resulting from this
- the barriers to networking and creation of alliances that mental illness *as impairment* can create

- the social construction of mental ill health as 'other' which continued to undermine the credibility of what mental health service users were seeking to achieve
- the politics and resourcing of partnership work
- and the unfulfilled quest to find an organizational solution to the challenge of establishing the independence and credibility of service user research.

Although these challenges have not all been overcome successfully, some progress has been made. The research panel did manage to stimulate research; projects have been completed successfully; and publications, conference presentations and tangible influences have been generated. The role of a support worker seems to have been very influential in this, not least in helping to maintain morale and commitment during times of challenge. The qualities and roles of support workers, issues we still know little about, merit much closer investigation in this context. In regard to the issue about independence it would now be timely to examine the influence of different organizational arrangements for hosting and sponsoring service user involvement in research. Basing service users in university departments or within the research arms of voluntary and charitable organizations might be one way of achieving independence, but with costs and consequences for access to service user peers.

The second narrative brought *ethical and methodological* concerns about the research interview sharply into focus. It can now be reported that RW has completed three successful interviews since writing this narrative. He considers that a major part of these is post-interview conversation with the interviewee. The aim of this is predominantly to chat person to person (as opposed to interviewer to interviewee) about any topic that comes to mind, so ensuring that all parties can relax in a convivial atmosphere before parting company. However, experience has also shown that interviewees are keen to talk about the interview process, so generating useful feedback.

By teaming up with another (similarly experienced) mental health service user researcher as a moral supporter in the field, a practical solution has been found to RW's vexing ethical interview dilemma. Not only will this supporter accompany the narrator when undertaking interviews, she will fulfil two linked roles. The first role is to act as a troubleshooter should the narrator's worst fears materialize during interviews, and, if necessary, negotiate termination and agreement to proceed on another occasion. The second role is more methodologically rooted, and concerned with acting as a 'second ear' during the interview. Being present in a passive, non-interventionist role, she will be well placed to validate constructions arrived at by the interviewer/narrator. In so doing she will also be in a position to provide moral reassurance, should it be needed, that these were not the product of the interviewer's own projections, especially those that might arise from his own experience of mental illness.

The ethical challenges embedded in these experiences are a reminder that decisions about ethics, in the UK at least, are primarily taken prior to the research (Ramcharan 2006), with far less scrutiny of what happens during the research itself. At the risk of suggesting further ethical regulation of an already highly regulated system of research governance in the UK, a code of practice working in the interests of service users, their allies and subjects needs to be developed so as to reassure everyone that ethics as practised in the field is just as ethical as ethics as intended. Mental health service user researchers, perhaps because of a sharpened awareness of human fallibilities and sensibilities deriving from their own experiences of mental ill health, have much to contribute to debates about research practice that is both ethically and methodologically sound.

The two narratives that form the core of this chapter show that, despite the inevitable challenges to be faced in the field, mental health service user researchers can accomplish a great deal in personal and project terms, supporting other accounts (Reeve et al. 2002; Trivedi and Wykes 2002; Allam et al. 2004). We are conscious that the experiences we have shared nevertheless represent a 'project in progress' and that, ultimately, inclusive research will need to be gauged by its contributions to knowledge, especially knowledge that can unlock windows to the richness, diversity and meaning of human experience.

9 Carers of people with mental health problems as co-researchers: reflections on the Partnerships in Carer Assessment Project (PICAP)

Julie Repper, Gordon Grant,
Monica Curran, Mike Nolan

Introduction

The Partnerships in Carer Assessment Project (PICAP) aims to provide a comprehensive understanding of the processes, experiences and consequences of assessing the needs of carers of people with mental health problems. Limited research has been undertaken into carer assessments, even less involving carers of people with mental health problems, so the views, experiences and priorities of such carers remain largely hidden (Arksey et al. 2002). In exploring aspects of assessment that carers consider important, we adopted a constructivist approach, involving carers in every aspect of the project (Rodwell 1998; Charmaz 2000). They played an active role, not only as 'subjects' sharing experiences of assessment, but also as co-researchers, working as part of the research team influencing the questions asked, the selection of participants, the analysis of data and the presentation of the findings.

Although UK health policy now requires 'consumer' or 'public' involvement in health care research, this generally refers to service users, as opposed to carers as researchers. This chapter describes how carers were involved in PICAP, their contributions to the research, and the lessons that we all learnt along the way. At the time of writing the detailed findings are not reported but selected excerpts illustrate key issues.

The Partnership in Carer Assessment Project

The Partnerships in Carer Assessment Project is a three-and-a-half-year study funded by the Department of Health (DoH) under its Service Delivery and Organization (SDO) programme. It uses a pluralistic (multi-phase, multi-method) approach (Bond 2000) to explore current assessment practice for diverse groups of carers of people with mental health problems across England. This involves four phases and an ongoing literature review. The phases are:

Phase 1:   Analysis of Local Implementation Team Plans for Standard 6 of the National Service Framework (NSF) for Mental Health to explore extant plans to develop and implement carer assessments.

Phase 2:   Carer Consultation events in nine different geographical areas involving around 80 carers with varied experiences of caring. These raised awareness of the research and gained carers' views about services for carers in each area, the parameters of carer assessments, inclusion and exclusion criteria and carers' views of 'good practice' in assessments.

Phase 3:   In-Depth Case Studies of nine carer assessment services examined how carers' needs are addressed at different levels of the organization, from strategy development, to involvement in service planning, to individual experience. Selection of sites was informed by phases one and two, reflecting: geographical and regional diversity; different types of Trusts (Primary Care, Mental Health and Partnership Trusts); and teams with acknowledged good practice. Case studies have included: documentary analysis of Trust Strategy, development plans and other relevant documentation; interviews with key individuals in selected Trusts; and in-depth interviews with carers about their experiences of the assessment processes, and with assessors about the implicit and explicit models they employ and the factors that both help and hinder their work with carers. Where possible the carer and assessor interviews have taken place shortly after initial assessment and six months later to give a longitudinal perspective.

   Analysis of data follows the principles of constructivist research (Rodwell 1998; Charmaz 2000) and, as will become clear, involved the carer researchers.

Phase 4:   As we write, Consensus Conferences are being planned with key stakeholders (carers, practitioners, managers from all of the participating sites) to allow detailed feedback and modification of draft principles of good practice and carer/assessor guides.

Although the broad shape of the project was predefined, the study design was emergent, with the results of each phase informing subsequent work. Consistent with the constructivist model, carers played a key role at all stages from development of the proposal to determining the methods and focus of data collection, analysis and dissemination. Before discussing the role of carers in the PICAP project, it is worth briefly considering the literature on carer involvement in research, with a particular focus on carers in mental health.

Carer involvement in mental health research

The role of carers in mental health is the focus of increased government attention. For example, the National Service Framework for Mental Health (DoH 1999) included a standard for supporting carers through assessment of their needs. In 2002, the DoH published guidance on developing services for mental health carers that are positive and inclusive, flexible and individualized, accessible and responsive, integrated and coordinated with mainstream services. Practical initiatives to enhance the involvement of carers as partners in mental health care include: the development of carer support services (for example Supporting Carers Better Programme, www.scbnetwork.org; and the Partners in Care Campaign run by the Royal College of Psychiatrists and the Princess Royal Trust for Carers, www.rcpsych.ac.uk/campaigns/pinc), carer education projects (for example the Meridan programme, www.meridanfamilyprogramme.com), and carer involvement leads in regional development centres (HASCAS 2005). However, initiatives to involve carers as partners in research have not developed at the same rate.

Although mental health service users have documented their role in all aspects of the research process (Faulkner and Morris 2003) and the Mental Health Research Network has published a strategy for the involvement of service users in research (MHRN 2004), there is no parallel strategy for carers. Pinfold and Hammond (2006) scoped the involvement of mental health carers in research, finding three relevant initiatives: the Institute of Psychiatry website (mentalhealthcare.org.uk) providing information about research into mental illness for carers; a carer research network is being set up to enable carers to work on research projects by Avon and Wiltshire Mental Health Trust; whilst the Alzheimer's Society runs the Quality Research in Dementia Network in which carers and people with dementia are actively involved in setting research priorities, awarding grants and assessing outcomes. However, no papers published in England describe carer involvement in research; one paper describes the experience of users and carers working collaboratively in a research project (Repper et al. 2003) and several 'Carer Focused Monitoring' groups have been developed to audit services following the User Focused Monitoring approach (Rose 2001). The National Co-ordinating Centre for

Service Delivery and Organization (NCCSDO) has commissioned a number of studies (of which PICAP is one) in its carer research programme (see www.sdo.lshtm.ac.uk/carers.htm) but, with the exception of PICAP, carers are the subjects of, rather than participants in, the research process. Rose et al. (2002) undertook a review of user and carer involvement in change management in mental health. They found few projects describing carer involvement, and only 25 per cent of papers referred to carers. It is therefore timely to consider carers' potential contribution to research and how this might be facilitated.

Carers as researchers

In 1996 the DoH established the Standing Advisory Group on the Involvement of Consumers in the NHS Research and Development Programme, later to become 'INVOLVE', to 'improve the ways in which healthcare research is prioritized, commissioned, undertaken and disseminated' (Steele 2004). Subsequently the *Research Governance Framework for Health and Social Care* (DoH 2001c) required consumer involvement at every stage of research, and greater transparency in reporting research; resulting in funders requiring bidders to demonstrate such involvement.

Usually 'consumer' refers to the general public as a whole: service users, their families and community members, but the guidance written on consumer involvement primarily refers to service users. They may be using services as diverse as primary care and/or cancer or mental health services; they may be a carer or a lay member of the public. If different people have different expectations, they may also have different priorities and preferences. In mental health, service users and carers often hold different views about mental health services (Perkins and Repper 1998) and have diverse experiences and motivations for getting involved in research. Whilst general principles may pertain, our experience of working alongside carers in research provides insights into the contributions that carers of people with mental health problems might make, and of their training and support needs. These should be seen in the context of good practice in consumer involvement more generally. However, as the PICAP experience illustrates, training and support needs vary depending on the socio-economic position, ethnic background, educational level, time available as well as the standard of health of the carer themselves. It takes time to build confidence, skills and trust with carers to enable them to develop into carer researchers who can explore the complex issues being investigated.

Good practice in consumer involvement

Guidelines for consumer involvement have been produced (see, for example, Folk Us, Baxter et al. 2001; Royle et al. 2001; INVOLVE, Hanley 2003; and the Mental Health Research Network, Faulkner 2004). These all cover similar areas including: the benefits of involvement in research; ethical issues, capacity-building; training; support; payment, and resources, and are essential considerations for researchers undertaking projects involving consumers. The first decision concerns the level of involvement required: consultation – obtaining consumers' views to inform decision-making; collaboration – ongoing partnership throughout the research process; or user-controlled research – where the locus of power and decision making lies with consumers (Hanley 2003 provides a description of the advantages and disadvantages of working at these three levels). The following discussion refers largely to collaborative research which was the approach taken in the PICAP.

Consumer involvement may benefit both the consumer researcher – increasing skills, confidence and future work opportunities – and the research process and findings (Hanley 2003). Consumers bring their experience of services/health problems, helping to ensure the study is relevant to clinical practice and to those using services (Trivedi and Wykes 2002; Hanley 2003; Allam et al. 2004). Their views can complement and challenge mainstream perspectives (Rose 2003) and influence the research subject, method, questions asked (Trivedi and Wykes 2002; Allam et al. 2004) and the indicators of success (Trivedi and Wykes 2002; Wykes 2003). Interviewees may be more likely to speak freely and honestly to another service user or carer than to a professional (Ramon 2000). Some evidence suggests that service users respond more fully when interviewed by someone with experience of using services (Polowycz et al. 1993; Clarke et al. 1999), and that response rates are higher, especially among groups that are generally hard to access (Fleischman and Wigmore 2000; Hanley 2003). However, it cannot be assumed that this is the case for carers. Although a marginalized group, they may actively wish to speak to professionals to make their experiences explicit, and they may have very different feelings about sharing their experiences or engaging with service providers.

To avoid 'tokenism' it is not sufficient simply to invite consumers onto the advisory panel of the research. Wherever funding, time and appropriate personnel are available, consumers should be involved in the initial planning stages of the research (Thorne et al. 2001; Faulkner and Morris 2003; Faulkner 2004). This is most successful where local expertise has been identified and relationships established. Rose (2003) emphasizes the importance of local capacity-building, with interested consumers receiving support to pursue research qualifications including the skills, language and confidence needed to join a team at the start of a project; and the capacity to negotiate aspects of the research whereby collaborators have a valuable contribution to make that requires genuine sharing of power (Trivedi and Wykes 2002; Faulkner and Morris 2003; Wykes 2003). This may create tension, particularly in mental health where service users may be seen as not able to make rational judgements owing to their 'madness' (Macran et al. 1999; Beresford 2002; Rose 2003) and carers may be viewed as having a biased view of services owing to their, often negative, personal experiences. It is just this diversity that is of value in collaborative research; if consumers agreed entirely with the professional researchers they would be contributing little to the research process. However, beyond a shared philosophy, practical issues of transparency, clarity of language, and accessibility must be considered so that non-professionals are able to make a full contribution.

There are some interesting accounts of research training provided for mental health consumers (Nichols 2001; Thorne et al. 2001; Nichols et al. 2003; Repper et al. 2003; Faulkner 2004; Lockey et al. 2004). Training is often specifically designed for a particular project but, in a review of such approaches, Lockey et al. (2004) identify several common features that seemed important: clarity about the aim and purpose of the project and the specific research tasks involved; a focus on demystifying research, particularly the language used; an interactive format so that all participants can contribute and recognize their own skills and experiences; and a safe, flexible and accessible environment. All authors emphasize the need to provide a thorough training to maintain the standards of research, some suggesting that training is also required by professional researchers to prepare them for working with consumers in research (Townend and Braithwaite 2002; Trivedi and Wykes 2002).

Finally, continuing support is essential to success (Allam et al. 2004; Faulkner 2004) in three areas: emotional, practical and supervision. Interviewing people who experience similar difficulties, or who have been through traumatic experiences, can be disturbing, and participants need to be prepared for this during training. Allam et al. (2004) suggest proactive contact following every interview to talk through any difficulties. In addition, the time pressure of the project may be stressful for people who are vulnerable and it is essential that they have access to support, and that timescales are both realistic and flexible. Practical support includes considerations of such things as transport, meeting times and payment. There are various ways in which payment can be organized but it is important that it is realistic. Allam et al. (2004) found that interviews took far more time than was anticipated if preparation, travel time and debriefing was allowed for. Restrictions on the amount of payment that people on benefits can receive may complicate issues, although useful guidance is provided by INVOLVE (2002). As well as payment for time, travel expenses and subsistence should be paid immediately or in advance. Other resources to be considered include access to office equipment, stationery and administration, these being problematic if consumers are working from home or at some distance from the research centre.

The PICAP research team members had experience of working with consumers, and several of the professional researchers, are, or have been, carers themselves. We were aware of the principles of good practice and endeavoured to maintain these standards throughout, but this was not without difficulties.

Involvement of carers in PICAP

Carers were involved at every stage and level of the PICAP. They were selected for their varying skills and experience, provided with appropriate levels of support and training, and made different contributions according to their different roles.

Advisory group

In developing the proposal representatives of different stakeholder groups were invited to join the project advisory group. The carer members of this group were selected for their ability to represent the viewpoint of carers of people with mental health problems. They included one regional carer lead who was also the carer of a sibling with serious mental health problems; another regional carer lead who worked exclusively with carers promoting their involvement in service planning and delivery; and a representative from the Alzheimer Disease Society with experience of working with carers in research. The draft proposal was sent to all members of the advisory group prior to submission but few changes were suggested. Ideally, with more time and available funding we would have developed and written the proposal with carer researchers. However the adoption of a flexible, evolutionary design and a constructivist approach ensured that carers' ongoing influence could be reflected.

Reference group

In order to elicit the views of service users and carers with concurrent experience of services, we approached an established user and carer group with experience of research to provide ongoing comment and suggestions. We met with this group before the project commenced and at six-monthly intervals in the initial stages to discuss our plans and gain their views. There are few sources of advice for working with reference groups in this way so we negotiated and agreed a plan for meetings including a clear purpose and payment. We sent all papers in advance of meetings. The group met to discuss their collective views before meeting with the research team. Following the initial meeting to discuss the overall project plan, we set an agenda which addressed specific questions – from us and them – to ensure that our meetings had a clear focus. Of particular use were their comments about the training of carer researchers. Since they had undergone research training themselves, they made valuable suggestions about our proposed training plan, particularly in interviewing practice using role play, and in providing additional time to discuss ethical issues. The group also raised interesting questions about inclusion criteria for the carers we would be interviewing. As the project progressed we found that we had less to discuss with the reference group as we had input from carers on all the study sites.

Consultation with carers

Early in the project we held a series of focus groups with carers in all regions of England. Carer leads from the National Institute of Mental Health (England) (NIMHE) regional offices helped us to identify carers who were aware of the views of other carers: for example people who led local carer groups or worked as carer representatives in service development. In addition invitations were sent out to local groups for any carers of people with mental health problems interested in talking about their experiences of assessment. The aim of the focus groups was to explore carers' views and experiences of assessment and their views of 'good practice' in assessments. Questions were deliberately open so that the carer participants in the groups could speak freely and fully. Interestingly, even though questions focused on *assessment*, in every group the carers spoke mainly about their experiences of *services*: assessments did not seem to be a priority for them. However the recent focus on 'carers' rather than 'services' and 'service users' is a departure for everyone – including carers. So it may well be that carers have relatively few experiences of assessment on which to draw. Notwithstanding this they made it clear that if services worked in an inclusive manner, valuing the experience and contribution of carers, then they did not feel separate assessments would be necessary. However, carers were able to identify features of good practice in assessments and could name some services where assessments were being implemented effectively. This informed the selection of case study sites, and the questions about how assessments were conducted. The views that carers expressed about assessments also led to a (successful) bid for further funding to extend the project by investigating service models which carers found particularly helpful. These included assertive outreach teams, psychosocial interventions, and the Family Group Conference service, all of which deliberately involved carers in all aspects of work but did not prioritize assessments.

Carers as researchers on case study sites

It was in this part of the study that we worked most intensively with carers. On each of the case study sites, between two and five carers were recruited, trained and supported to contribute to the development of carer interview schedules, undertake carer interviews, analyse transcripts and collaborate in the writing up and presentation of findings. This was approved by the Multi-Centre Research Ethics Committee (MREC) with no difficulties other than a require- ment that participants in the research were given a choice of interviewer: either professional researcher or carer researcher.

The process of working with carers developed iteratively with experience on each site informing the implementation on subsequent sites. Thus, for example, the research training was piloted on one site and amended before use on another site; the carer interview schedule developed on the first site pro- vided a template for the next site to adapt as they saw fit. Analysis was under- taken on each site independently to test the validity of the findings.

Each of the sites differed in terms of: methods and ease of the recruitment of carer researchers; support provided by local R&D office; skills and experience of the carers recruited; independence of the carers organizing and undertaking interviews; and participation of the carers in data analysis.

Recruitment of carer researchers

We began the recruitment process through carer leads in the NIMHE regional development centres. However, it became clear that although many carers were interested in improving services, very few carers had experience of research, so in all but one region we were 'starting from scratch'. In the region that was the exception two carers were recruited to work on the study who had training and experience of research and teaching. They were part of a regional carers' group who met regularly through their involvement in various service development, research and training initiatives. This demonstrates the poten- tial value of building capacity amongst local carers and supporting a group for ongoing involvement in relevant initiatives.

In all other sites we worked through the teams being studied, identifying local carer centres and sending or posting advertisements outlining the nature of the work to be done and the payment offered. The response to our invita- tions varied, but we did eventually identify between two and five carers in each site who remained interested in the project and joined the research training on offer. The majority of recruits were women aged 40 to 65 years who had spent several years caring for a child (now entering or in adulthood) with serious mental health problems. Most of the recruits had not previously done any research but they all had relevant experience of caring. There were some concerns expressed by local carer assessment services about issues of con- fidentiality: would local carers be willing to speak openly to carers they may already know? How would we select suitable carers for the project? These were pertinent questions. We had not set selection criteria because we intended to assess carers' suitability for the work throughout the training and assign work accordingly. This is discussed below.

Research governance procedures now require all researchers to have Criminal Records Bureau (CRB) clearance and honorary contracts. This was an onerous process for the carer researchers. Some mental health trusts had no system for signing off the CRB paperwork for non-employees and new systems had to be put in place which were lengthy and delayed interviewing. Honorary contracts required the completion of complex forms, citing of referees, and occupational health clearance. Carer researchers understandably needed help and reassurance during this process which necessarily took place soon after our first contact with them, before trusting relationships had been built up. This also proved a lengthy process, taking up to a year to complete. It disrupted the timing of interviews and meant that the gap between research training and commencing interviews was so long that revision sessions were required. In future, researchers who intend to involve consumers need to be aware of the complexity of this process and the implications for the timing of the research.

Training

Training was developed to reflect the requirements of the project and it drew on the format provided by Nichols et al. (2003) and Allam et al. (2004). It took place over three days, with time for some reading and rehearsal in between. Depending on their prior experience, some carer researchers opted not to follow the full programme.

Areas covered in training:

Session 1: Ground rules, introductions, what carers bring to the research, doing constructivist research, introduction to research, different kinds of research, stages of the research process, role of researchers, reliability and validity issues.

Session 2: Aims of PICAP, research design and methods, involvement of carers, case studies, interviewing carers in PICAP, analysing data, dissemination, your role as carer researcher.

Session 3: Qualitative research methods, qualitative research in PICAP, qualitative interviews, interviews with carers in PICAP, Open ended questions, qualitative interview questions for PICAP, building PICAP questions for carers, agreeing the PICAP interview schedule (see Charlesworth et al. 2004).

Session 4: Active listening, interviewing and distress, some interviewing problems and how to avoid them, difference in interviewing styles, thinking about tape recorders, using the PICAP interview schedule (see Charlesworth et al. 2004).

Session 5: Ethical issues and research governance, maintaining anonymity and confidentiality, providing information to participants, gaining informed consent, minimizing distress, organizing interviews and introducing PICAP, making arrangements to interview.

Session 6: Working safely, working in other people's homes and neighbourhoods, dealing with complaints, concerns and difficult events. Practicalities: expenses and finances, access to support, useful contacts.

A training manual was prepared and all carer researchers were given a copy. This provided an accessible description of the study, and an explanation of all the areas covered, including exercises to practise and test knowledge and a list of useful contacts and additional reading.

Early in the training, carers introduced themselves and their reasons for getting involved in the research. The majority wanted to do something to improve services and/or gain new skills. The project's focus on carers was a definite attraction for many of the carer researchers who stressed how their own experience of caring might help other carers in a similar situation. Although a small payment was made for most this was not a key incentive. Many carers were initially concerned about their ability to 'do' research. However, in the final review of the project, they all said they enjoyed their role and were keen to get involved in further research. It had increased their confidence, given them new skills, improved relationships between local carers, and had been 'interesting', a 'break', 'well paid' as well as 'worrying at times'. Although support had been offered following every interview, this was initially refused. In retrospect the carers said they thought that a phone call on every occasion may well have been helpful.

On every site, the carer researchers were able to use their experience of caring and of assessment to: understand the need for the research and the study design and methods; to amend the interview schedule and make the information sheet and invitation letters accessible; to articulate and apply ethical issues; and to understand the practicalities of interviewing. They had clear opinions and contributions to make. For example, the interview schedule followed a chronological sequence of events based on their own experiences of assessment and their priorities: how much choice, explanation and information they were given, whether they felt able to ask questions and raise issues. However, it was striking just how raw and painful were their past and ongoing experiences of caring. Accounts of their lives as carers took up a lot of time on research training days; every conversation triggered memories and sessions were often emotional. It was helpful to devote some time at the beginning of each day to share recent events and experiences. It was also useful to set ground rules for speaking one at a time, listening to each other, not making value judgements, and maintaining confidentiality within the group.

During the second day of training we discussed interview skills and practised active listening. Although initially reluctant, carers found role play was the most helpful way of rehearsing active listening skills (such as following up issues that interviewees mentioned, responding to comments to open up the discussion, acknowledging responses and encouraging respondents to give more detail). Carers worked in threes, playing carer, interviewer and observer, each giving feedback before 'de-roleing' and then feeding back to the larger group what had been learnt. Many continued to find it difficult to detach from their own experiences and remained focused on the respondent's account. It is difficult to witness someone else's distress, particularly when you identify strongly with the feelings, and even more so when your role is not to offer solutions or suggestions, but rather just to listen. The carer researchers, used to having an active role, wanted to volunteer their own experiences, suggestions and ways they had coped. Repeated practice and feedback helped them to remain 'other focused'. A list of local resources was provided for carers that interviewers could discuss with them at the end of the interview. In this way interviewees were not abandoned without help.

Perhaps hardest of all was achieving a balance between disclosing enough information about themselves to facilitate the interviewee in telling their story, and disclosing too much; taking over or leading the interview. We were employing carers as researchers because of their caring experience but it is still not clear how they can use this experience most effectively during interviews. All interviewees knew that they were being interviewed by another carer, and interviewers gave some more details about their personal situation when introducing themselves before the interview. During the interview, they were encouraged to use non-verbal cues to convey agreement and familiarity, and brief comments ('I know what you mean', 'I've been there', 'it is awful when that happens') to show empathy. However, no blanket rule can be made about how to answer direct questions asked of them (such as 'I'm terrified at times – are you?', 'Has your son ever been sectioned?'). Some carers were reluctant to talk about the person they cared for as this compromised their privacy; others found it hard to know when to stop talking about their own situation. For this purpose it was useful to work in pairs, monitoring the amount and appropriateness of self disclosure and giving each other feedback.

In all but one area (where the carer researchers had considerable previous experience), we found that the planned three days' training were not sufficient so we provided additional days to practise skills until the majority of carers felt confident and able to undertake interviews independently. Some continued to lack confidence, and some found interviewing so difficult that they worked with the professional researcher. This begs questions about the selection of consumer researchers. We did not set selection criteria: if people considered themselves to be a carer for someone with mental health problems and were interested in the project then we invited them to join the training. However, it may be more appropriate to think about relevant selection criteria, bearing in mind that carers from more deprived areas, who may not be used to training intensively and have differing, educational backgrounds are likely to need prolonged contact and support if they are to be enabled to take part. Not surprisingly, carers with experience of research were more confident and found the skills easier to pick up. Most of the difficulties were overcome by training, by targeting areas in which they lacked confidence, and by careful complementary pairing of researchers. However, it became clear that a certain level of literacy was necessary, and some understanding of research and the role of the researcher were helpful.

Undertaking interviews

The carers were working at some distance from the research centre so local systems for organizing interviews were established. This was complicated as carers often did not have access to an office or administration; they needed to rent local rooms to undertake interviews, and they had to access funds to pay for things like postage, stationery and transport. Arrangements differed on each site. One group of four carer researchers working on a south coast site will be described as an example. On this site, one of the carer researchers, a retired teacher, volunteered to organize interviews. This involved:

- maintaining clear records of the names, addresses and contact numbers of each of the ten interviewees and keeping this locked in her home
- contacting interviewees, writing initially, then speaking on the phone to negotiate a convenient time and place for interview, then texting them the day before interviews to remind them
- arranging interviewers for each interview, and calling them following interviews to check for any difficulties
- contacting the professional researcher if problems arose
- completing records: dates at which interviewees were first contacted, interviewers, dates and places of interviews and dates at which tape was sent for transcription, returned, sent to interviewee and so on
- booking venues for the interviews and ensuring that everything required was available.

On three occasions the interviewers were concerned about the distress of interviewees and asked their permission to let the carer assessors know their situation. This was agreed and the carer assessors were pleased to have been informed. The carer researchers attended the same carer support group as many of the interviewees but this did not appear to have a positive or negative effect on the interviews. Without exception, all ten interviewees on this site spoke in detail, and agreed to talk at three-monthly phone interviews and when visited again for the six-month follow-up interview.

Interviews were particularly challenging in more deprived inner-city areas where the interviewees often lived in potentially threatening circumstances. On this site carer researchers were accompanied by, and worked together with, a professional researcher. The experience of working on this site raises ethical and methodological questions about expecting consumer researchers (with just five days' training) to undertake interviews in such complex situations. This suggests the need to tailor expectations and support to the unique demands of differing contexts rather than having a 'one size fits all' approach.

On the first interview site, all interviewees were given a choice of interviewers. Interestingly, all ten asked to be interviewed by a professional interviewer. Although they were interviewed by a professional researcher a carer researcher observed the interview. Following a carer researcher's suggestion, on subsequent sites interviewees were given a choice of interviewer but informed that unless they specifically requested otherwise, they would be interviewed by a carer researcher. No one specifically requested not to have a carer researcher. It is interesting to note that although carer interviewers felt they established a good relationship with interviewees, the interview transcripts of professional interviewers differed from those conducted by carer interviewers: they were considerably longer and more detailed. This is understandable. Interviewees often introduced issues relating to service provision, types of interventions and local services that were followed up by professional interviewers who had greater knowledge of mental health and more confidence moving away from the interview guide.

Analysis of data

Carers were involved in the analysis of transcribed data on three of the study sites, receiving copies of the interviews from their site and meeting with a professional researcher to discuss the interviews. Analysis was carried out independently by different professional and carer researchers on each site, but there was striking consistency in the themes identified. The professional researchers are writing up a report for each site and undertaking cross-case analysis, but the overall findings and recommendations will be returned once again to all participants. All stakeholders will be invited to a central consensus conference where the final report and emerging guidance for the assessment of carers will be discussed until agreement is reached.

Reflecting on our experiences

The PICAP is one of very few projects to collaborate with carers at every level and stage of the research. It has been a valuable learning exercise, raising as many questions as answers about carers as researchers.

As far as possible established good practice was followed. Carers were selected for different phases of the research according to their skills and experience. However, there is a scarcity of carers already trained in research skills which meant that training and support needed to be more intensive than was planned. The relative ease with which experienced carer researchers worked in the region where an established group existed reinforces the recommendations of Rose (2003) that effort needs to go into capacity-building and ongoing support of local carer researchers. In some areas this may mean providing intensive and/or prolonged support and in-depth training that is sensitive to ethnic and cultural differences if potentially excluded carer researchers are to have the opportunity to contribute. Further engagement with carer researchers is already being planned by the Mental Health Research Network which is producing a carer involvement strategy, but to be effective this will need to develop a variety of models for engaging with carers.

Although training was provided for carer researchers this had variable success. Where recruits gained the skills and confidence to work independently as a group, with a self-selected co-ordinator, the experience was successful and both interviewees and interviewers expressed satisfaction with the process. But some recruits did not acquire sufficient confidence and competence to act independently and were accompanied by a professional researcher throughout. However, this was not a 'one way street' and the professional researcher relied on the support and the knowledge of the local carer researchers to make links within a primarily working-class and multi-ethnic community. Whilst service users prefer interviews by another service user, and speak more freely to them, this may not necessarily be the case for carers. Given the choice, some chose to speak to professional researchers. Such interviews tended to generate fuller responses, possibly due to the interviewers' additional confidence and knowledge of the mental health system. To be fair, carer researchers had very limited research training compared with professional researchers, but it raises questions about the best means of using carers as interviewers as the time and resources invested in the process may not always pay dividends. Careful thought needs to be given to the selection process and to recruits' potential ability to work independently. On the other hand, it needs to be recognized that carers and professional researchers can have an interdependent relationship, where each brings unique knowledge and skills to the situation.

Training in research skills clearly needs to fit potential researchers for purpose. We placed an emphasis on qualitative interviewing skills. It was active listening that proved most difficult for carers who were often immersed in their own painful experiences. Practice using paired role play was helpful in giving trainees feedback about their performance. Ethical issues such as confidentiality, managing distress, reporting concerns, and providing support following the interview proved important. Like Lockey et al. (2004), we found that an interactive process of discussion based on real experience was useful. But additional training was needed before we made decisions about trainees' ability to work independently in a safe, ethical and effective manner.

Carers perhaps contributed most to the planning and analysis stages of the research, rather than to interviewing. Their experiences of caring and of using services were particularly helpful in the consultation exercise which influenced the selection of study sites and the questions asked about services on those sites. Carers were also very helpful in the development of the interview schedule, information sheets and introduction letters for use with carers; their insights into what it is like to be a carer gave us additional sensitivity when inviting carers to participate in the research.

Finally, carers were helpful in the analysis of interview data. They read the transcripts and together suggested themes, categories and worked up a coding framework. However, their interpretation of the interviews did not differ from that of the professional researchers who categorized the data independently. Whilst this demonstrates the validity of the findings, it also suggests that the carers were not bringing new insights to the data in this particular instance.

Conclusion

It is often assumed that carers of people with mental health problems have the same support needs as service users when engaging in research as partners. Yet, carers clearly have a very different experience of services from service users themselves and different views of what services should provide and to whom (see Perkins and Repper 1998). Their particular perspective and experience of caring can be helpful in determining research priorities and carer-specific research questions, accessing carers for research, and in designing interview schedules for use with carers. Yet, our experience of working with carers in PICAP suggests that carer interviewers may have different training needs from service users and that carer interviewees may not gain the same benefits from interviews with other carers as service users appear to gain from interviews by their peers (Polowycz et al. 1993). Clearly the advantages of carers interviewing need to be balanced against limitations. Particular consideration needs to be given to the recruitment, and selection of carer researchers, their training and support. Questions remain about levels of self-disclosure. Some personal information needs to be disclosed for carer researchers to establish their common identity with the interviewee, yet there is a danger of them taking over the interview, compromising the privacy of the 'cared for' person, as well as raising issues of privacy between carers themselves. Care needs to be taken to avoid transforming the research interview into a peer support event.

The PICAP has raised a series of important questions about using carers as researchers, the benefits gained and the challenges to be addressed if diverse groups of carer researchers are to be enabled to make the most appropriate contribution.

Acknowledgement

We would like to acknowledge the contribution of all the people who worked on the project and those who participated in interviews.

10 Involving children, young people and parents in knowledge generation in health and social care research

Veronica Swallow, Jane Coad,
Ann Macfadyen

Introduction

Children and young people[1] make up 19 per cent of the UK population (ONS 2004) and it is clearly important to consider their views when developing and evaluating child health and social care services. Just as policy and practice initiatives have led to greater adult involvement in service delivery and research in recent years, children and their families are increasingly engaged in planning, implementing and evaluating the care and services they receive (DfES 2004a). This chapter focuses on the child and family perspective, particularly the challenges and rewards of participatory approaches with this group, and the implications for knowledge creation.

Using three case studies from our research and development experience, we outline a pragmatic framework illustrating different approaches to engaging children and their parents. This framework comprises three activities – planning, implementing and evaluating – with each case example consisting of one activity. In addressing issues such as the balance of power between adults and children, ethical and legal considerations, time and resources, we argue that involving children and their parents can have several benefits. These include: greater understanding of family perspectives; enabling participants' voices to be heard; ensuring that policy and practice initiatives reflect the views of those most closely affected by them; and providing practitioners with a sound basis from which to develop partnership-based services.

The growth of techniques for engaging children and their parents has generated global interdisciplinary interest and now constitutes an important area of study in the social sciences. This has implications for professionals, policy-makers and researchers wishing to gain insight into family perspectives, to inform services and facilities that meet their needs (Farrell 2005). However, successful participation depends on the development of strategies that engage with and promote meaningful input from children and their parents.

Background to children's and parent's involvement in knowledge development

Since the 1990s, there has been a rapid increase in activities related to children's participation in the statutory, voluntary and community sectors across the UK. These have been partly in response to Article 12 of the *United Nations Convention on the Rights of the Child* (UN 1989) and partly the result of policy imperatives exhorting active decision-making by children and their families on matters that affect them (DfES 2004a, 2004b; DoH/DfES 2004). Voluntary and community sector organizations have developed good practice for involving children (NECF 2004), and professional organizations have started producing guidelines for their members (RCPCH 2000; BERA 2004; DfES 2004a; RCN 2004). Each of these drivers has differing implications for how participation and knowledge construction is understood and enacted by citizens or consumers.

In conventional knowledge development, children's perspectives have been filtered through interpretations offered by adults, usually parents/guardians and/or researchers. This has been increasingly criticized for its failure to account for children's insights and perspectives of their social worlds (Christensen and James 2000; Jones 2004). Sociologists of childhood and children's rights advocates argue that researchers have both an ethical and practical responsibility to consider children's marginalized positions in relation to adults during all stages of the research process (Christensen and James 2000). As part of this shift, the use of participatory methodologies has been advocated within the fields of childhood studies, social policy, health and social care (Christensen 2004; Coad and Lewis 2004).

As children are usually members of a wider family new steps are being taken to capture the family as a unit of analysis in research involving them (Knafl and Deatrick 1990; Robison and Krauss 2003; Wang and Pies 2004). Grey (2003) for instance describes how family units were involved in investigating social exclusion, poverty, health and social care (Robison and Krauss 2003). Meanwhile, Hayes (1997) points out that although such studies contribute significantly to our understanding of family life, they only scratch the surface of what health and social care professionals and families need to know to design effective care. Researchers and professionals often work in relative isolation from each other and we still know very little about how families function (Hayes 1997). This isolation may be compromising coordinated attempts to develop a knowledge base.

Participatory methodologies encourage children and their parents to contribute as equal partners to knowledge development, rather than simply supplying their views during data collection. Proponents argue that this helps to reduce power imbalances in the researcher – researched relationship, as both parties are recognized as active participants in the research process, and consequently exercise greater control. Constructivist enquiry requires a position of mutuality between researcher and participant and it is therefore important for researchers to develop a partnership with participants (Meiers and Tomlinson 2003; Mills et al. 2006).

Many researchers now acknowledge children's capacity, including very young children, to be involved in research about their lives (Christensen and James 2000). The issue then becomes one of the skills needed, rather than competence, and some authors have advocated that if the family is to be involved the family members need to be given appropriate training and support (Kirby et al. 2003; Clark 2004; Kirby 2004).

Involving children and their parents in research therefore requires differing approaches to planning, implementing and evaluating projects than those used with adult research participants. We now consider some of the main issues, drawing on our respective research experiences to illustrate these. In the first section VS focuses on planning research projects involving children and parents and considers the key legal and ethical issues around consent/assent, confidentiality, anonymity and factors influencing recruitment. Next, AM explores the negotiation of access to research participants, power relationships between the researcher and children and the need for creativity and flexibility in data collection. Finally, JC discusses evaluation and outcomes of the research, impact factors and rewards for children following their involvement in research.

Planning to involve children and parents in research

When planning a research project involving children and parents, researchers must consider the legal and ethical implications. Children and adults have the same rights to confidentiality and anonymity (UN 1989; Masson 2000; RCN 2004) and the importance of involving children in decisions about whether or not to take part in research is increasingly recognized (Morrow and Richards 1996; Alderson 1997; Coyne 1998; DoH 2001c; Allmark 2002), for, as a powerless group in society, they are not in a position to challenge the way in which research findings about them are presented (Morrow and Richards 1996). A child-centred approach is widely promoted (MRC 1991; RCPCH 2000; RCN 2004) although codes of research ethics for children have only recently been developed (Allmark 2002).

The main precursor to modern ethical review processes for research is the legacy of appalling things done in the past to people, including children. The Nuremberg trials revealed horrifying research conducted on wartime captives when no regulation, apart from those relating to conventional treatments, existed regarding testing on humans (Kennedy and Grubb 2000; Allmark 2002; Shields and Twycross 2003). The Nuremberg Code was developed in 1946 (BMJ 1996) to regulate research and mandated that voluntary consent from research participants be obtained. Paradoxically this meant that research could not be conducted with those considered 'incompetent' to consent, including children. In 1964 the Helsinki declaration (WMA 2000) modified the Nuremberg Code, permitting research on 'incompetents' under strict controls, including that research proposals should be submitted to independent research committees for approval. The declaration, however, was not legally enforceable and so was not always implemented, with some health care researchers arguing that they could be relied upon to act ethically without the need for 'state interference' (Weindling 1996).

However, Beecher (1966) revealed the publication of unethical clinical research in several reputable journals, some involving children. As a result of these cumulative events: 'Reputable journals now insist that the research they publish has been subject to ethical review; ethical committees exist throughout the western world and researchers are subject to control by many ethical codes' (Allmark 2002: 9). In reviewing proposals, research ethics committees are now required to consider three main criteria: welfare of participants; respect for the dignity; and rights of participants (DoH 2001c; Allmark 2002).

Using an example from a recently completed qualitative study (Swallow 2006) investigating how children and their families learned to manage the child's chronic illness following referral to a Children's Kidney Unit, I will illustrate some of the principles followed when planning and conducting such a study and address the main legal, ethical and recruitment issues. When seeking consent from children and young people I was guided by the literature reported above and information from the Central Office for Research Ethics Committees (see Table 10.1).

I was also guided by published assessments of the age at which children become adults. These have varied over the years. However, the UK Children Act (DoH 1989) indicates that a child is any person under the age of 18 years and Kennedy and Grubb (2000) define three stages of childhood according to UK Case Law:

- children of 'tender years' who lack capacity to consent to health care treatment
- Gillick Competent children who are under 16 years and have developed sufficient maturity to consent to some or most health care procedures
- those aged 16 and 17 years who according to the Family Law Reform

Table 10.1 Guidelines for researchers: information sheets and consent forms: version 2.0 – 22 November 2005 COREC

Arrangements will vary according to the type of study proposed, according to ethical considerations and applicable law.

(i) Studies governed by the European Union Clinical Trials Directive 2001/20/EC
- Written consent must be given by parents or those with legal responsibility for the child, but children should *also* give their assent (the voluntary permission given by one who is old enough to understand and know if they want to take part or not).
- Where the parent is competent to decide for their child but unable to read or write, an impartial witness could sign the consent form to say that the information sheet has been read to the parent and verbal consent has been given.

(ii) Studies NOT governed by the European Union Clinical Trials Directive 2001/20/EC
- UK law is *untested* with regard to the legal age of consent to take part *in research* (as opposed to treatment) and it is therefore possible to apply the principle of 'Fraser' (formerly known as 'Gillick') competence for research in the UK. This can be summarized: children who are felt to be competent to understand the research proposal and thus make decisions can give consent on their own behalf.

Act (DoH 1987) are assumed to be as competent as adults unless there are grounds to suggest otherwise.

These definitions helped to inform recruitment to the study in which the age of child participants ranged from 3 months to 15 years on entry to the study.

There is also an important distinction between the concepts of consent and assent in research with children. Consent is permission given by one with legal authority such as a parent or guardian, whilst assent is voluntary permission given by one with no legal status (Lamprill 2002; Coad and Lewis 2004), in this instance a child. Competence to make a decision is critical in determining the age of assent (UN 1989) but needs to be assessed carefully, as does the context in which competence is gauged. The Law Lords decreed that children who are competent to make informed and wise decisions can give valid consent on their own behalf (Gillick 1986). However, this ruling related to treatment rather than research participation and Lamprill (2002: 2) points out that 'It would be a foolhardy investigator who consented a child into a trial against parental wishes.'

The study reported here was not a clinical trial but I was mindful that competence needs to be assessed carefully (BMA 2001), that information from those who know and love the child is of great importance (although this may of course be subjective) and that consent is a process not an event and should be constantly reassessed as children mature. In this study, there was no potential for physical harm and any possibility of psychological exploitation was minimized using the guidelines for conducting research with children (MRC 1991; RCPCH 2000; RCN 2003). As far as possible, the principles of benefi-cence, non-maleficence, respect for autonomy and justice were observed (Beauchamp and Childress 1994; Brykczynska 1994; Alderson 2005) and child-ren's rights were respected at all times in line with the *United Nation Convention on the Rights of the Child* (UN 1989). So every effort was made to: avoid inva-siveness and intrusions into family life by arranging interviews at a time and place convenient to the child and parents; interview the child without the parents present if that was their wish; and to try to ensure that any benefits arising from the study were greater than any potential disadvantages to the child and family.

In addition, I was conscious that conducting research interviews of a potentially sensitive nature soon after the child was referred to the Children's Kidney Unit may have caused distress to family members; I was guided by the Senior Nurse about the most appropriate time to approach families. This was also a concern for Alderson (2005) when conducting research with par-ents in intensive care baby units. She acknowledged the need to keep away from parents who looked particularly anxious, even though this can make projects longer and harder to complete. I applied similar principles to avoid approaching families too soon after referral in order not to cause additional stress that may have negatively influenced the quality of response I obtained from them.

In phase two of this study, data were collected through repeated inter-views over 18 months. Because of the time between interviews, I reaffirmed consent (verbally) with participants before each interview and reassessed chil-dren's ability to consent for themselves where they had not initially done so. Interviews lasted between 30 minutes and 2 hours (the average being 1 hour and 20 minutes). Mothers, fathers and children were given the opportunity to be interviewed separately or conjointly. There is a lack of consensus in the literature about the most effective approach to take; with most reported accounts from parents in studies of children with chronic disease being from mothers (Hayes 1997). There are a small number of reported studies about differences between mothers' and fathers' accounts and some suggest that we should be cautious about making generalizations from one parent to another (Hayes 1997; Wysocki and Gavin 2004), while others (Pelchat et al. 2003; Burgess 2005) imply that the paucity of accounts from fathers may be because mothers tend to be the primary carers and so are more likely to be available to participate in research, or they may in fact be more interested in research.

In this case study, the approach used was consistent with the traveller metaphor proposed by Kvale (1996) that falls within the constructivist research model, where knowledge is not given but is created and nego-tiated. Thus the interviewer is regarded as the traveller who journeys with the respondent. The meanings of the respondents' stories are developed as the traveller interprets them. Through conversation, the interviewer leads the respondent to new insights. There is a transformative element to the journey and the researcher is an active player in the co-construction of meaning and knowledge with the participants. Therefore, I saw myself as an active player in the development of data and of meaning, rather than simply a 'pipeline' through which knowledge was transmitted (Holstein and Gubrium 1997).

There are issues to consider before entering the field, particularly relating to control and negotiation of access (Coad and Lewis 2004). Commonly, access occurs through adult gatekeepers, predominantly parents, head teachers, programme managers, and key workers such as health, play and social care workers (Barker and Smith 2001). Pragmatic advice on negotiating access and preparation before entering the field is discussed by a number of researchers (James and Prout 1997; Johnson et al. 1998; Christensen and James 2000; Lewis and Lindsay 2000). There is also a further consideration here. If establishing relationships with children means that children are invited to participate in research planning meetings at an early stage, there may then be repercussions for the use of the children's time (for example, can you justify taking children away from school or from leisure activities?). In the next section AM discusses data collection involving children.

Implementing research involving children and young people

Data collection is very different when working with children than it is with adults. Experience with both groups has highlighted that, whilst some principles apply to both (giving clear explanations regarding their involvement in a study, valuing their time and effort, giving feedback on the findings), the practicalities of engaging children have to be carefully planned in advance, but also require flexibility and quick, creative thinking.

These issues are illustrated by lessons learned from interviewing 4- and 5-year-old children who were undergoing minor inpatient procedures in hospital (Macfadyen 1997). Examples from other experiences of research and consultations with older children are also given, to demonstrate the need to use strategies which are appropriate to the children involved.

In the study involving 4 and 5 year olds, children were visited the week prior to admission, within 48 hours following discharge, and two weeks later. The aim of the study was to gain insight into their experiences. Consent was obtained both from the children and their parents at the beginning of the study and on an ongoing basis. For children, a verbal explanation, describing the aims of the project and outlining their participation (with options to withdraw at any point) was given. In subsequent projects, I have used information sheets (written using language appropriate for the children), or posters (displayed in the areas where a consultation was taking place). The advice of children in the wording/layout of these has always been useful.

To try to ensure that the children felt comfortable, and because I thought that they might be more honest about their experiences away from the hospital, they were visited in their own homes. The visits were organized to suit the child and family – most visits took place after school, or at weekends. A common issue with this arrangement was the presence of other children, as the majority of the interviews took place in the family living room. The provision of paper and coloured pencils for all the children present meant that they were happily occupied, but positioning the child involved in the study slightly away from the others meant that the conversation was clearer for subsequent transcription.

The conversations were tape-recorded on a child's tape recorder and the child was invited (after some basic instructions) to take control of this, pressing the start and stop buttons when they wished. This gave the child as much control as possible, potentially reducing the power balance between myself and the child. In order to familiarize the child with the equipment, they recorded their voice and listened to it being played back before the interview started; a valuable lesson here was to ask the children in the room (who all wanted a go) just to say their name, age and favourite colour, or this part of the proceedings could become a lengthy concert!

To engage them in conversation, children were asked to draw a picture (initially of what they thought hospital would be like, then of their experiences in hospital) which they were asked about whilst they were drawing. Hill et al. (1996) promote art as a stimulus to conversation and I found this was the case with the younger children. In subsequent consultations with children I have found activity sheets (with pictures and coloured borders) are a useful tool to stimulate conversations about their experiences and opinions (Figures 10.1, 10.2 and 10.3). They particularly liked A5 booklets with different questions and activities, which can be made using greeting card making software. Older children have responded well to attractively laid out questionnaires with different types of questions (rating scales or open questions) which can be used both to collect information and as a stimulus for further discussion (Macfadyen 2006).

Engaging a child in activity is an effective way of establishing rapport in a relatively short time, and I found that doing something alongside the child made the interviews more natural conversations. Both because I did not want to influence what the children drew, and owing to my lack of artistic ability, I took along some pictures (basic line drawings of a child standing outside a hospital) and coloured them in as we talked. I have also found that having alternative strategies to stimulate conversation is useful, as have others (Docherty and Sandelowski 1999). When one child was too tired to draw (following discharge), we read a book about a child going into hospital and

A booklet to help you tell us about being ill
and how we can help you

Figure 10.1   Example 1 of activity sheets used with children.

compared this experience to their own. In a later study designed to evaluate young people's experiences of respite care, we took along some photographs (of activities in which the young people had previously been involved) to the focus group, in case the conversation dried up and we needed something to stimulate further discussion (Swallow et al. 2006).

Using activity during the research conversation helps a child feel relaxed, and provides them with a legitimate alternative when they do not want to talk. They can then change the subject quite easily if they wish. It can also give them time to think about their answers. Activities can be particularly helpful during focus group discussions, either as an ice-breaker, or as part of data collection. Varying activities have been identified in the literature, including drawing, concept mapping, taking or discussing photographs, video, graffiti wall, role play, drama and storytelling (Faulkner 1996; Hill et al. 1996; Miller 1996, 1998; Doorbar and McClarey 1999; Save the Children 2000; Clark and Moss 2001; Coad et al. 2004). Strategies used to ascertain the views of

If you draw a picture of the best ward there could be, what would be in it?

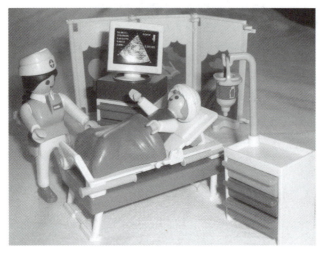

Figure 10.2 Example 2 of activity sheets used with children.

What things make coming to hospital not so bad?

Figure 10.3 Example 3 of activity sheets used with children.

individual children have included the use of drawings or pictures followed by discussion, journals and diaries, ICT, creative writing (letters and poetry) and individual interviews (Miller 2000; Save the Children 2000; Gettings and Gladstone 2001; Barker and Weller 2003; Carney et al. 2003).

If the activity involves drawing, I have found that using good quality paper and a choice of sharp pencils or nice paints/felt tipped pens encourage children's participation. I have always used colours which are washable from clothes/furniture when I have taken them to a child's home. Children are often proud of their art work and may be used to writing their name on it. To preserve anonymity the best strategy is to suggest that they put their name on the back of the paper. Whilst the use of drawing can be a useful prompt, or data collection tool, it may extend the interview time greatly; some children take great care with their colouring-in.

Children's consent (or assent) should be reaffirmed on an ongoing basis, and should clarify that they can stop whenever they wish. During the conversation they can be asked 'Have you had enough?', 'Do you want to do something different?' Some researchers have used a card system, where the child is given different coloured cards to hold up when they wish to stop or change subject. Individual children may use their own strategies to change the direction of the conversation by, for example, asking for a drink or starting another activity.

Feedback is an important part of acknowledging the children's views, and can be done in a number of ways. With the 4 and 5 year olds I gave a verbal explanation to the children, and sent a thank you letter, addressed to them. Strategies which we have used to give feedback to older children include brief summaries of the findings, newsletters or posters (Coad and Lewis 2004; Macfadyen 2006).

Can involving children and young people in health care research improve outcomes?

So far we have drawn on projects illustrating the importance of careful planning and implementation. However, several recent literature reviews have noted that literature around the impact or outcome of involving children as service users is largely absent (Lightfoot and Sloper 2002; Cavet and Sloper 2004; Coad and Houston 2006; Coad and Shaw 2006). The limited literature available shows that there are many potential benefits from involving children, such as their personal learning, development of new skills and increased confidence. Adults involved in participatory initiatives can also benefit through increasing their knowledge and understanding about children and the views they hold, which can subsequently inform personal practice (Sloper and Lightfoot 2003; Kirby 2004; Coad and Shaw 2006). Unfortunately, there is currently little evidence that children's involvement has had a significant sustainable impact on health care service provision (Coad and Houston 2006). Where improvement occurs, it tends to be local but does appear to have an impact on professionals, either those directly involved in the project and later readers, by making them more aware of children's lives (Morrow 2001a, 2001b).

There is clearly a need for more work in this area and here JC draws on a project which sought to illustrate how children can make a difference to outcomes. Coad and Coad (2005) ascertained children's views across a broad range of ages and abilities about a purpose-built Children's Unit in a new hospital planned to open in 2006. The approach was driven by the opinions of the children obtained through the use of child-friendly multi-methods, based on a combination of interviews; drawing; artwork and questionnaires identifying aspects of child-friendly services such as preferred decor, colour and environmental textures. Twelve older children and young people (aged 10–16) acted as an 'advisory expert group' to the project. The group was given supportive ongoing training, and with carefully planned adult support, developed all data collection tools and validated data analysis. The intention was for them to contribute to the research process by gaining insights into other children's perspectives, but it was also hoped to impact directly on the planning and design of the Children's Unit.

There are challenges in involving children in the research process. From the outset, ground rules were agreed. All the research took place in a convenient location, at hours that fitted around school (or, in one case, college) and at a pace appropriate to the needs and abilities of those involved. At each meeting we discussed: the need for the project; the different roles of the children/ adult researchers; time commitment and positive personal benefits of their involvement, such as projects being used for school/GCSE work. Payment for children's participation has been debated in the literature, but is contentious, owing to parental attitudes and potentially negative effects on welfare benefits of adding cash to the household income (Jones 2004). In this project, the children's 'advisory expert group' was asked about preferences in this context. This led to a decision that vouchers of their choice should be given once the project was complete.

The study comprised two phases; Phase 1 consisted of 60 semi-structured interviews and Phase 2 of questionnaires. Whilst the adult research team collected the data, the children's 'advisory expert group' informed the design, piloting and verification of the interview schedule for Phase 1. After the interviews, the children's 'advisory expert group' supported analysis and helped to develop the questionnaire for Phase 2 (Coad and Evans 2007). Full ethical approval was given by the Local Research Ethics Committee (LREC).

What was the impact?

This case study actively involved children as participants in an 'advisory expert group' to explore their views and preferences about the new hospital environment. We now draw on this experience and other literature to consider the potential impact of involving children as service users in health care research.

One contentious issue concerns decision-making, which, regardless of age, depends upon the context and the decision-maker/s (usually adults) power base and/or resources. Consequently, how decisions are framed and supported is crucial to involving children of all ages and abilities. In the present case study, following the completion of the project the children's 'advisory expert group' and some participants become increasingly vocal about what they wanted for their Children's Unit, which raised issues that were difficult for the adults. One example was the cost, relative to the funding available, of some of the children's desires for the unit and the hospital. The children's 'advisory expert group' considered that it was vital to engage participants, staff and service users in resolving this problem. It was subsequently agreed that decisions were required about what was essential and what was desirable. For example, it was recognized that some of the desirable options, like a 'mood room' for adolescents, would require help from voluntary organizations and internal fund-raising activities. Some readers may feel that this was an unacceptable compromise but resolution involved communicating fully with the children and families, being honest and asking for help with solutions. Kirby and Bryson (2002) support such an approach, noting that involving children can have a negative effect if their expectations are raised unrealistically and they later find out that their views have been ignored.

Another concern was that it was probably the most articulate children who volunteered to be part of the children's 'advisory expert group'. This is difficult to resolve as it was a self-selected group and in a time-limited project the 12 volunteers were warmly welcomed. Many research projects find that it is the most articulate and accessible who are over-represented (Coad and Twycross 2006). Whilst a limitation in terms of democratic representation, this small and well-informed group was able to have considerable impact, which we charted using clear audit trail so they were able to see the 'fruits of their labours'.

For example, the group was invited to contribute to writing the final report and to make presentations. This is important as formalized structures such as writing reports and dissemination do not usually provide channels for the creative expression of children's needs, views and ideas (Kirby and Bryson 2002). Indeed, when children's views are written up, presented and often ignored by adults, this serves to decrease children's self-esteem and may stop them getting involved again. We need to be conscious of this when involving children as service users, but it should not deter us from seeking such involvement (Cavet and Sloper 2004; O'Malley 2004). When done well, involvement breeds involvement, as a quote from one of the 'advisory expert group' illustrates:

> If all groups did what Jane did with us, I think a lot more kids like me could be involved because they made each bit very simple without making you feel stupid. The way they presented it and talked about it . . . it was easier to understand and then what we said was listened to and we wrote our bit into her bit in the report and it felt cool y'know . . . to be asked and to be listened to . . .

Evaluating the impact of giving children 'choice and voice' on service delivery and planning is important. Wright et al. (2005) undertook a follow-up study 'one year on' to evaluate how organizations that had involved children in planning services were following up. Whilst staff considered their current participation practice as inclusive, when asked to describe the profile of the children involved in the consultation, most were white, able-bodied young adults (Wright et al. 2005). There was little evidence of what had changed or improved in the organization following the consultation. For our study no evaluation has yet taken place but a youth council within the Trust has been established, comprising 25 young people who meet regularly to inform the Trust regarding children's services.

Wright et al. (2005) concluded that policy, research and practice are often at different stages, and that an organizational cultural change about children's involvement is difficult to sustain. This is often the case when both agendas and processes are controlled by adults with little consideration of their salience to children, with the assumption that notions of partnership, participation and citizenship are shared. However, I have found that children are more likely to participate if, through experience, they learn that they can voice their problems and concerns, knowing they will be taken seriously and responded to, with appropriate service improvements made. The success of attempts to involve children are heavily dependent upon the development of strategies, which not only meaningfully engage children but also show them, individually and collectively as a group, that what they say has an impact on improving outcomes.

Conclusion

Involving children, young people and families in the construction of knowledge can be both challenging and rewarding for researchers and participants. Increasingly, participants report satisfaction from their involvement in constructivist research and value the opportunity to contribute to new understandings about services. By drawing on our own research experiences to illustrate key strategic actions, we have offered some insights into the planning, implementation and evaluation of participatory research. The challenges of recruiting participants of different ages with varying levels of understanding have been addressed and the importance of involving even quite young children in the consent process has been emphasized. In addition, we have demonstrated the value of reaffirming consent as children become more developmentally mature.

Creative participatory methodologies and a flexible but adaptable approach have been shown to encourage active participation of children and parents in the knowledge development process rather than simply eliciting their views during the collection of data. These techniques can readily be used and adapted by researchers with little or no previous experience of collecting data from children or parents. The importance of using findings obtained from participatory research and evaluating the impact of these findings on services and practice development has been emphasized. Failure to do so can lead to a reduction in self-esteem by the children and young people who willingly participated in the research but who might later feel that their views have been ignored. Consequently, they may be unwilling to take part in future research. Nevertheless, a constructivist approach can, we believe, help to reduce the power imbalance often inherent in research involving children and parents. Therefore, our experience leads us to suggest that participatory approaches to involving children and parents can enable their individual and collective voices to be uncovered in a way not possible using non-participatory approaches.

Acknowledgement

We would like to thank Bethany for allowing us to use her rainbow drawing in the activity sheets illustration.

Note

1. For conciseness throughout this chapter the term 'children' is used when referring to 'children and young people' and the term 'parent' when referring to 'parent/guardian'.

11 Engaging community leaders and students in rural American community-based participatory research

Gene W. Marsh, Kristine Morgan Reimer, Lauren Clark

Background

Universities and neighbouring communities often diverge in their social and economic experiences, to the consternation of community residents and academics. Commonly, university staff are from the upper tiers of educational, social and economic classes, whereas the surrounding neighbourhoods and businesses may reflect working-class or poverty-level households. Race and ethnic composition of the university and community may also differ. Tensions can arise when community residents view the university as unsympathetic to local social problems, or focused on intervening rather than engaging with communities to identify needs and potential solutions. Unique opportunities arise from community–campus differences, and finding ways to facilitate joint working on common research and community interests has led to community-based participatory research (CBPR).

The goal of a CBPR approach is to enhance both research and population outcomes. Community-based participatory research is defined as 'an approach that combines research methods and community capacity-building strategies to bridge the gap between knowledge produced through research and translation of this research into interventions and policies' (Viswanathan et al. 2004: 1–2). This approach is designed to 'ensure and establish structures for participation by communities affected by the issue being studied, representatives of organizations, and researchers in all aspects of the research process to improve health and well-being through taking action, including social change' (Viswanathan et al. 2004: 4–1). The principles of CBPR include the following:

- acknowledging community as a unit of identity
- building on strengths and resources within the community
- facilitating a collaborative, equitable partnership in all phases of research, involving an empowering and power-sharing process that attends to social inequalities
- fostering co-learning and capacity-building among all partners
- integrating and achieving a balance between knowledge generation and intervention for the mutual benefit of all partners
- focusing on the local relevance of public health problems and on ecological perspectives that attend to the multiple determinants of health
- involving systems development using a cyclical and iterative process
- disseminating results to all partners and involving them in the wider dissemination of results
- involving a long-term process and commitment to sustainability (Israel et al. 2005).

In this chapter we introduce the CBPR approach and illustrate its application by describing a rural community assessment. This was conducted by local public health nurses, community leaders, and the professors and graduate students at a nearby university, being a shared endeavour between the local community and nurse-researchers. The public health nursing professors and graduate students at the University of Colorado at Denver and Health Sciences Center have worked with counties in Colorado for over a quarter-century to complete such community assessments. These partnerships benefit all concerned: professors gain a community 'laboratory' to teach students how to assess a community; students benefit from observing and participating in interdisciplinary public health dialogue about community organization, resources and multiple needs, they learn how to identify community issues and recommend strategic action aimed at improving the health of residents, whilst honing their qualitative and quantitative research skills; and rural county public health officials and public health nurses benefit from having an influx of academic expertise and students eager to assist with the community assessment process.

Identifying the target community

In 2003, Chaffee County in south-central Colorado was the selected community for a four-month community assessment clinical practicum for nursing graduate students. This particular assessment offers an instructive window into the process and outcomes of a CBPR research experience in community assessment.

Community-based health research begins with the moral premise that researchers should engage community residents as full, participating members of the research team. Community residents are more than passive participants in research and are actively engaged in the process as they embody community values that pertain to health and care delivery, possess knowledge about local health behaviours and resources, and apply skills to solve problems. Their expertise matters. Another premise is that CBPR produces action-oriented results for solving problems in which the community is invested. As such, communities function as 'co-investigators', in the words of a US government report on CBPR (Viswanathan et al. 2004). Their involvement spans problem definition, data collection and analysis, dissemination and application of results.

The CBPR process can be subdivided into three main components (Viswanathan et al. 2004): first, co-learning by both researchers and community collaborators so that the expertise and insights unique to each can be shared and studied; second, sharing in decision-making; and third, mutual ownership of the processes and products of the research enterprise. For the purpose of our community assessment, we have combined these main ideas with steps to achieve them, as outlined by Israel et al. (2005):

- Co-learning to foster expertise and insight is facilitated through the steps of partnership formation and community assessment and diagnosis. Community assessment can have a broad meaning referring to preliminary assessment to inform problem identification. In the example we present, community assessment defines the scope of the study we conducted.
- Sharing in decision-making occurs when the academic research team and community members define the field of data collection and agree on the main issues resulting from data collection and analysis. In community assessment, this culminates in agreement about the diagnoses of the community's strengths and themes.
- Mutual ownership of the processes and products of the community assessment enterprise can be assessed through documentation and evaluation of the partnership process, and by feedback, interpretation, dissemination and application of the results.

An example of CBPR will unfold as we describe the three major steps and processes and how we applied them within the target community of Chaffee County, Colorado, USA. However, first we provide a brief overview of Chaffee County and its public health infrastructure.

Chaffee County is located in south central Colorado amidst sprawling plains and majestic mountains with several peaks exceeding 14,000 feet. This diverse land is home to 16,242 residents (Chaffee County nd). Chaffee County was settled in the late eighteenth century when Spanish and French explorers travelled up the Arkansas River Valley. Early industry included trading and gold mining. Mining continued to be a large source of income. As coast-to-coast settlement continued, the railroad was extended through Chaffee County in the 1880s. Chaffee County was particularly desirable for settlers because of its beautiful valley location (Figure 11.1).

Two towns in the upper Arkansas Valley are the most developed in Chaffee County: Buena Vista and Salida. Initially Buena Vista was a lawless town, over-run by saloons and gamblers. The town of Salida originated as a stagecoach stop running from Cañon City to Leadville, Colorado. Yet, building the railroad defined the town. Two significant events changed the culture of the county in the late twentieth century: the decline in mining and the decline of the rail-road. The mining industry was hit with lay-offs, followed by mine closures in the 1980s creating a severe recession. The people of Chaffee County and their leaders have since developed new employment opportunities in construction, recreation, real estate and prison industries. Today people are drawn to the county for its beauty, versatility and small-town atmosphere. The county has been described as 'a gem with many facets' (Marsh et al. 2004).

Chaffee County currently is in the midst of change: demographically, socio-economically and culturally, which its government has attempted to remain informed of and responsive to. Within Chaffee County, the Department of Health and Human Services oversees delivery of public health and

Figure 11.1   A typical scene in Chaffee County (photograph: Elizabeth W. Bush).

social services, public health being managed by the local Board of Health comprised of three elected county commissioners. Local public health staff receive technical assistance and programme support through the Colorado Department of Public Health and Environment (CDPHE), which also funds Chaffee County's core public health functions. In the USA, the core functions of the public health system are assessment, assurance and policy development (IoM 1988). The CDPHE assures that these core functions are conducted at the county level throughout Colorado. Counties receiving state funding for public health nursing services have to conduct a community health assessment every five years and to base annual service planning on the needs revealed in the local assessment.

Community-based participatory research often begins when researchers initiate dialogue with members of a target community to study a population or community-based health issue. This community assessment began when Chaffee County Public Health staff expressed interest in obtaining a thorough, objective assessment of their community. The local public health director obtained county commissioner approval to contact the University of Colorado at Denver and Health Sciences Center, School of Nursing (SON) and request the opportunity to partner with the SON to undertake the Chaffee County Community Health Assessment. Annually, the SON receives requests for assistance with the CDPHE-mandated community assessments, as rural counties are often under-resourced and have limited human and financial capacity to conduct a broad assessment. Community assessments are conducted as part of a one-semester, public health practicum called 'Community Analysis', that is a component of the SON graduate curriculum in Public Health Nursing.

Implementing the CPBR process

Co-learning to foster expertise and insight

Following agreement to partner the community, their representative, in this case, the local public health director/public health nurse, contacted the course coordinator at the SON, requesting that Chaffee County be considered for the 2003 community analysis course. The course professor chose the target community based on the potential for building successful community academic partnerships, the likelihood of students and professors having an excellent CBPR field experience, and the community's commitment to future health-oriented action.

Negotiating the scope of work with community leaders is a critical first step, and begins about six months prior to the community analysis course. As course professors we evaluate the potential of each community requesting assistance, and consult with the director of nursing from CDPHE to consider the characteristics of potential target communities and assess their needs and resources. Co-learning to foster expertise and insight involves two steps: building mutual trust and sharing expertise and insight.

Building mutual trust

Building trust begins when the two course professors travel to the community about three months prior to the semester and meet with community representatives. This allows both the insider (community) and outsider (academic) partners to: discuss the scope of work; establish trust and respect; and create a positive environment engendering enthusiasm for the project. Fortuitously, the academic partners were quite familiar with one of the inside partners, the Director of Chaffee County Public Health being a graduate of the university's Nursing Doctorate Programme. Identifying a community leader that bridges the insider/outsider gap is a bonus that greatly facilitates trust-building.

At a lunch planned by the Director of Public Health, we met key stakeholders, community leaders and government officials. Light-hearted introductions and friendly conversation created a congenial opportunity for building trust. Some communities, like Chaffee County, react positively to outside academicians studying their community, and support from the Board of Health and the Director of Public Health set the stage for open access to community residents and life ways. The community's responsiveness to outsiders is critical to a successful CBPR approach, as students are more likely to be welcomed, accepted and respected by the community and 'cut a little slack' whilst they develop skill in the CBPR process.

Sharing expertise and insight

Academic partners are the natural experts on the CBPR process, and are expected to describe how they will arrive at credible findings whilst assessing the community. Conversely, community partners are experts on community characteristics and are instrumental in fine-tuning the process so that it is comfortable for their community, and predictive of success. In sharing expertise and insight amongst both partners, we began by discussing the Community as Partner Framework (Anderson and McFarlane 2004) that would guide our work, and provided reports from our previous CBPR studies to help community partners visualize the final product.

Theoretical framework

The Community as Partner Framework (Anderson and McFarlane 2004) was selected to guide the community health assessment of Chaffee County. The framework was first developed in 1988 and has evolved over time. It depicts a systems approach whereby system equilibrium results in the promotion and preservation of a healthy community. Central to the framework is engaging the community, as partner, and using the five steps of the nursing process

(Anderson and McFarlane 2004): assessment, diagnosis, planning, implementation and evaluation.

Community residents are the prime focus. Their demographic characteristics, values, beliefs and history form the foundation for the assessment. Health is defined broadly, and eight subsystems depict those factors that affect the health of the community and are likewise influenced by community members. The eight subsystems are health and social services; politics and government; safety and transportation; education; economics; communication; recreation; and physical environment (Anderson and McFarlane 2004). Table 11.1 depicts areas of assessment for each subsystem.

The Community as Partner Framework examines stressors that produce tension and disequilibrium in the community and responses to stressors that may be either strengths or limitations. Strengths represent community assets and community member resiliency within each subsystem. Limitations represent potential areas for improvement. The assessment team draws conclusions and suggests recommendations for strengthening the equilibrium of subsystems based on community action (Marsh et al. 2004).[1]

Table 11.1 Community as partner subsystems and assessment focal areas

Subsystem	Focus of assessment
Health and social services	Primary health care, public health services, emergency care, long-term care, specialty care, social service, mental health, and other health services
Politics and government	Political activities of the community, governmental infrastructure, political affiliations, community's pattern of interaction with the local political and governmental systems
Safety and transportation	Public and private mobility systems available to the community. Freedom from harm in everyday community life, protective services, fire department and police force
Education	Community public and private schools, educational opportunities, other educational resources such as adults' learning opportunities and services such as libraries, continuing education programmes
Economics	Goods and services available to the community. Also, employment rates, job availability, resource allocation, industry, businesses, and community economic stability
Communication	Formal and informal methods used to disseminate information between groups and individuals within the community
Recreation	Availability of fun and leisure activities and determining activities residents prefer
Physical environment	Appearance and quality of man-made and natural components of the community, for example, land use, housing, pollution, and water quality

Source: Anderson and McFarlane 2004

Following our presentation of the assessment framework and proposed methods, residents and community leaders offered colourful and detailed descriptions of the community. We asked community leaders about potentially vulnerable sub-populations, and they identified a small Spanish-speaking part of their community, and their two population centres in a vast and rugged land mass of 1013 square miles. The population centres are the more northern town, Buena Vista and the southernmost town, Salida. Community partners requested that we equitably represent the population of the whole county. We knew that we would need to remain flexible to new ideas and needs voiced by the community. Time spent in preparation is always important, but with CBPR it is critical and without full acceptance and a solid community–academic partnership, it can fail.

Sharing in decision-making

Following these presentations, we collaborated on customizing the CBPR process to fit the needs of Chaffee County whilst also meeting the requirements of CDPHE for credible final report including recommendations for community action. Dates for a three-day field trip when students would immerse themselves in rural county life and collect data from multiple sources were agreed and expectations for both sides discussed.

Clarifying the responsibilities of community and academic partners in a signed memorandum of understanding (MOU) is helpful for future reference. For example, we asked the county to provide meeting space, an operations centre, communication assistance, press releases prior to our arrival, publicity about our 'county sponsored' activities, access to most community organizations, permission to undertake surveys in public venues, and an on-call resource person to provide quick information and responses to questions. Most importantly, we requested a list of about 100 willing key informants, individuals knowledgeable about an area of community life, with whom students could arrange a 45- to 60-minute interview.

As we discussed the issues, our partners' enthusiasm grew as they realized they were instrumental to success. They began envisioning ideal scenarios such as conducting focus groups with special populations, translating the survey into Spanish, school-wide activities and guest appearances in classes. We reminded our enthusiastic partners that our students were in a mentored, supervised learning environment, unlike paid consultants, and were required to complete their work in one semester, over 135 hours. We therefore encouraged communities to augment our data collection efforts with their own.

Together we identified three sources of data to collect, analyse and synthesize for the community assessment. Primary data would be collected by our assessment team specifically for this CBPR and would include key informant interviews and primary informant surveys using a convenience sample of community residents. Our students would develop the data collection tools with community partners' input. Secondary data, that existed prior to the start of the CBPR, would be retrieved from large databases accessed via the Internet, county publications, newspapers, previous reports and other available resources. Community members were helpful in identifying such secondary sources of data previously unknown to us.

Fostering expertise and insight, and shared decision-making continued throughout the entire process as data were collected, analysed, synthesized and disseminated back to the community for validity checks prior to writing the final report. Having worked with the community we needed to repeat the initial steps with our students prior to data collection.

Engaging students in CBPR methods

The first class and course orientation occurred five weeks prior to the scheduled field experience. We required our 28 students to become familiar with the Community as Partner Framework (Anderson and McFarlane 2004) through assigned readings. All students joined one of two work teams. The first group covered the core domain and eight subsystems of the Community as Partner Framework. They would write the chapters for the core domain and eight subsystems by synthesizing secondary data, and key informant and survey primary data, and summarize the strengths and limitations of each subsystem, making recommendations for community action. The second group represented specialized tasks that occurred throughout the semester, including: developing the key informant interview guide and preparing students to conduct key informant interviews; developing the survey, overseeing and assisting other students with data entry, data cleaning and analysis; writing the introduction to the final report; describing overarching themes, writing the assessment conclusions, and executive summary; preparing the final presentation in slideshow format and presenting it to the community at the project's conclusion; critiquing and editing the final report.

Our community partners were invited guests at our second class. The Public Health Nurse (PHN) presented vivid descriptions of her community and its people, enlivening Chaffee County life by telling stories about noteworthy residents, folk heroes and humorous events. She infused the process with realism and hooked the students on this educational adventure, whilst emphasizing how much the community partners valued the students' efforts. Students recognized the professional commitment required of them.

The remaining pre-field work classes were devoted to developing data collection tools, key informant interview guides, a community health survey and demographic profile. Community input was solicited for each of the data collection tools and revisions reflected concerns of community partners.

Students gained familiarity with protocols for data collection and expectations of the field experience.

Sources of data

The core domain and eight subsystems of the Community as Partner Framework were used to organize data collection as well as for writing the final report and preparing the final presentation for the community. Primary data were collected during the three-day field experience. Secondary data were collected throughout the semester.

Key informant interviews

An exploratory method was used to obtain perceptions of community life from knowledgeable individuals in the community, based on a list of more than 100 potential key informants compiled by community leaders. Informants were recruited based on their knowledge and expertise with community issues or leadership positions within the community, for example, educators, health care providers, emergency and protective service providers, clergy, local elected officials, long-term citizens, and parents. All key informants received a letter from the Public Health Director inviting their participation and each student was assigned a minimum of three key informants to contact and arrange a 45- to 60-minute interview. Once key informants were identified, the workgroup developed a standardized semi-structured interview guide to elicit key informants' perceptions about the community. In all, 76 key informants participated in interviews.

Primary informant surveys

A survey was used to collect data referencing the core domain, eight subsystems (Anderson and McFarlane 2004) and questions specific to Chaffee County. For example, for the core domain related to 'culture', survey respondents were asked to indicate their level of agreement with the following statement: 'The community is sensitive to the needs of the different races and cultures in Chaffee County.' Each student was responsible for collecting a minimum of ten surveys from a convenience sample of community residents. However, the first debriefing revealed that students had not diversified throughout the county as expected, and had collected most of their data in only one of the two population centres. To correct this sampling bias, students collected a similar number of surveys from the second population centre, bringing the total number of surveys to 424 and equitably representing both population centres. Similar demographic data were collected on both the key informant and survey samples.

Secondary data

Students collected secondary data from a variety of sources. These comprised previously collected data such as census records (US Census Bureau at http://www.census.gov) and Behavioral Risk Factor Data from the state health department website (http://www.cdphe.state.co.us/hs/brfss/), minutes from town meetings; local newspapers, informational flyers, community reports and numerous other sources.

Data analysis methods

Key informant interviews – the professors guided students in the analysis of key informant interviews using traditional ethnographic principles, and supported by an online course software platform (WebCT)[2] modified by the professors for asynchronously coding and categorizing data with a large group of students.

Time constraints and class expectations prohibited transcribing interviews. Working within their unique subsystem groups and with their subsystem-specific data, students reviewed tapes and field notes and extracted note-worthy comments and quotes. They assigned substantive or interpretative codes to each comment or quote. Codes were clustered into beginning categories and defined with a provisional category definition. Student-created category definitions were compiled across the core domain and all subsystems, resulting in a working codebook to use in coding the remaining subsystem data from their interviews.

Quotes and key statements across all interviews were posted to the appropriate category. Students responsible for unique subsystems then compiled and downloaded all of the quotes and noteworthy statements that contributed to their defined categories. They used these data to develop and write their final chapters. An advantage of the online data analysis process is that it supports group learning. Students can communicate with one another about the data they are posting. They can challenge existing category definitions prompting revisions and suggest additional categories based on their own emerging data. In addition, their professors can drop into group discussions of the analysis-in-progress and clarify questions.

Primary informant surveys – each student entered his or her survey data into a computerized database file. The survey work team cleaned and analysed survey data descriptively using the Statistical Package for the Social Sciences 13.0 (SPSS). The computer printout of statistical results was provided to each work team for the purpose of interpreting subsystem results and writing the final chapters.

Overarching themes – finally, in a lengthy face-to-face class lasting several hours, students debated, discussed, negotiated and, finally, reached consensus on the overarching themes that emerged from all of the data. These themes were used to frame the conclusions about the full study and to generate recommendations for community action. The five overarching themes from the Chaffee County community assessment appear below:

- Diversity is both a strength and a challenge.
- Changes in the community evoke varied perceptions.
- Chaffee County residents have a strong sense of community.
- Economic strengths, disparities, fluctuations and affordability factors affect daily life.
- Gaps in community resources and services affect residents' well-being.

Preparing the final presentation and written report

Armed with an academic semester's worth of data, students submitted their draft chapters of the final report to their professors and to the Presentation Task Group. The Presentation Task Group used the chapters to develop and produce a slideshow presentation that was presented publicly to the community at the course conclusion. The final class was a dry run of the presentation. Community partners were invited and participated as the students fine-tuned their facts and information. The course professors, students and community partners are always astonished at the amount of information that we have provided. We often feel a bit overwhelmed and tired in the final stretch, but the lasting rewards are great.

Mutual ownership of the processes and products

Mutual ownership of the processes and products of the community assessment enterprise can be assessed through documentation and evaluation of the partnership process and by feedback, interpretation, dissemination and application of the results.

Dissemination of results and evaluation of the CBPR process characterizes the final phase of the community assessment study. At this point, the academic partners begin to pull back from their involvement with the community. In contrast, the community leaders embark upon the challenge of developing and implementing a community action plan using many of the community assessment findings and recommendations.

Dissemination of results

Based on input from community representatives, course professors and students, the final slideshow presentation underwent quick refinement. Students from the presentation task group returned to the community and presented the full report to the original community leaders, government officials, stake-holders, key informants, members of the general public and fellow students. The final presentation was a notable event, and a culmination of the mutual process and ownership of the CBPR project. Students had pride in their product, and they strived to be accurate and credible. They recognized the potential impact of their work on future community health directions, decisions and resource allocations. We assured them that we would help field difficult questions from the community, but we knew they were well prepared, and our intervention was unlikely. Nevertheless, for students it was a time of high anticipation that later gave way to celebration of the quality of their work and the contribution they had made to future efforts to improve the community's health.

Community feedback necessitated minor final revisions to the written report. For example, a member of the parks and recreation department indicated that we had incorrectly reported the number of county parks. We corrected that. The local coroner informed us that the county's suicide rate was most likely inflated due to non-residents from the city choosing to end their lives in a beautiful environment. Although the fact seemed grim, the distinction was important in evaluating the prevalence of mental health problems and treatment resources in the community. Correcting these inaccuracies increased community ownership and readers' acceptance of the final report.

Following the public forum, students refined and resubmitted their chapters. Over the years, we have learned the importance of hiring an editor to help synthesize the final report, check the accuracy of references and format the report consistently throughout. This time-consuming process required another month or two before the final written report (usually about 200 pages in length) was printed and disseminated.

Evaluating the CBPR process

Evaluating the CPBR process allows us continually to refine our methods and adopt students' creative ideas. By the conclusion of the course, students' initial enthusiasm, experienced prior to the field trip, has waned, and given way to relief from having survived the rigorous, demanding process, reflecting the time-intensive nature of CBPR research. The course exceeds the usual workload expectations of professors and students in other courses, and yet, it is perhaps the most rewarding course we have taught because of the real-world mutual experience with communities that leads to successful political advocacy for change in health care delivery. The professor role requires enthusiasm, expertise with qualitative and quantitative research methods, knowledge about rural communities in Colorado, and the national and state public health infrastructure, negotiation and mediation skills with students and community members, and the ever-present reminder that our students represent the highly visible and political interface between the university and local communities. We believe that the benefits outweigh the limitations, especially when anecdotal reports from graduates indicate that this was the most valuable of their graduate educational courses. Students laud the real-world experience of working with peers, communities, health care and political systems, and presenting their work in written and oral report forms for public debate.

Benefits to students and professors

Community-based participatory research requires professors to evaluate and refine their own expertise in working with communities in public health practice sites. Students reap the secondary benefits, refining and applying their quantitative and qualitative research skills, and gaining expertise in retrieving, managing, analysing and synthesizing large amounts of data. No other experience affords the opportunity for them to synthesize 'real' data, and they recognize the effort essential for assuring credibility. Rarely, do they attempt shortcuts. Students also gain insight into local politics, public health roles, and in population focused care, service learning and social justice research.

Benefits to the State of Colorado

Community-based participatory research demonstrates a valuable contribution from the university to rural communities of Colorado, promoting role development for the future public health nursing workforce and enlightening student nurses about opportunities in rural Colorado. For the Colorado Department of Public Health and Environment, the community assessment documents trends and changes in rural communities and provides valuable data on which to base higher-level funding decisions.

Benefits to the community

The biggest winner in CBPR is the community, the process stimulating citizens and government to prioritize needs strategically and apply the results. Community-based participatory research stimulates inter-professional collaboration amongst existing community health service partners, helping them to appreciate broad areas of concern and to target areas for community capacity-building. Whilst meeting the mandate from the CDPHE for a five-year assessment, the final report also provides a detailed snapshot of the community's health, strengths, limitations and future recommendations for action, providing essential facts strengthening future funding proposals. Unexpected findings are unearthed that attract the attention of county government officials. For example, we discovered and reported that amongst single parent, female head of household families, 32 per cent subsisted below the US poverty level (US Census Bureau 2000). County commissioners were surprised at the size of this vulnerable group on their doorstep. This, and other socio-economic findings, caught their attention and motivated them to examine county socio-economic data more thoroughly.

Applying the results

The forces of change in Chaffee County are well identified. Our information on community stressors was not new. However, documenting the impact that these factors have on the community is often new, factual and commands attention. Findings confirmed that the county was experiencing a period of rapid economic change, with mining and agriculture, the mainstays of the community for decades, having been replaced by construction and tourism jobs. This trend is expected to continue over the next ten years and the incongruence between the supply and demand in the job market is leading to negative consequences for the working class (Marsh et al. 2004).

Chaffee County Public Health has utilized the health assessment to challenge traditional views of community health. The data have been utilized by county officials to enhance economic development efforts and planning. Most notable, Chaffee County Public Health has utilized the data to demonstrate the health care disparities experienced by the county's uninsured people. This example provides a clear illustration of the process of applying the community assessment results.

According to Healthy People 2010 (US Department of Health and Human Services 2000) having health insurance and regular primary care providers predict quality health care. The community health assessment revealed that an estimated 25 to 33 per cent of Chaffee County residents lacked health insurance. Of the 424 residents surveyed, 43 per cent indicated that they sought care through the local hospital emergency room. Additionally, 42 per cent of key informants did not believe that all residents in Chaffee County were able to access necessary health services (Marsh et al. 2004).

Public health is often viewed as a 'gap-filler' for primary care services for underserved populations. Locally, Chaffee County Public Health was not equipped to provide 'quality access to health services' through direct service delivery any more than the national public health system can provide primary care services to the estimated 44 million uninsured individuals in the USA. Whilst the public health system is not able to handle current uninsured and underinsured residents, the private sector also is unable to absorb the rising costs of persons in need of care.

The community health assessment confirmed that many jobs within the rising tourism and construction fields do not provide benefits such as health insurance. Over the next five to ten years, as the population of the county continues to grow, so will the number of uninsured and underinsured county residents. Additional demographic data revealed that Chaffee County is experiencing an increasing number of undocumented immigrant families who do not have health insurance and are ineligible for government health plans such as Medicaid. Therefore, health issues faced by many children, pregnant women and individuals remain untreated unless an emergency.

Whilst growth has occurred amongst some population segments (for example, retired people and second-home owners), school district figures indicated that families are leaving Chaffee County at a rate of 5 to 7 per cent annually because they cannot afford to live in the community (Chaffee County School District, R-32-J, personal communication 2004). Poverty rates for families and children exceed the state average and are increasing. The average wage is more than a third lower than the state average, yet housing prices continue to rise (Marsh et al. 2004). Paradoxically, some families cannot leave owing to a lack of financial resources for mobilization. These combined trends have resulted in a shrinking middle class for Chaffee County.

The community health assessment revealed that the median age of the county is greater than the state median and expected to increase at a rate higher than the state due to the affluent 'baby-boomers' that are settling in the county. Unless Chaffee County engages in strategic planning, the disparities between the 'haves' and the 'have-nots' including access to adequate health care are predicted to widen over the next ten years.

Health care resources include a local medical centre, private practice providers, Planned Parenthood and public health. Major gaps exist in access to affordable care as evidenced by the number of families who cite the emergency room as their 'primary care provider', and the number of key informants (65 per cent) who cite lack of health insurance as the number one health concern in the county (Marsh et al. 2004). Few providers offer a sliding scale or publicize free or reduced cost services to uninsured and underinsured residents.

Based on the community health assessment and other data, medical centre representatives, small businesses owners, individuals, social service agencies, government officials and private providers have all voiced concern about access to affordable care in Chaffee County. County health providers and other stakeholders are motivated and ready to address disparities in health care access and to redesign systems that have lost pace with escalating health care costs over the past 15 years.

In response to the community health assessment results, a diverse group of community stakeholders began meeting in 2004 to examine the feasibility of offering a sliding scale clinic to the uninsured residents of Chaffee County. With the support and collaboration of key stakeholders, Chaffee County utilized the Community Health Assessment data to support a funding proposal to the Colorado Trust Partnerships for Health Initiative. A five-year grant of $75,000 annually was awarded to address access to care in the community through a variety of steps culminating in the opening of the Chaffee People's

Clinic. In 2006, the citizens of Chaffee County, the regional medical centre, the County Commissioners and many local health providers helped facilitate the startup of the Chaffee People's Clinic, a non-profit sliding-scale clinic for uninsured persons living and working in Chaffee County.

Conclusion

Community-based participatory research is an evolving methodology that involves forging and sustaining academic–community partnerships. In this chapter we presented a case example of CBPR drawn from our years of experience in teaching public health nursing and research methodology at the University of Colorado. The rural Colorado community exemplifies a CBPR setting that is typical of communities that embrace healthy change and welcome academic expertise in launching the change process. Examples of the phases of CBPR – co-learning to foster expertise and insight, sharing in decision-making, and mutual ownership of the processes and products of community assessment – have been illuminated with professors', students' and community members' experiences. Although CBPR can be a lengthy and tedious process, the benefits are rewarding and can often stimulate community and political changes that yield positive community health outcomes.

Notes

1. This approach is one of several community health assessment frameworks used in the USA, and is particularly effective for conveying the concepts of public health nursing. Since conducting the Chaffee County assessment we have adopted a more recent approach, Mobilizing for Action through Planning and Partnerships (MAPP) that was developed by the Centers for Disease Control (CDC) and the National Association of County and City Health Officials (NACCHO). The CDPHE now mandates the use of the MAPP framework for county health assessments. Further information on MAPP may be obtained from the NACCHO website (http://www.naccho.org).
2. WebCT was originally developed by Murray W. Goldberg who built a system to assist web-based learning environments. In 1999, WebCT was acquired by Universal Learning Technology, and in 2006, WebCT was acquired by Blackboard_Inc. The merger terms with Blackboard, will result in phasing out the WebCT name in favour of the Blackboard brand (http://en.wikipedia.org/wiki/WebCT, n.d.).

12 Conclusions: realizing authentic participatory enquiry

Mike Nolan, Elizabeth Hanson, Gordon Grant, John Keady

> Our world does not consist of separate things but of the relationships we co-invent.
>
> (Bradbury and Reason 2003: 206)

> . . . instead of the categorical distinctions between an undifferentiated lay understanding and an equally undifferentiated expert, the proposal is for a more relational view. This would enable the local knowledge of workers, the experiential knowledge of people with chronic illness, the variable distribution of expert knowledge amongst health professionals, and the challenges posed by lay activists to expert science to be recognized.
>
> (Hodgson and Canvin 2005: 54)

In the preceding case studies many of the authors used metaphors involving some form of movement to capture their experiences: Swallow et al. talked of being a 'traveller'; in order to provide a sense of momentum for her unfolding life story MQ likened her personal theory to a motor vehicle; McClimens et al. compared how official accounts of a fictional car crash serve to silence many voices, as do traditional approaches to research; Tolson et al. reflect on their 'shared journey' with co-participants. These metaphors were adopted entirely independently; so is this simply a remarkable coincidence, or does it signal something more significant and shared? We would like to think the latter, believing that the case studies provide many key insights with important implications for advancing participatory research in health and social care. What then do the case studies say about voices, values and evaluation, and what lessons can we learn from them about the theory and practice of user participation in health and social care research? In this chapter we provide our own interpretations and reflections, and link these back to some of the issues we raised in Chapter 1.

Before doing so we feel it is helpful to reflect upon the richness and diversity of the case studies, as they varied considerably on several dimensions. For example, some focused very clearly on working with small groups of people to create essentially 'individual' knowledge based on biography and life history (Keady et al.; Koch and Crichton), which could nevertheless be used to inform both care delivery and contribute to collective understanding. Others provided either individual accounts of users' experiences as researchers (Shields et al.), or partisan accounts of academics working to engage users as researchers (McClimens et al.). User groups also included the reflections of practitioners as participatory users (Hanson et al.). Some case studies concentrated on the participation of certain groups of users in research, such as: carers of people with mental health problems (Repper et al.); children and parents (Swallow et al.); and relatives and staff in care homes for older people (Davies et al.). Expanding the notion of participation yet further there was also a focus on engaging with communities as participants (Marsh et al.) or generating insights that could lead to the development of national guidelines (Tolson et al.).

There was also diversity in the range of user roles that were described, from co-constructors of personal narratives (Keady et al.; Koch and Crichton) to co-researchers in a shared endeavour (McClimens et al.; Repper et al.; Shields et al.; Swallow et al.), to participants in varying forms of action orientated enterprises (Davies et al.; Hanson et al.; Marsh et al.; Tolson et al.). Not surprisingly, therefore, methodological approaches also differed including: narrative accounts (Keady et al.; Koch and Crichton); reflexive accounts (Hanson et al., McClimens et al.; Shields et al.), and multi-method approaches (Davies et al.; Hanson et al.; Marsh et al.; Repper et al.; Swallow et al.; Tolson et al.).

Notwithstanding such diversity, the accounts also shared several important features, notably:

- the use of innovative methodological approaches to enable, as far as possible, the full participation of traditionally silenced or muted voices
- a focus on developing partnerships and a commitment to co-construction and co-learning
- acknowledgement of the importance of developing and sustaining relationships to the success (or otherwise) of participatory research
- some, but not all, described barriers within traditional institutions that generally hindered their efforts.

All of the above have important implications for the voices that are heard, the values that are seen as important, and the way that the effectiveness of participation can be evaluated. Our reflections on these issues constitute the main focus of this chapter.

Prior to this, however, we would like to highlight the importance of ensuring sufficient time, resources and thorough preparation for the success of any participatory endeavour. The literature clearly stresses the need for:

- sufficient time and resources for effective participatory research with users (Clark et al. 2005; Minogue et al. 2005; Steel 2005)
- a focus on training and preparation for *everyone* involved (Reed et al. 2004; Beresford 2005; Dewar 2005; Fleming 2005; Hodgson and Canvin 2005; Minogue et al. 2005; Owen 2005; Roche et al. 2005; Clough et al. 2006). Such preparation and training is not about 'expert' researchers imparting their wisdom to 'novice' users, but rather about pooling and sharing the combined expertise of everyone (Dewar 2005; Owen 2005; Clough et al. 2006). A range of training is described, varying from a few sessions to a two-year programme with university validation (Clough et al. 2006)
- attention to practical issues. For example, how will employment and payment be handled, and what implications do these have for users who may be in receipt of benefits? How are role expectations established, and is there a need for a more formal 'job' description (see Clark et al. 2005; Roche et al. 2005 for interesting discussions)
- ongoing support for all those involved (Faulkner 2004; Beresford 2005; Clark et al. 2005; Dewar 2005), at several levels: emotional; practical; in conducting the research itself (Faulkner 2004).

The stories recounted in the case studies, and our own experiences over a number of years, would amply reinforce the above.

Time and resources are clearly crucial, and the need for considerable investment of both should not be underestimated. The benefits of careful planning were described in several of the case studies, particularly the importance of establishing clear aims from the outset. Of course such aims cannot be set in stone, especially when engaging in the type of constructivist work underpinning many of the studies, where designs emerge and evolve over time. This requires a delicate balance between clarity, creativity and flexibility. However, allowing sufficient time is essential. Marsh et al., for example, talk of the several months of careful planning and consultation that preceded their work in Chaffee County, Colorado. Both Repper et al. and Swallow et al. stress the need to set up and establish mechanisms for participation, and to take unexpected delays into account, particularly in complex projects spanning several sites where research governance issues need to be addressed. These currently impact on all research in health and social care, but seem particularly intrusive for those studies involving users. The amount of effort required should not be underestimated, nor should its potential impact, with McClimens et al. describing it as 'energy sapping'. Such 'energy' is a very important resource for participatory work, and time must be allowed for people to regain energy so that the process does not grind to a halt.

Another facet of time that requires careful consideration is patience – things will not happen quickly, nor may changes seem particularly dramatic. For example, Davies et al. talk of the three years' investment they made when introducing changes to 67 Birch Avenue. Their progress appeared painfully slow at times, and it was only when the collective changes made were considered that they realized how much had been achieved. Conversely, the sense of frustration in McClimens et al.'s exclamation of *two* years to produce an article is almost palpable. Taking a longer-term view is therefore essential, with the success of the ACTION project building on over ten years of work, and Marsh et al. talk of 25 years' experience of involving differing communities in participatory work. The other key investment of time is that required to establish relationships. These experiences raise some thorny questions about the kind of infrastructure required to support pre-protocol work that fully engages service users and user or carer researchers, and who should be responsible for funding this, bearing in mind the long lead times that may be necessary to work on proposals, and without any guarantees of success. The hidden costs of this activity, for academic researchers, are written off in the main by their employers – universities. User and carer researchers do not typically share this luxury, so they are left in most cases to bear this cost themselves.

Many of the case studies also emphasized the benefits of sufficient initial and ongoing training. This again has time implications, but the results more than justify the investment. The case studies reflect the messages from the literature, highlighting that initial training is not simply about developing skills, although this is vital; it is also about identifying shared values and goals. The case studies by Davies et al. and Tolson et al. clearly demonstrate the importance of agreeing values from the outset and, Tolson et al. in particular, stress the emergence of a team spirit as integral to this. However, caution also needs to be sounded, for if such team-building does not include everyone, then it can be difficult for those not involved from the outset to 'break' into the group. So Tolson et al. describe how the Communities of Practice (CoP) they set up for practitioners were reluctant to let older people join later. On reflection they acknowledge that early engagement with all groups is essential, again an issue to which we will return.

Beyond a shared vision, several case studies consider the challenges of ensuring that the skills and knowledge needed to engage as researchers are available to everyone. Repper et al. and McClimens et al. consider this in relation to users actively engaging in data collection, admitting that they may have underestimated the complexities involved. For researchers experienced in the process it is all too easy to lose sight of their own initial fears and apprehensions. This is well illustrated by Marsh et al., who described how even nurses on the final year of their undergraduate programme required extensive training and support. How much more daunting might this be for those entirely new to the process? Despite prior experience of working with users as researchers, Repper et al. would admit that they failed fully to anticipate the considerable initial training and ongoing support required.

Practical issues concerning employment and other bureaucratic processes were clearly implicated in several of the case studies. This was perhaps most tellingly illustrated by McClimens et al. in the case of people with learning difficulties, and Shields et al. for people with mental health problems. Here it seems that 'systems' conspire against the success of user participation or, at the very least, minimize its scope because of their failure to provide needed support, or to trust in the abilities of those 'labelled as having learning disabilities' (McClimens et al.). This seems reminiscent of the 'system induced setbacks' described by Hart (2001), whereby a significant proportion of the difficulties people with stroke experience in the community are directly attributable to health and social systems themselves. Clearly such structural and institutional impediments need to be recognized and addressed. Conversely, the success of the ACTION project, and Paul and Fredrik's ability to expand their roles, would not have been possible without support and encouragement from the wider management structure at several levels. Such commitment is another prerequisite for successful participatory working.

On a more practical, but nevertheless important, level, Repper et al. reflect on the benefits that would have been gained by having a clearer vision of the roles of carer researchers, and a better recruitment strategy from the outset.

Perhaps most important of all is the question of ongoing support at emotional, practical, methodological and ethical levels. The emotional demands on everyone involved in participatory work are considerable, and we will touch on this at a number of points in this chapter when we consider the 'relational' nature of participatory work. The case studies by Hanson et al. and Tolson et al. capture the practical support required when engaging older people as participants using ICT as the interface. However, the benefits both in terms of the project and personally were more than worth the efforts expended. Several case studies attest to the need for innovative methodologies and support to ensure that the voices of traditionally silenced or muted groups such as children, especially young children (see Swallow et al.) or people with dementia (Keady et al., Koch and Crichton) or learning difficulties (McClimens et al.) may be heard. Ethics are a major consideration in all forms of research, but are especially important in user-focused participatory approaches, as eloquently captured in the reflections in the case study by Shields et al.

Having flagged up the above issues, we return to several of them later, but now we turn our attention once more to considerations of voice, values and evaluation.

In reflecting on her experiences of establishing a centre for the participation of older people in Edinburgh, Dewar (2005) identified a series of questions that she considered important to address if the theory and practice of participatory research are to advance. These were:

- the need to develop greater insights about involvement in research, both practical, such as what level and type of support to provide, and theoretical
- to explore further the concept of 'equal' but 'different' partnerships and how they can work
- to consider both processes and outcomes, especially what types of knowledge have been produced, and whether they are really more 'realistic or authentic'
- to share and learn from experiences across different user groups
- to raise debates with funders and ethical committees about how involvement can be improved.

We feel that the case studies have something to say about each of these issues. We have already touched on some of them, such as the need for time and planning and the importance of addressing the structural impediments to participation. We will elaborate further on others later. We now explore a number of the above questions under the headings of voice, values and evaluation.

Voice – need anyone 'shout the loudest'?

In the opening chapter we noted the tensions within the participatory research literature about whether the enterprise should be essentially 'user controlled' or based on some form of partnership (for us the phase of consultation is important in certain contexts, but would not constitute participatory research). One set of voices suggested that the 'gold' standard should be emancipatory, user-controlled research (Minkler and Wallerstein 2003; Turner and Beresford 2005), anything else being seen as 'undesirable' (Turner and Beresford 2005). Offering an alternative perspective, several groups of 'users' themselves do not necessarily want such a degree of control (Dewar 2005; Clough et al. 2006), preferring instead a joint and shared undertaking. It is clear from the case studies that the model used in every instance involved the formation of varying forms of partnerships with users. This is not to say that there is no place for 'user-controlled' studies, but it seems paradoxical that those who assert that anything else is undesirable ignore the wishes of user groups for whom partnership ways of working is their preferred option.

The literature suggests that partnerships should ideally be equal (Dewar 2005), collaborative (Marsh et al. 2005), active (Hanley et al. 2004) or real

(Hulatt and Lowes 2005). In considering the case studies it is clear that they all reflected a collaborative and active engagement with users, but not all could be considered equal. But is this necessarily inappropriate and, moreover, what does equal or real mean in this context? After their experience of working with people 'labelled as having learning disabilities', McClimens et al. conclude that perhaps it is time to be honest enough to recognize that not all partnerships can be equal. However, this does not necessarily mean that the 'researcher' is the 'senior' partner. For example, Paul and Fredrik readily acknowledge that in their early days of working with ACTION the partnership was unequal, with themselves being mentored by Barbro, the more experienced and knowledgeable user. The other case studies also describe varying degrees of partnership that were not necessarily equal throughout. So, for instance, Keady and colleagues in working to co-construct personal theories with people with dementia used a dramaturgical metaphor and suggested that in the early stages the 'director' of the presentation was the academic researcher but that, as their experience grew and the person with dementia became more confident in articulating their story, the roles became reversed. In the latter stages of dementia Koch and Crichton talk of working together with the person's wider social network in order to 'curate' their story, thereby ensuring that it continued to act as the key reference point informing their future care.

At the community level Marsh et al. illustrate how the varying actors involved each contributed their own unique expertise and knowledge in compiling a complete picture. For example, the local coroner was able to add his knowledge of the reasons for the apparently high suicide rate in the county, providing a possibly more telling interpretation.

Partnerships tend to work best when people bring differing skills, experiences and expertise that are all equally valued as contributions. This for us provides a more meaningful definition of an 'equal' partnership in the context of user participation in research. It is not that everybody contributes the same thing, or even different things in equal measure. Rather it is about ensuring that what people contribute is seen to be of equal value, with an accompanying recognition that without everyone's input the partnership would diminish.

Other dimensions of partnerships that are raised in the literature suggest that users should be involved at every stage of the process (Marsh et al. 2005) and that partnerships should be experienced as equally satisfying for everyone involved (Hodgson and Canvin 2005). The case studies raise questions about the first of these points. For example, based on their experiences McClimens et al. go as far as to suggest that active involvement of users at every stage is little more than a 'comfortable delusion'. Several of the case studies also challenge the notion that involvement at all stages is necessary, desirable or productive. For example, both Repper et al. and Swallow et al. engaged users (carers of people with mental health problems in the former case and children in the latter) at many stages but questioned the wisdom of their involvement in data collection (in this case interviewing). Swallow et al. did not use children to carry out interviews and, whilst Repper et al. did use carers as researchers, this was not always successful. For some carers the prospect was simply too daunting and they lacked the confidence to undertake the interviews. They were therefore accompanied by an experienced researcher. In other instances interviews conducted by carer researchers were found to be less detailed and potentially missing important information when compared to interviews carried out by academic researchers. Moreover, carer researchers sometimes did not know how much of themselves to reveal, and found this process threatening. The case study by Shields et al. describes how Ray found the ethics of interviews a potential minefield for the user researcher, but with appropriate support he was able to go on and conduct the interviews. Again we are not suggesting that user researchers should never collect data, just that careful consideration of the benefits and drawbacks is required before a joint decision is taken. The study by Clough et al. (2006) clearly indicates the benefits of using older people to collect data, but then, these individuals had been through a two-year training programme. Dewar (2005) cautions that in our desire to be inclusive we should neither lose sight of the skills and experiences that academic researchers bring, nor the time it takes to acquire these. The evidence from our case studies would lead us to agree with this point of view.

The question of whether everyone considers the partnership as 'equally satisfying' is an interesting one. Hodgson and Canvin (2005) contend that, owing to imbalances of power and a lack of 'insider knowledge' by users, it is not possible for them to find the process of participation equally satisfying. We would not necessarily agree. Certainly this may be the case when 'traditional' scientific research is considered, but this is not our focus here. The question of whether people find things satisfying is, in any case, largely subjective and therefore ultimately individual. Moreover, if we accept that differing types of knowledge and expertise contribute to a full understanding, then no one has privileged 'insider' knowledge, but everyone has differing knowledge from which everybody can learn. Herein lies the nub of the issue.

The literature suggests that participatory research should be characterized by a process of co-learning (Minkler and Wallerstein 2003; Faulkner 2004; Dewar 2005) and, based on the case studies and our own experience, this is certainly something to which we would subscribe. Each of the case studies in their own way provides examples of co-learning, whereby something new was jointly created during the process, and where participants gained new insights about themselves and others. A few examples will illustrate this point. Marsh et al. aimed explicitly to maximize co-learning in order to foster expertise and insights, and provide an account of how this was achieved. In the process the students learned much about both themselves and the realities of living in rural Colorado. Similarly, the residents of Chaffee County not only learned something important and new about their community, but also gained a better understanding of the students, and of the value of fostering links with an academic institution. Paul and Fredrik's testimony captures the valuable lessons they learned about themselves, about family carers, and their contribution to enhancing the understanding of their colleagues. It is also quite clear how, over time, Paul and Fredrik, the carers and older people all learned much from each other and, in so doing, enriched all their worlds. This, for us, is the sort of 'living knowledge' to which Bradbury and Reason (2003) refer. However, there is also a role for theoretical knowledge here, with Paul and Fredrik appreciating that the theory underpinning the ACTION project ('carers as experts', Nolan et al. 1996) helped to give direction and meaning to their work. This illustrates how Bradbury and Reason's four ways of knowing (experiential knowledge, presentational knowledge, propositional knowledge and practical knowledge) combine to produce something that is far more than the sum of its parts.

At this point readers may like to reflect back on the various case studies for themselves, and see if they can identify differing examples of co-learning.

Of course, this type of co-learning is an integral, if sometimes implicit, component of participatory research. On the other hand, in some instances there is an explicit intention to generate new knowledge. This was certainly the case with the work of Keady et al. Using an innovative methodological approach of 'Co-Constructed Inquiry' (CCI) they eloquently describe how they engaged with a person with early dementia and their family carer, and explicitly embarked on a journey to create a 'personal theory' of the dementia experience that would help to preserve personhood and give renewed purpose and meaning to life. Whilst this involves theory building, the result is a personal 'theory' that differs markedly from the detached theory of traditional science. There is not space here to engage in debate about the nature and value of theory, but such 'personal theories' are increasingly important. They can be used to enhance the agency of disadvantaged groups, such as people with dementia, and when this is no longer possible, they can help to shape appropriate support by the process of 'curation', thereby giving voice to previously 'unauthored' stories (Koch and Crichton). More work using CCI is being undertaken with people with stroke and Parkinson's disease, and should provide further valuable insights into living with these conditions.

But Keady et al. go further and, without in any way undermining the value of personal theory, they point to the benefits of constructing 'collective theory' wherever possible by fully engaging with users. Others have argued that we need to explore ways of helping users to engage in theory-building (Hodgson and Canvin 2005) and to consider how to move from individual to collective knowledge (Beresford 2005). 'Co-Constructed Inquiry' may well offer one such means. This attests to the value of seeking to build an 'extended epistemology', with theories being anchored in people's experience and providing them with renewed insights that help them to 're-see their world' (Bradbury and Reason 2003). We feel that the case studies provide several examples of this, so we shall return to this point when we consider evaluation.

Voice, then, does not involve anyone 'shouting the loudest', but is rather about creating partnerships and ways of working that potentially allow everyone's voice to be heard. As Steel (2005) argues, this is more about 'interdependence' which turns attention to the 'relational practices' of participatory enquiry (Bradbury and Reason 2003). This raises the question of values.

Values in participatory research: a relationship-centred approach

As we noted in the opening chapter, several commentators reflected on the 'relational' dimensions of participatory research, talking of the importance of interdependence and reciprocity (Bradbury and Reason 2003; Dewar 2005; Steel 2005; Clough et al. 2006). Such relationships seem essential to the success of participatory research (Morgan and Harris 2005). The case studies more than reinforce such a position.

Hanson et al. talk of developing 'meaningful and reciprocal relationships', whilst others refer to relationship-building being integral to the conduct of participatory research and of using 'relationship-centred keys' to unlock meaning (Keady et al.). The early efforts expended by Marsh et al. in establishing and maintaining relationships paid obvious dividends and were essential to the success of their project. Tolson et al. adopted an explicitly relationship-centred approach that attended in particular to 'the social niceties that grease everyday interactions'. However, not everything always runs smoothly, and Shields et al. caution about being prepared for 'relational difficulties'. McClimens et al. are unequivocal in stating that enabling partnerships or emancipatory research 'starts and falls with the relationships that develop with new research colleagues'.

If positive relationships are essential to participatory research then how such relationships can be facilitated is an important consideration. Here we would like to draw on extensive work that has been undertaken in the area of caring relationships, and consider the potential value of applying a relationship-centred approach (Tresolini and the Pew-Fetzer Task Force 1994), underpinned by the 'Senses Framework' (Nolan 1997; Davies et al. 1999; Nolan et al. 2002, 2006). This model was explicitly referred to in two of the case studies (Davies et al.; McClimens et al.), with Davies et al. using the senses to underpin their development work, whilst McClimens et al. used them as a device to reflect upon their engagement with people labelled as having learning disabilities. The value base described by Tolson et al. is also predicated on a relationship-centred model.

The idea of relationship-centred care emerged as the result of a major reconsideration of the bases of the health care system in the USA in the 1990s, which concluded that if the needs of people with chronic conditions are to be adequately addressed then the focus has to shift from an acute biomedical orientation to one that places the nature and quality of people's relationships at the centre of therapeutic activity (Tresolini and the Pew-Fetzer Task Force 1994). Concurrently work was under way to explore the nature of relationships in care settings for older people (Nolan and Grant 1993; Nolan et al. 1996; Nolan 1997), from which the 'Senses Framework' emerged. This framework was subsequently further elaborated upon and extensively tested in several major studies, always with the active participation of older people, family carers and paid carers (see Davies et al. 1999; Nolan et al. 2001, 2002, 2004, 2006). The basic premise is that if older people are to receive excellent care, then they need to experience six senses: a sense of security; a sense of belonging; a sense of continuity; a sense of security; a sense of achievement; and a sense of significance. However, in order to deliver such care, staff and family members also have to experience the senses themselves. An environment in which all major groups experience the 'senses' is termed an 'enriched' environment, one in which the senses are absent for one or more groups is termed an 'impoverished' environment (Brown 2006; Nolan et al. 2006). Table 12.1 provides a brief overview and summary of the senses.

Table 12.1   The six senses in the context of caring relationships

A sense of security	
For older people	Attention to essential physiological and psychological needs, to feel safe and free from threat, harm, pain and discomfort. To receive competent and sensitive care
For staff	To feel free from physical threat, rebuke or censure. To have secure conditions of employment. To have the emotional demands of work recognized and to work within a supportive but challenging culture
For family carers	To feel confident in knowledge and ability to provide good care (To do caring well – Schumacher et al. 1998) without detriment to personal well-being. To have adequate support networks and timely help when required. To be able to relinquish care when appropriate
A sense of continuity	
For older people	Recognition and value of personal biography; skilful use of knowledge of the past to help contextualize present and future. Seamless, consistent care delivered within an established relationship by known people

Table 12.1 continued

For staff	Positive experience of work with older people from an early stage of career, exposure to good role models and environments of care. Expectations and standards of care communicated clearly and consistently
For family carers	To maintain shared pleasures/pursuits with the care recipient. To be able to provide competent standards of care, whether delivered by self or others, to ensure that personal standards of care are maintained by others, to maintain involvement in care across care environments as desired/appropriate
A sense of belonging	
For older people	Opportunities to maintain and/or form meaningful and reciprocal relationships, to feel part of a community or group as desired
For staff	To feel part of a team with a recognized and valued contribution, to belong to a peer group, a community of gerontological practitioners
For family carers	To be able to maintain/improve valued relationships, to be able to confide in trusted individuals to feel that you're not 'in this alone'
A sense of purpose	
For older people	Opportunities to engage in purposeful activity facilitating the constructive passage of time, to be able to identify and pursue goals and challenges, to exercise discretionary choice
For staff	To have a sense of therapeutic direction, a clear set of goals to which to aspire
For family carers	To maintain the dignity and integrity, well-being and 'personhood' of the care recipient, to pursue (re)constructive/reciprocal care (Nolan et al. 1996)
A sense of achievement	
For older people	Opportunities to meet meaningful and valued goals, to feel satisfied with one's efforts, to make a recognized and valued contribution, to make progress towards therapeutic goals as appropriate
For staff	To be able to provide good care, to feel satisfied with one's efforts, to contribute towards therapeutic goals as appropriate, to use skills and ability to the full
For family carers	To feel that you have provided the best possible care, to know you've 'done your best', to meet challenges successfully, to develop new skills and abilities
A sense of significance	
For older people	To feel recognized and valued as a person of worth, that one's actions and existence are of importance, that you 'matter'
For staff	To feel that gerontological practice is valued and important, that your work and efforts 'matter'
For family carers	To feel that one's caring efforts are valued and appreciated, to experience an enhanced sense of self

Source: adapted from Nolan 1997; Davies et al. 1999; Nolan et al. 2001

The senses may be applied to any care environment but the factors needed to create and sustain them vary by context.

Our argument here is that similar 'senses' may create an 'enriched environment' for participatory research. Steel (2005) argues that it is not possible for others directly to empower users. Rather the goal should be to create an environment in which they can empower themselves. Such an environment can be captured by the 'senses', but to be 'enriched' these senses should be experienced by all participants. So key questions become:

- How do we create an environment in which both users and academic researchers feel 'safe' to engage in a participatory research? Users may feel threatened by the language and perceived complexity of the 'research' process, and intimidated by the power differentials that they encounter. On the other hand, participatory approaches can also threaten researchers' own sense of security, moving them out of their comfort zone and exposing their limitations. For as Warren and Cook (2005: 183) note 'fundamentally involving research users in a purposeful and extensive way challenges the very foundation of how we are used to doing research projects'. We have already alluded to the importance of early and ongoing support for everyone involved. This support may come from unexpected sources, with Ray describing how the help he received from a support worker was the 'best therapy and counselling' he had received throughout his illness.

  The potential impact of the intensive engagement required of researchers should not be underestimated either, with Ashburner et al. (2004) calling for the use of more psychodynamically informed approaches. A similar sentiment was expressed by Tee and Lathlean (2004: 542) who argue that researchers engaging in participatory research require 'high levels of personal awareness and skill to navigate the interpersonal, relational and group dynamics that may arise'.

- How do we create an environment in which both carers and academic researchers experience a sense of belonging? Both groups often come to the enterprise with differing values and beliefs, with different linguistic codes and traditions. Hodgson and Canvin (2005) argue that the language of science may effectively exclude users and is likely to foster a sense of alienation rather than belonging. As Zgola (1999) notes, if people are to communicate well they have to share a similar set of concepts and language. Even those writing about emancipatory research often do so in an alienating language (Turner and Beresford 2005). There is clearly a need to adopt an accessible language (Owen 2005; Steel 2005; Turner and Beresford 2005) if users are to enter the 'social world' of the researcher (Hodgson and Canvin 2005). However, perhaps it might be more productive to talk about creating a new shared world with a common set of concepts and values. We have found that the 'senses' speak to very different groups in meaningful ways, thereby helping to create and sustain a sense of shared belonging, and of purpose (see below).

- How do we create an environment in which users and academic researchers experience a sense of continuity? Continuity requires the linking of the past, present and future, each informing the other. The work of Keady et al. and Koch and Crichton, in this volume, have at their heart the maintenance of continuity. But to achieve this requires continuity of relationships over time. This was clear in the case of Paul and Fredrik, who describe their six-year engagement with family carers and older people. The implications of this for the funding of participatory research are obvious. But it also raises ethical issues of how to 'end' relationships without the user feeling abandoned. The case studies provide few answers for this, but experience of ACTION suggests that the ongoing use of ICT provides one means whereby users can maintain links and continue to enjoy ongoing relationships if they so wish.

- How can users and academic researchers experience a shared sense of purpose? This reinforces the importance of early engagement and full discussion of intended roles and relationships so that everyone agrees expectations, and shares a sense of purpose, being clear about what they have to offer and what they might gain. This is essential to user and academic researchers having a sense of achievement, which, for us, is primarily about enjoying a productive partnership characterized by co-learning and, where appropriate, action for change. We will elaborate upon this in the final section on evaluation.

- How can users and academic researchers have a sense of significance? This is possibly the most important sense of all, and is about both users and academic researchers feeling that what they do is valued and accorded status. This is often easier for academic researchers, but not necessarily for those academics engaged in participatory research. This type of work often fails to meet the accepted 'canons' of high-quality academic work, as the following quote from Owen (2005: 173) illustrates:

> Much research effort continues to be shaped and governed by the reward structures and performance management systems which prevail in higher education: in particular the Research Assessment Exercise which takes place periodically. It remains the case that conventional, single-authored books and articles attract more recognition than the relatively time-consuming and often smaller-scale collaborative partnerships which are acknowledged

to facilitate user-involvement. In principle, it would be quite feasible to alter this emphasis, and, for example, to build in specific research assessment criteria which recognize and reward partnership working between user networks and university departments.

The problem is exacerbated by the fact that the scientific community controls and formalizes the boundaries of acceptable (that is, fundable and publishable) enquiry (Ray and Mayan 2001) and this hegemony needs to be challenged before the true significance of participatory work is properly established, and a wider definition of what counts as valued knowledge is accepted.

Interestingly the debate about evidence-based practice is beginning to recognize that the application of knowledge (however defined) is itself essentially relational (Brehaut and Juzwishin 2005; Clark and Kelly 2005), with the concept of 'brokering' being increasingly applied (Brehaut and Juzwishin 2005).

Brokering recognizes the relational aspects of applying knowledge and is about bringing the right players together, and creating and sustaining relationships in order that they can engage in collaborative problem-solving, so it is a process that: 'links decision makers and researchers, facilitates their interactions so that they are able to better understand each other's goals and professional cultures, influence each other's work, forge new partnerships and promote the use of research based evidence in decision making' (Brehaut and Juzwishin 2005: 12).

Whilst the emphasis above is placed on bringing policy-makers and researchers together, the same logic would apply to participatory research. It seems to us that the role of a 'broker' could be essential to create the sort of enriched environment in which partnerships can flourish. Bradbury and Reason (2003) argue that one of the keys to evaluating the 'quality' of participatory research is the extent to which there is a full dialogue about what is meant by quality.

Evaluating the quality of participatory research

Debates about the relative merits of differing approaches to gauging the quality of research generally continue to appear regularly in the academic literature. This is also the case for participatory approaches. We referred to the criteria for 'good' participation suggested by Clough et al. (2006) in the introductory chapter and these have much to commend them.

Working from within a participatory action research (PAR) paradigm Bradley and Reason (2003) identify what they call five key 'choice points' for participatory methods. They recognize that the relative emphasis placed on these choices will vary across projects, but argue that all participatory studies should at least consider five issues:

- Quality as relational praxis – does the study fully involve others and does it take a 'relational stance'? This reflects the arguments we have made above, supporting the importance of relationships in participatory enquiry.
- Quality as a reflexive or practical outcome – is the study potentially useful or capable of application? This mirrors PAR's commitment to action or change, and again is consistent with the literature on user participation which suggests that, as a minimum, it should result in the development of better services or the experience of better services (Beresford 2005; Warren and Cook 2005).
- Quality as a plurality of knowing – which reflects the value placed on considering multiple forms of knowledge as valid. For this to be effective Bradbury and Reason (2003) contend that methodology must also be relational, and anchored in people's experiences.
- Quality as engaging is 'significant' work – that is likely to make a difference to people's lives.
- Enquiry towards enduring consequence – is the work likely to lead to real and lasting changes to the infrastructure of society, that is, does the study have 'transformational' potential?

These criteria resonate with much of what has been written in this volume, and might be usefully applied to studies ranging from the individual accounts of living with dementia (Keady et al.) to engagement with entire communities (Marsh et al.), or participation that is intended to generate national guidelines to stimulate best practice in health care (Tolson et al.). Each of these studies could, in their own way, be evaluated using the criteria suggested by Bradbury and Reason (2003).

Here we would like to revisit the modified authenticity criteria as developed and applied in the ÄldreVäst model (Magnusson et al. 2001; Nolan et al. 2003a) and explore their potential as an evaluative framework. Readers will recall that, in developing the ÄldreVäst Sjuhärad Centre, the authenticity criteria originally proposed by Guba and Lincoln (1989) appealed as an evaluative framework but that the language was considered inaccessible. The broad intent of the criteria was therefore retained but the phrasing modified so as to be more understandable to a wider audience. The modified criteria became:

- Equal Access.
- Enhanced Awareness of own position/values.
- Enhanced Awareness of the position/values of other groups.
- Encourage Action – does the study generate insights that might encourage change?
- Enable Action – does the study provide the means to promote or stimulate change?

The ways in which these criteria are applied was also changed. Originally they were designed to focus mainly on the research process (Rodwell 1998), but at ÄldreVäst Sjuhärad they are used to identify key issues at the planning, process and product phase of a study. This approach has proved very useful in forward planning, concurrent monitoring and retrospective evaluation. Equal access is a key consideration at each stage, particularly when frail or traditionally excluded users are being engaged.

The case studies have thrown up several issues about ensuring equal access at the planning stages. We have already noted the importance of ensuring that sufficient time and resources are made available in preparing for a participatory study, and this is vital to ensuring equal access. However, even with adequate preparation equal access is difficult to achieve. For example, are some groups involved before others, and what effect might this subsequently have? Both Tolson et al. and Davies et al., in reflecting back on what they had learned, acknowledged that they should have engaged older people at an earlier stage. Furthermore, Swallow et al. and McClimens et al. point out that it is often the most articulate people who volunteer to take part. Overcoming this may require additional support and resources.

However, as Keady et al. demonstrated, engaging traditionally excluded groups, such as people with dementia, is possible at an early stage with innovative methodological approaches. Moreover, the potential for technology to involve individuals at great distance, and with significant disability, has been well demonstrated by Hanson et al. and Tolson et al.

As we have pointed out several times, ensuring equal access at all stages depends on careful training and preparation that involves everybody concerned. This not only helps to identify the relative contribution of all participants, but is essential to agreeing a shared set of goals and expectations.

This brings attention to the beliefs and value systems of participants, and can 'kick-start' reflections about self and others that have the potential to begin 'enhancing' awareness for all concerned. In our experience the earlier this process begins the better.

It is also important to decide at an early stage whether the project has the explicit goals of encouraging and enabling action, that is, is the study action orientated or not? Not all participatory models explicitly attempt to introduce change, but all should have the potential to do so. We return to this issue when we consider the products of research.

In terms of the process of research the literature would suggest that participatory models should engage users at all stages from the initial planning, through the conduct of the research, to the dissemination and utilization of findings. Earlier we have suggested that there may be advantages and disadvantages to users engaging in data collection. Again, this will depend on the nature of the study. If the study is explicitly action orientated then everyone involved will contribute to the process, as this is an integral element and essential to success. On the other hand, when users may, for example, be conducting interviews in a more traditional project, then the position is not so clear-cut. In all cases, however, the importance of adequate ongoing support and reflection cannot be overstated. For example, Ray was able to overcome his ethical concerns with appropriate support, and those carer researchers who lacked the confidence to conduct interviews themselves were able to contribute by attending alongside an experienced researcher, as in Repper et al.'s case study.

The case studies also highlight the potentially inhibitory effects of relatively simple procedural issues. For instance, Davies et al. struggled to attract relatives to their 67 Birch Avenue action group, but when they abandoned the use of minutes and replaced these with an informal noticeboard, and badged the meeting a coffee morning, both attendance and participation increased dramatically, so that now the group is effectively organized by relatives. This simple illustration sends powerful messages about the role of formal structures in limiting participation, as illustrated by both McClimens et al. and Shields et al.

The need for innovative and unconventional methodological approaches, as discussed by Swallow et al., Hanson et al., Tolson et al. and Keady et al., is also important in ensuring equal access to the research process. Encouragement to participate, and enthusiasm for the project, are also prerequisites. Take the case study described by Marsh et al. The students were initially daunted by the prospect of going out into the wider, and relatively alien, community of rural Colorado until a key member of that community came along, spoke to them and 'infused the process with realism and hooked the students on their educational adventure'.

We have referred to how being involved in research can enhance people's awareness of their own situation, and those of others, at several points already, and do not intend to do so again here. Encouraging and enabling action of one sort or another is also integral to the research process.

It is when attention is turned to the products of the research that issues of equal access again become particularly significant for, if the products are not equally accessible, then their potential to enhance awareness or encourage and enable action is severely compromised.

In theory the products of research have never been more accessible, with the Internet opening up knowledge to a wider audience than ever. Indeed, initiatives such as ACTION are based on this wider accessibility. However, it is one thing for research findings to be fully accessible physically, quite another for them to be intellectually accessible and presented in a language that people can understand and relate to. As Owen (2005) noted earlier, the reward systems in traditional science promote publication in 'peer-reviewed' journals which require 'insider' (Hodgson and Canvin 2005) knowledge of a particular kind. This is exclusionary. Several commentators call for research findings to be presented in a language that is more widely accessible (Owen 2005; Steel 2005; Turner and Beresford 2005). This, it is suggested, will allow users to enter the 'social world' of the researcher (Hodgson and Canvin 2005). However, perhaps the responsibility should be the other way around, and the onus placed on researchers to enter the 'social world' of the user, not as a 'smash and grab' data collector, but with a commitment to widespread knowledge dissemination. Marsh et al. describe the importance of careful production of their final report for the community so that it appealed to a broad church, and as Koch and Crichton note, there is a need to write with an awareness of the audience for, if the narrative is not engaging, the audience will ignore it.

Surely the days when an academic audience writes primarily for itself and continues to determine the 'boundaries of acceptable (that is, fundable and publishable) inquiry' (Ray and Mayan 2001) should be numbered. Fortunately there are signs of progress with, for example, the Quality Research in Dementia (QRD) programme of the Alzheimer's Society that engages carers and people with dementia in identifying priorities and commissioning research, and the Department of Health Learning Disability Research Initiative (LDRI) that engaged people with learning disabilities as co-commissioners, peer reviewers, advisers and, in some cases, as researchers (Grant and Ramcharan 2002, 2006).

There is also a role for involving users far more in the dissemination of research (Stevens et al. 2005). The type of brokering activity that we referred to earlier suggests that there is now growing awareness amongst researchers about engaging the policy community more fully, and there is considerable potential for the use of such approaches if modified to suit the needs of differing user groups.

If the products of research are more widely accessible, then their potential to enhance awareness and encourage or enable action is improved significantly. The 'transformational' potential (Bradbury and Reason 2003) of research should not be confined to those intimately involved in participatory work, but extend to everyone by providing 'vicarious' experience from which we all might learn. Such vicarious experience might be provided in several forms: a 'curated' account of the biography of a person with dementia (Koch and Crichton); a 'collective' theory of living with dementia (Keady et al.); a report on a communities 'state of health' (Marsh et al.); or in the production of national guidelines for 'best practice' (Tolson et al.). Herein lies the true power of participatory work.

The journey continues

> This means a willingness to listen, to learn, and to change and compromise – from everyone – is essential to the success of user involvement.
>
> (Faulkner 2004: 6)

Our aim in this volume has been to raise awareness, further debate, and potentially add new insights into the theory and practice of participatory research with the users of health and social care services. In attempting to do so we have drawn on the relevant literature but have relied primarily on the accounts of others who have provided their diverse experiences of working with users in very differing contexts. Despite this diversity we believe that shared messages have emerged and, in bringing these messages together, we have suggested that a relationship-centred approach to participation, as reflected in the 'Senses Framework', might provide the means of creating an 'enriched' environment in which participatory research can truly flourish. Faulkner's quote above captures the importance of letting go of preconceived ideas and being willing to 'listen, to learn, and to change and compromise'. These all seem essential. In their case study Keady et al. posed a set of questions that also seem very pertinent, and we would like to end with these. Anyone contemplating engaging in participatory work with users might therefore like to reflect on the following:

- Is this for me?
- Am I comfortable with opening up (at least part of) my life?
- What am I hoping to achieve by taking part?
- Do I think (or at least am I willing to try to think) creatively and imaginatively?

Your answers will indicate if you are willing to start on a journey that might change you and your views of research for ever.

References

Abell, S., Ashmore, J., Beart, S. et al. (2007) *Including everyone in research*: The Burton Street Research Group. *British Journal of Learning Disabilities*, 35(2): 121–4.

Alderson, P. (1997) Children as research subjects: science, ethics and law, *Nursing Ethics*, 4(2): 174–6.

Alderson, P. (2005) Designing ethical research with children, in A. Farrell (ed.) *Ethical Research with Children*. Maidenhead: Open University Press.

Allam, S., Blyth, A.S., et al. (2004) Our experience of collaborative research: service users, carers and researchers work together to evaluate an assertive outreach service, *Journal of Psychiatric and Mental Health Nursing*, 11(3): 368–73.

Allmark, P. (2002) The ethics of research with children, *Nurse Researcher*, 10(2): 7–19.

Alzheimer, A. (1907) Über eine eigenartige Erkankung der Hirnrinde, *Allgemeine Zeits Psychiatry, Psychisch-Gerichtlich Medicine*, 64: 146–8.

Alzheimer's Society (2002) *The Mini-mental State Examination (MMSE). A Guide for People with Dementia and their Carers*. Alzheimer's Society quality research in dementia information sheet 436. London: Alzheimer's Society.

Anderson, E.T. and McFarlane, J. (2004) *Community as Partner: Theory and Practice in Nursing*, 3rd edn. Philadelphia, PA: Lippincott, Williams and Wilkins.

Arksey, H., O'Malley, L., Baldwin, S., Harris, J. and Mason, S. (2002) *Consultation Report: Services to Support Carers of People with Mental Health Problems*. www.sdo.lshtm.ac.uk/mentalhealthcarers.htm (accessed 6 December 2006).

Ashburner, C., Meyer, J., Johnson, B. and Smith, C. (2004) Using action research to address loss of personhood in a continuing care setting, *Illness, Crisis and Loss*, 12(1): 23–37.

Aveyard, B. and Davies, S. (2006) Moving forward together: evaluation of an action group involving staff and relatives within a nursing home for older people with dementia, *International Journal of Older People Nursing*, 1(2): 95–104.

Barker, J. and Smith, F. (2001) Power, positionality and practicalities, *Ethics, Place and Environment*, 4: 142–7.

Barker, J. and Weller, S. (2003) 'Never work with children?': the geography of methodological issues in research with children, *Qualitative Research*, 3(2): 207–27.

Barnes, M. (1999) *Public Expectations: From Paternalism to Partnership, Changing Relationships in Health and Health Services*. Policy Future for UK Health, No. 10. London: Nuffield Trust.

Barnes, M. (2002) Bringing differences into deliberation? Disabled people, survivors and local governance, *Policy and Politics*, 20(3): 319–31.

Barnes, M. and Walker, A. (1996) Consumerism versus empowerment: a principled approach to the involvement of older service users, *Policy and Politics*, 24(4): 375–93.

Barnett, E. (2000) *Including the Person with Dementia in Designing and Delivering Care: 'I Need to be Me!'*. Vancouver, BC: University of British Columbia Press.

Baxter, L., Thorne, L. and Mitchell, A. (2001) *Small Voices, Big Noises*. Exeter: Washington Singer Press.

Beauchamp, T.L. and Childress, J.F. (1994) *Principles of Biomedical Ethics*. Oxford: Oxford University Press.

Beecher, H. (1966) Ethics and clinical research, *New England Journal of Medicine*, 274: 1354–60.

Benner, P. (1984) *From Novice to Expert: Excellence and Power in Clinical Nursing Practice*. Menlo Park, CA: Addison-Wesley.

Beresford, P. (2002) User involvement in research and evaluation: liberation or regulation, *Social Policy and Society*, 1(2): 95–105.

Beresford, P. (2005) Theory and practice of user involvement in research: making the connection with public policy and practice, in L. Lowes and I. Hulatt (eds) *Involving Service Users in Health and Social Care Research*. (pp. 6–17.) London: Routledge.

Bernard, W.T. (2000) Participatory research as emancipatory method: challenges and opportunities, in D. Burton (ed.) *Research Training for Social Scientists*. London: Sage.

Bond, J. (2000) The impact of staff factors in nursing home residents, *Aging and Mental Health*, 4(1): 5–8.

Booth, J., Tolson, D., Hotchiss, R. and Schofield, I. (in press) Using action research to construct national evidence-based nursing care guidance for gerontological nursing, *Journal of Clinical Nursing*, 16(5): 945–53.

Bowers, B.J. (1988) Grounded theory, *National League for Nursing Publications*, 15: 33–59.

Bradbury, H. and Reason, P. (2003) Issues and choice points for improving the quality of action research, in M. Minkler and N. Wallerstein (eds) *Community-Based Participatory Research for Health*. San Francisco, CA: Jossey-Bass.

Brehaut, J.D. and Juzwishin, D. (2005) *Bridging the Gap: The Use of Research Evidence in Policy Development*. Edmonton: Health Technology Assessment Unit and Alberta Heritage Foundation for Medical Research.

British Educational Research Association (BERA) (2004) *Research Ethics Guidelines*. London: British Educational Research Association.

British Medical Association (BMA) (2001) *Consent: Rights and Choices in Health Care for Children and Young People*. London: BMJ Books.

British Medical Journal (BMJ) (1996) The Nuremberg Code, *British Medical Journal*, 313: 1448.

British Sociological Association (BSA) (2002) *Statement of Ethical Practice for the British Sociological Association*. (Appendix updated 2004.) www.britsoc.co.uk (accessed 10 July 2006).

Brody, H. (2003) *Stories of Sickness*, 2nd edn. New York: Oxford University Press.

Brown, J. (2006) Student nurses' experience of learning to care for older people in enriched environments: a constructivist inquiry. PhD thesis, University of Sheffield.

Bruner, J. (2002) *Making Stories: Law, Literature, Life*. Cambridge, MA: Harvard University Press.

Brykczynska, G. (1994) Implications of the Clothier Report: the Beverly Allitt case, *Nursing Ethics*, 1(3): 179–81.

Buggy, T., Andrew, N., Tolson, D. and McGhee, M. (2004) Evolution of a virtual practice development college for nurses, *ITIN – the Official Journal of the British Computer Society Nursing Specialist Group, Part of the British Journal of Computing*, 16(3): 4–11.

Burgess, A. (2005) *Fathers and Public Services. Daddy Dearest? Active Fatherhood and Public Policy*. London: Institute for Public Policy Research.

Bury, M. (1982) Chronic illness as biographic disruption, *Sociology of Health and Illness*, 4: 167–82.

Burton Street Research Group (in press) Researching together, *British Journal of Learning Disabilities*.

Butler, C. (2002) *Postmodernism: A Very Short Introduction*. Oxford: Oxford University Press.

Candlin, C.N. (1997) General editor's preface, in B.-L. Gunnarsson, P. Linell and B. Nordberg (eds) *The Construction of Professional Discourse*. London: Longman.

Carney, T., Murphy, S. et al. (2003) Children's views of hospitalization: an exploratory study of data collection, *Journal of Child Health Care*, 7(1): 27–40.

Cavet, J. and Sloper, P. (2004) The participation of children and young people in decisions about UK service development, *Child: Care, Health and Development*, 30: 612–31.

Chaffee County (nd) *Colorado's Headwaters of Adventure*. http://www.colorado-headwaters.com/chaffee_county/profile.cfm (accessed 20 September 2006).

Chappell, A.L. (2000) Emergence of participatory research methodology in learning disability research: understanding the context, *British Journal of Learning Disabilities*, 28: 38–43.

Charlesworth, G., Poland, F. and Vaughan, S. (2004) Volunteer Befriender Training Guide Pack used in the BECCA ('Befriending and Costs of Caring') project.

Charmaz, K. (1990) Discovering chronic illness: using grounded theory, *Social Science and Medicine*, 30: 1161–72.

Charmaz, K. (1991) *Good Days, Bad Days: The Self in Chronic Illness and Time*. New Brunswick, NJ: Rutgers University Press.

Charmaz, K. (1995) Body, identity and self: adapting to impairment, *Sociological Quarterly*, 36: 657–80.

Charmaz, K. (2000) Grounded theory: objectivist and constructivist methods, in N.K. Denzin and Y.S. Lincoln (eds) *Handbook of Qualitative Research*, 2nd edn. Thousand Oaks, CA: Sage.

Charmaz, K. (2006) *Constructing Grounded Theory: A Practical Guide Through Qualitative Analysis.* London: Sage.

Christensen, P. (2004) The health-promoting family: a conceptual framework for future research, *Social Science and Medicine*, 59(2): 377–87.

Christensen, P. and James, A. (2000) *Research with Children: Perspectives and Practices.* London: Falmer Press.

Clare, L. (2003) Managing threats to self: awareness in early stage Alzheimer's disease, *Social Science and Medicine*, 57: 1017–29.

Clare, L., Markova, I. et al. (2006) Awareness and people with early-stage dementia, in B. Miesen and G. Jones (eds) *Caregiving in Dementia – Research and Applications*, Vol. 4. London: Routledge.

Clark, A. (2004) The Mosaic approach and research with young children, in V. Lewis, M. Kellett, C. Robinson, S. Fraser and S. Ding (eds) *The Reality of Research with Children and Young People.* London: Sage.

Clark, A. and Moss, P. (2001) *Listening to Young Children. The Mosaic approach.* London: Joseph Rowntree Foundation and National Children's Bureau.

Clark, G. and Kelly, L. (2005) *New Directions for Knowledge Transfer and Knowledge Brokerage in Scotland.* Research Findings No. 1/2005, Scottish Executive.

Clark, M., Lester, H. and Glasby, J. (2005) From recruitment to dissemination: the experience of working together from service user and professional perspectives, in L. Lowes and I. Hulatt (eds) *Involving Service Users in Health and Social Care Research.* London: Routledge.

Clarke, A., Hanson, E. and Ross, H. (2003) Seeing the person behind the patient: enhancing the care of older people using a biographical approach, *Journal of Clinical Nursing*, 12: 697–706.

Clarke, C., Scott, E. et al. (1999) Effects of client interviews on client reports of satisfaction in Mental Health Services, *Psychiatric Services*, 50(7): 961–3.

Clarke, C.L. and Wilcockson, J. (2002) Seeing need and developing care: exploring knowledge for and from practice, *International Journal of Nursing Studies*, 39(4): 397–406.

Clough, E. (2005) Foreword, in J. Burr and P. Nicolson (eds) *Researching Health Care Consumers, Critical Approaches.* Basingstoke: Palgrave Macmillan.

Clough, R., Green, B., Hawkes, B., Raymond, G. and Bright, L. (2006) *Older People as Researchers: Evaluating a Participative Project.* Report for the Joseph Rowntree Foundation.

Coad, J. and Coad, N. (2005) An exploratory study into children and parents' views of their hospital environment. Unpublished report, Coventry and Warwickshire NHS Trust.

Coad, J. and Evans, R. (2007) Reflections on practical approaches to involving children and young people in the data analysis process, *Children and Society* (forthcoming).

Coad, J. and Houston, R. (2006) *Involving Children and Young People in the Decision-*

making Processes of Health Care Service: A Literature Review. London: Action for Sick Children.

Coad, J. and Lewis, A. (2004) *Engaging Children and Young People in Research: A Systematic Literature Review for The National Evaluation of The Children's Fund.* London: Department for Education and Skills.

Coad, J. and Shaw, K. (2006) Defining choice in children's services. *A Scoping of Children and Young People's Choice in Planning and Delivery of Health Care Services: Systematic Literature Review and Report.* Birmingham: Birmingham and Black Country PCT (BBCPCT).

Coad, J. and Twycross, A. (2006) Editorial: User involvement is not just a box to be ticked, *Paediatric Nursing,* 18(6): 3.

Coad, J., Horsley, C. et al. (2004) *Participatory Workshops for Indicators Report.* Birmingham: NECF.

Cohen-Mansfield, J., Golander, H. and Arnheim, G. (2000) Self identity in older persons suffering from dementia: preliminary results, *Social Science and Medicine,* 51: 381–94.

Cohen-Mansfield, J., Parpura-Gill, A. and Golander, H. (2006) Salience of self identity roles in persons with dementia: differences in perceptions among elderly persons, family members and caregivers, *Social Science and Medicine,* 62(3): 745–57.

Cotrell, V. and Schulz, R. (1993) The perspective of the patient with Alzheimer's disease: a neglected dimension of dementia research, *Gerontologist,* 33(2): 205–11.

Coupland, N., Nussbaum, J.F. and Grossman, A. (1993) Introduction: discourse, selfhood, and the lifespan, in N. Coupland and J.F. Nussbaum (eds) *Discourse and Lifespan Identity.* Newbury Park, CA: Sage.

Cowdell, F. (2006) Preserving personhood in dementia research: a literature review, *International Journal of Older People Nursing,* 1: 85–94.

Coyne, I.T. (1998) Researching children: some methodological and ethical considerations, *Journal of Clinical Nursing,* 7(5): 409–16.

Crichton, J.A. (2003) Issues of interdiscursivity in the commercialisation of professional practice: the case of English language teaching. Unpublished doctoral thesis, Macquarie University.

Crichton, J.A. and Koch, T. (forthcoming) Living with dementia: curating self identity. *Dementia: The International Journal of Social Research and Practice.*

Curran, J., Gurevitch, M. and Woollacott, J. (1982) The study of the media: theoretical approaches, in M. Gurevitch, T. Bennett, J. Curran and J. Woollacote (eds) *Culture, Society and the Media.* (Part 1, 'Class, Ideology and the Media'.) London: Methuen.

Davies, S. (2001) Relatives' experiences of nursing home entry: a constructivist inquiry. Unpublished PhD thesis, University of Sheffield.

Davies, S. (2003) Creating community: the basis for caring partnerships in nursing homes, in M.R. Nolan, G. Grant, J. Keady and U. Lundh (eds) *Partnerships in*

Family Care: Understanding the Caregiving Career. Maidenhead: Open University Press.

Davies, S., Nolan, M.R., Brown, J. and Wilson, F. (1999) *Dignity on the Ward: Promoting Excellence in Care*. London: Help the Aged.

Davies, S., Powell, A. and Aveyard, B. (2002) Developing partnerships in care: towards a teaching nursing home, *British Journal of Nursing*, 11(20): 1320–8.

Davies-Quarrell, V. (2005) The ACE approach to facilitating wellbeing for younger people with dementia and their families, *Signpost*, 9(2): 19–23.

Department for Education and Skills (DfES) (2004a) *Every Child Matters: the Next Steps*. London: Department for Education and Skills.

Department for Education and Skills (DfES) (2004b) *National Evaluation of the Children's Fund. Children, Young People, Parents and Carers' Participation in Children's Fund Case Study Partnerships*. London: Department for Education and Skills.

Department of Health (DoH) (1987) *The Family Law Reform Act*. London: The Stationery Office.

Department of Health (DoH) (1989) *The Children Act*. London: The Stationery Office.

Department of Health (DoH) (1997) *The New NHS: Modern, Dependable*. London: The Stationery Office.

Department of Health (DoH) (1999) *Caring About Carers: A National Strategy for Carers*. London: HMSO.

Department of Health (DoH) (2001a) *The Expert Patient: A New Approach to Chronic Disease Management for the Twenty-first Century*. London: The Stationery Office.

Department of Health (DoH) (2001b) *National Service Framework for Older People: Modern Standards and Service Models*. London: The Stationery Office.

Department of Health (DoH) (2001c) *Research Governance Framework for Health and Social Care*. London: Department of Health.

Department of Health (DoH) (2005) *Everybody's Business: Integrated Mental Health Services for Older Adults*. London: The Stationery Office.

Department of Health (DoH) (2006) *Best Research for Best Health*. London: The Stationery Office.

Department of Health/Department for Education and Skills (DoH/DfES) (2004) *Every Child Matters – National Service Framework for Children, Young People and Maternity Services*. Nottingham: Department for Education and Skills.

Dewar, B.J. (2005) Beyond tokenistic involvement of older people in research – a framework for future development and understanding, *International Journal of Older People Nursing*, 14(3a): 48–53.

Dewar, B. (2006) Promoting positive culture in care homes, in Help the Aged, National Care Homes Research and Development Forum (eds) *My Home Life: Quality of Life in Care Homes*. London: Help the Aged.

Dewing, J. (2002) From ritual to relationship: a person-centred approach to consent in qualitative research with older people who have dementia, *Dementia: The International Journal of Social Research and Practice*, 1(2): 157–71.

Docherty, S. and Sandelowski, M. (1999) Focus on qualitative methods. Interviewing children, *Research in Nursing and Health*, 22(2): 177–85.

Doorbar, P. and McClarey, M. (1999) *Ouch! Sort it Out: Children's Experiences of Pain*. London: Royal College of Nursing.

Elliott, J. (2005) *Using Narrative in Social Research: Qualitative and Quantitative Approaches*. London: Sage.

Ellis, K. (2000) User involvement, community care and disability research, in H. Kemshall and R. Littlechild (eds) *User Involvement and Participation in Social Care*. London: Jessica Kingsley.

Epp, T.D. (2003) Person-centred dementia care: a vision to be refined, *The Canadian Alzheimer Disease Review*, 5(3): 14–18.

Eraut, M. (1994) *Developing Professional Knowledge and Competence*. London: Falmer.

Farrell, A. (ed.) (2005) *Ethical Research with Children*. Maidenhead: Open University Press.

Faulkner, A. (2004) *Capturing the Experience of Those Involved in the TRUE Project. A Story of Colliding Worlds*. www.invo.org.uk (accessed 6 December 2006).

Faulkner, A. and Layzell, S. (2000) *Strategies for Living: A Report of User-led Research into People's Strategies for Living with Mental Distress*. London: Mental Health Foundation.

Faulkner, A. and Morris, B. (2003) *Expert Paper on User Involvement in Forensic Mental Health Research and Development*. Liverpool: National Programme on Forensic Mental Health Research and Development.

Faulkner, M.S. (1996) Family responses to children with diabetes and their influence on self-care, *Journal of Paediatric Nursing*, 11(2): 82–93.

Finch, J. (1984) It's great to have someone to talk to: the ethics and politics of interviewing women, in C. Bell and H. Roberts (eds) *Social Researching*. London: Routledge and Kegan Paul.

Fleischman, P. and Wigmore, J. (2000) *Nowhere Else to Go. Increasing Choice and Continuity within Supported Housing for Homeless People*. London: Single Persons' Homeless Unit.

Fleming, J. (2005) Foster carers undertake research into birth family contact: using the social action research approach, in L. Lowes and I. Hulatt (eds) *Involving Service Users in Health and Social Care Research*. London: Routledge.

Folstein, M.F., Folstein, S.E. and McHugh, P.R. (1975) Mini-mental state: a practical guide for grading the cognitive state of patients for the clinician, *Journal of Psychiatric Research*, 12: 189–98.

Foster, C. (2003) *The Ethics of Medical Research on Humans*. Repr. edn. Cambridge: Cambridge University Press.

Fox, N., Hunn, A. and Mathers, N. (2001) *New Horizons: GMH 6010 Research Methods*. Sheffield: Institute of General Practice and Primary Care, University of Sheffield.

Garro, L.C. and Mattingly, C. (2000) Narrative as construct and construction, in

C. Mattingly and L.C. Garro (eds) *Narrative and the Cultural Construction of Illness and Healing*. Berkeley and Los Angeles, CA: University of California Press.

Gergen, K. (1991) *The Saturated Self: Dilemmas of Identity in Contemporary Life*. New York: Basic.

Geronurse website of the Gerontological Nursing Demonstration Project. www.geronurse.com (accessed on 28 September 2006).

Gettings, D. and Gladstone, C. (2001) *Using ICT Based Questionnaires in Attempting to Gain the Views of Students with Severe Learning Difficulties*. ESRC. Birmingham, University of Birmingham.

Gillick v West Norfolk and Wisbech Area Health Authority and Department of Health and Social Security (1986) AC112, (1985) 3 WLR 830, (1985) 3 All ER 402 HL.

Glaser, B.G. (1978) *Theoretical Sensitivity*. Mill Valley, CA: Sociology Press.

Glaser, B.G. (2002) Constructivist grounded theory? *Forum: Qualitative Social Research* (online journal), 3(3). www.qualitative-research.net/fqs-texte/3-02/3-02glaser-e.htm (accessed 12 December 2006).

Glaser, B.G. and Strauss, A.L. (1967) *The Discovery of Grounded Theory: Strategies for Qualitative Research*. Chicago, IL: Aldine.

Golander, H. and Raz, A.E. (1996) The mask of dementia: images of 'demented residents' in a nursing ward, *Ageing and Society*, 16: 269–85.

Goodley, D. and Moore, M. (2000) Doing disability research: activist lives and the academy, *Disability and Society*, 11: 333–48.

Gould, N. (2006) An inclusive approach to knowledge for mental health social work practice and policy, *British Journal of Social Work*, 36: 109–25.

Grant, G. and Ramcharan, P. (2002) Researching 'valuing people', *Tizard Learning Disability Review*, 7(3): 27–33.

Grant, G. and Ramcharan, P. (2006) User involvement in research, in K. Gerrish and E.A. Lacey (eds) *The Research Process in Nursing*, 5th edn. Oxford: Blackwell.

Grant, G., Courtney, D., King, S., Minogue, V. and Walsh, M. (2006) Accounting for research: the difficulties posed for user-centred research, *Mental Health and Learning Disabilities Research and Practice*, 3(1): 5–19.

Greenwood, D.J., Whyte, W.F. and Harkavy, I. (1993) Participatory action research as a process and as a goal, *Human Relations*, 46(2): 175–91.

Grey, B. (2003) Social exclusion, poverty, health and social care in Tower Hamlets: the perspectives of families on the impact of the Family Support Service, *British Journal of Social Work*, 33(3): 361.

Grypdonck, M.H.F. (2006) Qualitative health research in the era of evidence-based practice, *Qualitative Health Research*, 16(10): 1371–85.

Guba, E.G. and Lincoln, Y.S. (1989) *Fourth Generation Evaluation*. Newbury Park, CA: Sage.

Gubrium, J.R. (1993) *Speaking of Life: Horizons of Meaning for Nursing Home Residents*. Newbury Park, CA: Sage.

Gubrium, J.F. and Holstein, J.A. (1997) *The New Language of Qualitative Method*. Oxford: Oxford University Press.

Hadden, S.C. and Lester, M. (1978) Talking identity: the production of 'self' in interaction, *Human Studies*, 1: 331–56.

Ham, M., Jones, N., et al. (2004) 'I'm a researcher!' Working together to gain ethical approval for a participatory research study, *Journal of Learning Disabilities*, 8(4): 397–407.

Hanley, B. (ed.) (2003) *Involving the Public in NHS, Public Health and Social Care Research: Briefing Notes for Researchers*, 2nd edn. Eastleigh: INVOLVE.

Hanley, B., Bradburn, J. et al. (2004) *Involving the Public in NHS, Public Health, and Social Care Research: Briefing Notes for Researchers*. www.invo.org.uk/publication_guidelines.asp (accessed 14 February 2007).

Hanson, E., Magnusson, L., Nolan, J. and Nolan, M. (2006a) Developing a model of participatory research involving researchers, practitioners, older people and their family carers, *Journal of Research in Nursing*, 11(4): 325–42.

Hanson, E., Nolan, J. et al. (2006b) *COAT: The Carers Outcome Agreement Tool: A New Approach to Working with Family Carers*. Getting Research into Practice (GRiP) Report No. 1, University of Sheffield.

Harris, P. and Keady, J. (2006) Editorial, *Dementia: The International Journal of Social Research and Practice*, 5(1): 5–9.

Harris, P.H. and Sterin, G.J. (1999) Insider's perspective: defining and preserving the self of dementia, *Journal of Mental Health and Aging*, 5(3): 241–56.

Hart, E. (2001) System induced setbacks in stroke recovery, *Sociology of Health and Illness*, 3(1): 101–23.

Hayes, V. (1997) Families and children's chronic conditions: knowledge development and methodological considerations, *Scholarly Inquiry for Nursing Practice: An International Journal*, 11(4): 259–90.

Health and Social Care Advisory Service (HASCAS) (2005) *Making a Real Difference: Strengthening Service User and Carer Involvement in NIMH(E)*. London: HASCAS.

Help the Aged and the National Care Homes Research and Development Forum (2006) *My Home Life: Quality of Life in Care Homes*. London: Help the Aged.

Henri, F. and Pudelko, B. (2003) Understanding and analysing activity and learning in virtual communities, *Journal of Computer Assisted Learning*, 19: 474–87.

Hill, M., Laybourn, A. et al. (1996) Engaging with primary-aged children about their emotions and well-being: methodological considerations, *Children and Society*, 10: 129–44.

Hill, R., Hardy, P. and Shepherd, G. (1995) *Perspectives on Manic Depression: A Survey of the Manic Depression Fellowship*. London: Sainsbury Centre for Mental Health.

Hodgson, P. and Canvin, K. (2005) Translating health policy into research practice, in L. Lowes and I. Hulatt (eds) *Involving Service Users in Health and Social Care Research*. London: Routledge.

Holst, G. and Hallberg, I.R. (2003) Exploring the meaning of everyday life for those suffering from dementia, *American Journal of Alzheimer's Disease and Other Dementias*, 18(6): 359–65.

Holstein, J. and Gubrium, J. (1997) Active interviewing, in D. Silverman (ed.) *Qualitative Research: Theory, Method and Practice*. London: Sage.

Holstein, J. and Gubrium, J. (2000) *The Self We Live By: Narrative Identity in a Postmodern World*. New York: Oxford University Press.

Holstein, J.A. and Gubrium, J.F. (2004) The active interview, in D. Silverman (ed.) *Qualitative Research: Theory, Method and Practice*, 2nd edn. London: Sage.

Holter, I.M. and Schwartz-Barcott, D. (1993) Action research: what is it? How has it been used and how can it be used in nursing? *Journal of Advanced Nursing*, 18: 298–304.

Hubbard, G. (2004) Users or losers: does the rhetoric of user involvement deliver? *Research Policy and Planning*, 22(1): 53–6.

Hulatt, I. and Lowes, L. (2005) Introduction, in L. Lowes and I. Hulatt (eds) *Involving Service Users in Health and Social Care Research*. London: Routledge.

Humphries, B. (2003) What *else* counts as evidence in evidence-based social work?, *Social Work Education*, 22(1): 81–91.

Hunt, P. (1981) Settling accounts with the parasite people, *Disability Challenge*, 2: 37–50.

Hurtley, R. (2003) Job satisfaction and motivation for staff in long-term care. Unpublished MSc thesis, University of Surrey.

Institute of Medicine (IoM) (1988) *The Future of Public Health*. Washington, DC: National Academy Press.

INVOLVE (2002) *A Guide to Paying Members of the Public Who Are Actively Involved in Research*. (Revised in 2003.) Eastleigh: INVOLVE.

INVOLVE (2004) *Involving the Public in NHS, Public Health and Social Care Research: Briefing Notes for Researchers*. Eastleigh: INVOLVE.

Ironside, P.M., Scheckel, M. et al. (2003) Experiencing chronic illness: co-creating new understandings, *Qualitative Health Research*, 13(2): 171–83.

Israel, B.A., Eng, E., Schulz, A.J. and Parker, E.A. (2005) Introduction to methods in community-based participatory research for health, in B.A. Israel, E. Eng, A.J. Schulz and E.A. Parker (eds) *Methods in Community-Based Participatory Research for Health*. San Francisco, CA: John Wiley and Sons.

James, A. and Prout, A. (1997) *Constructing and Deconstructing Childhood: Contemporary Issues in the Sociological Study of Childhood*. London: Falmer Press.

Jennings, B.M. and Loan, L. (2001) Misconceptions among nurses about evidence-based practice, *Journal of Nursing Scholarship*, 33(2): 121–7.

Johnson, V., Ivan-Smith, E. et al. (1998) *Stepping Forward. Children and Young People's Participation in the Development Process*. Filey: Intermediate Technology Publications.

Jones, A. (2004) Children and young people as researchers, in S. Fraser, V. Lewis,

S. Ding, M. Kellett and C.R.C. London (eds) *Doing Research with Children and Young People.* Maidenhead: Open University Press.

Karp, D. (1997) *Speaking of Sadness: Depression, Disconnection, and the Meanings of Mental Illness.* Oxford: Oxford University Press.

Karp, D. (2000) *The Burden of Sympathy: How Families Cope with Mental Illness.* Oxford: Oxford University Press.

Keady, J. and Bender, M. (1998) Changing faces: the purpose and practice of assessing older adults with cognitive impairment, *Health Care in Later Life: An International Research Journal,* 3(2): 129–44.

Keady, J. and Williams, S. (2005) Co-constructing the early experience of dementia using the CCI approach. Paper presented to the Alzheimer's Europe Conference, Kilarney, Ireland, June.

Keady, J., Ashcroft-Simpson, S., Halligan, K. and Williams, S. (in press) Admiral nursing and the family care of a parent with dementia: using autobiographical narrative as grounding for negotiated clinical practice and decision-making, *Scandinavian Journal of Caring Sciences.*

Kelly, M. and Field, D. (1996) Medical sociology, chronic illness and the body, *Sociology of Health and Illness,* 18: 241–57.

Kelly, T.B., Tolson, D., Schofield, I. and Booth, J. (2005a) Describing gerontological nursing: an academic exercise or prerequisite for progress? *International Journal of Nursing Older People,* 14(3a): 1–11.

Kelly, T.B., Lowndes, A. and Tolson, D. (2005b) Advancing stages of group development: the case of virtual nursing community of practice groups, *Groupwork,* 15(2): 7–28.

Kelly, T.B., Schofield, I., Booth, J. and Tolson, D. (2006) The use of on-line groups to involve older people in influencing nursing care guidance, *Groupwork,* 16(1), 69–94.

Kennedy, I. and Grubb, A. (2000) *Medical Law.* London: Butterworth.

Kiernan, C. (1999) Participation in research by people with learning disability: origin and issues, *British Journal of Learning Disabilities,* 29(2): 51–5.

Killick, J. and Allan, K. (2001) *Communication and the Care of People with Dementia.* Buckinghamshire: Open University Press.

King, T. (2003) *The Truth about Stories: A Native Narrative.* In the 2003 Massey Lecture (compact disc in a series of four). Canadian Broadcasting Corporation Audio IDEAS.

Kirby, P. (2004) *A Guide to Actively Involving Young People in Research: For Researchers, Research Commissioners and Managers.* Eastleigh: INVOLVE.

Kirby, P. and Bryson, S. (2002) *Measuring the Magic: Evaluating and Researching Young People's Participation in Public Decision-making.* London: Carnegie Young People Initiative.

Kirby, P., Lanyon, C. et al. (2003) *Building a Culture of Participation: Involving Children and Young People in Policy, Service Planning, Delivery and Evaluation.* Research report. London: Department for Education and Skills.

Kitson, A. (2002) Recognising relationships: reflections on evidence-based practice, *Nursing Inquiry*, 9(3): 179–86.

Kitwood, T. (1990) The dialectics of dementia: with particular reference to Alzheimer's disease, *Ageing and Society*, 10: 177–96.

Kitwood, T. (1997) The experience of dementia, *Ageing and Mental Health*, 1(1): 13–22.

Kitwood, T. and Bredin, K. (1992) Towards a theory of dementia care: personhood and well-being, *Ageing and Society*, 12: 269–87.

Kleinman, A. (1988) *The Illness Narratives: Suffering and the Human Condition*. New York: Basic Books.

Knafl, K.A. and Deatrick, J.A. (1990) Family management style: concept analysis and development, *Journal of Pediatric Nursing*, 5(1): 4–14.

Koch, T. and Kralik, D. (2006) *Participatory Action Research in Health Care*. Melbourne: Blackwell Science.

Kvale, S. (1996) *Interviews: An Introduction to Qualitative Research Interviewing*. Thousand Oaks, CA: Sage.

Lamprill, J. (2002) Asking for children's assent to take part in clinical research, *Good Clinical Practice Journal*, 9(8): 1–4.

Lave, J. and Wenger, E. (1991) *Situated Learning: Legitimate Peripheral Participation*. Cambridge: Cambridge University Press.

Leeson, G.W., Harper, S. and Levin, S. (2004) *Independent Living in Later Life: Literature Review*. Report of research carried out by the Oxford Institute of Ageing, University of Oxford, on behalf of the Department of Work and Pensions. www.dwp.gov.uk/asd/asd5/ih2003–2004/IH137.pdf (accessed 30 August 2006).

Lewis, A. and Lindsay, G. (eds) (2000) *Researching Children's Perspectives*. Buckingham: Open University Press.

Lewis, J. (2001) What works in community care?, *Managing Community Care*, 9(1): 3–6.

Lieblich, A. (1996) Some unforeseen outcomes of conducting narrative research with people of one's own culture, in R. Josselson (ed.) *Ethics and Process in the Narrative Study of Lives*. Thousand Oaks, CA: Sage.

Lightfoot, J. and Sloper, P. (2002) Having a say in health: involving young people with a chronic illness or physical disability in local health services development, *Children and Society*, 29(1): 15–20.

Lincoln, Y.S. and Guba, E.G. (2000) Paradigmatic controversies, contradictions and emerging confluences, in N.K. Denzin and Y.S. Lincoln (eds) *Handbook of Qualitative Research*. Thousand Oaks, CA: Sage.

Lockey, R., Sitzia, J. et al. (2004) *Training for Service Users in Health and Social Care Research: A Study of Training Priorities and Participants' Experience (TRUE) Project*. Worthing: Worthing and Southend Hospital NHS Trust.

Macfadyen, A. (1997) *A Phenomenological Study into the Experiences of Young Children Undergoing Minor, In-patient Procedures*. London: RCN Institute.

Macfadyen, A. (2006) Consultation with paediatric oncology service users. Unpublished report, Newcastle upon Tyne NHS Hospitals Trust.

Macran, S., Ross, H. et al. (1999) The importance of considering clients' perspectives in psychotherapy research, *Journal of Mental Health*, 8(4): 325–37.

Magnusson, L. (2002) The Swedish ACTION project 2000–2002. Unpublished final report to the Ministry of Social Affairs (in Swedish, English summary available from the author).

Magnusson, L. and Hanson, E. (2005) Supporting frail older people and their family carers living at home using information and communication technology: a Swedish case study cost analysis, *Journal of Advanced Nursing*, 51(6): 645–57.

Magnusson, L., Nolan, M.R., Hanson, E., Berthold, H. and Andersson, B.-A. (2001) Developing partnerships with older people and their family carers: the ÄldreVäst Sjuhärad model, *Quality in Ageing – Policy, Practice and Research*, 2(2): 32–8.

Magnusson, L., Hanson, E. and Nolan, M.R. (2005) The impact of information and communication technology on family carers of older people and professionals in Sweden, *Ageing and Society*, 25(5): 693–714.

Malterud, K. (2001) The art and science of clinical knowledge: evidence beyond measures and numbers, *The Lancet*, 358: 397–400.

Marsh, G., Clark, L. et al. (2004) Chaffee County community health assessment. Unpublished report, University of Colorado at Denver and Health Sciences Center, School of Nursing, Nursing Doctorate Program, Denver, CO.

Marsh, P., Fisher, M., Mathers, N. and Fish, S. (2005) *Developing the Evidence Base for Social Work and Social Care Practice, Using Knowledge in Social Care Report*. London: Social Care Institute for Excellence.

Marx, K. and Engels, F. (1947) *The German Ideology*. New York: International Publishers [1845].

Masson, J. (2000) Researching children's perspectives: legal issues, in A. Lewis and G. Lyndsey (eds) *Researching Children's Perspectives*. Buckingham: Open University Press.

Maurer, K., Volk, S. and Gerbaldo, H. (1997) Auguste D and Alzheimer's disease, *The Lancet*, 349: 1546–9.

McAdams, D.P. and Janis, L. (2004) Narrative identity and narrative therapy, in L.E Angus and J. McLeod (eds) *The Handbook of Narrative and Psychotherapy: Practice, Theory and Research*. London: Sage Publications.

McCall, M.M. (2000) Performance ethnography: a brief history and some advice, in N.K. Denzin and Y.S. Lincoln (eds) *Handbook of Qualitative Research*, 2nd edn. Thousand Oaks, CA: Sage.

McCormack, B., Manley, K. and Garbett, R. (2004) *Practice Development in Nursing*. Oxford: Blackwell.

McKenzie, K. and Harpham, T. (2005) *Social Capital and Mental Health*. London: Jessica Kingsley.

Mead, G.H. (1934) *Mind, Self, and Society.* Chicago, IL: Chicago University Press.

Medical Research Council (MRC) (1991) *Working Party on Research on Children.* London: Medical Research Council.

Meiers, S.J. and Tomlinson, P.S. (2003) Family-nurse co-construction of meaning: a central phenomenon of family caring, *Scandinavian Journal of Caring Sciences,* 17(2): 193–201.

Meininger, H. (2005) Narrative ethics in nursing for persons with intellectual disabilities, *Nursing Philosophy,* 6(2): 106–18.

Mental Health Research Network (MHRN) (2004) *Service User Involvement in the UK Mental Health Research Network: Guidance for Good Practice.* London: MHRN Service User Research Group (England).

Merighi, J.R., Ryan, M., Renouf, N. and Healy, B. (2005) Reassessing a theory of professional expertise: a cross-national investigation of expert mental health social workers, *British Journal of Social Work,* 35: 709–25.

Merriam, S.B. and Caffarella, R.S. (1991) *Learning in Adulthood.* San Francisco, CA: Jossey-Bass.

Mienczakowski, J. (1995) The theater of ethnography: the reconstruction of ethnography into theater with emancipatory potential, *Qualitative Enquiry,* 1(3): 360–75.

Miller, J. (1996) *Never too Young – How Young Children Can Take Responsibility and Make Decisions. A Handbook for Early Years Workers.* London: The National Early Years Network and Save the Children.

Miller, J. (1998) 'No fun in Bilsthorpe', *Social Action Today,* 7: 9–11.

Miller, S. (2000) Researching children: issues arising from a phenomenological study with children who have diabetes mellitus, *Journal of Advanced Nursing,* 31(5): 1228–34.

Mills, J., Bonner, A. and Francis, K. (2006) Adopting a constructivist approach to grounded theory: implications for research design, *International Journal of Nursing Practice,* 12(1): 8–13.

Mills, M. (1997) Narrative, identity and dementia: a study of emotion and narrative in older people with dementia, *Ageing and Society,* 17(6): 673–98.

Mills, M.A. and Coleman, P.G. (1994) Nostalgic memories in dementia: a case study, *International Journal of Aging and Human Development,* 38(3): 203–19.

Milroy, L. (1987) *Observing and Analysing Natural Language: A Critical Account of Sociolinguistic Method.* Oxford: Blackwell.

Milroy, L. and Gordon, M. (2003) *Sociolinguistics: Method and Interpretation.* Oxford: Blackwell.

Minkler, M. and Wallerstein, N. (2003) Introduction to community based participatory research, in M. Minkler and N. Wallerstein (eds) *Community-Based Participatory Research for Health.* San Francisco, CA: Jossey-Bass.

Minogue, V., Boness, J., Brown, A. and Girdlestone, J. (2005) The impact of service user involvement in research, *International Journal of Health Care Quality Assurance,* 18(2): 103–12.

Morgan, H. and Harris, J. (2005) Strategies for involving service users in outcomes focused research, in L. Lowes and I. Hulatt (eds) *Involving Service Users in Health and Social Care Research*. London: Routledge.

Morrow, V. (2001a) Using qualitative methods to elicit young people's perspectives on their environments: some ideas for community health initiatives, *Health Education Research*, 16(3): 255–68.

Morrow, V. (2001b) Young people's explanations and experiences of social exclusion: retrieving Bourdieu's concept of social capital, *International Journal of Sociology and Social Policy*, 21(4/5/6): 37–63.

Morrow, V. and Richards, M. (1996) The ethics of social research: the United Nations Convention on the Rights of the Child, *Children and Society*, 10(2): 90–105.

National Audit Office (2003) *Progress in Making E-Services Accessible to All: Encouraging Use by Older People*. London: The Stationery Office.

National Evaluation of the Children's Fund (NECF) (2004) *National Evaluation of the Children's Fund. Children, Young People, Parents and Carers' Participation in Children's Fund Case Study Partnerships*. London: Department for Education and Skills.

National Institute for Health and Clinical Excellence. www.nice.org.uk (accessed 28 September 2006).

Nettleton, S. and Watson, J. (1998) The body in everyday life: an introduction, in S. Nettleton and J. Watson (eds) *The Body in Every Day Life*. New York: Aspen Publications.

NHS Quality Improvement Scotland (NHSQIS) (2004) *Working with Older People towards Prevention and Early Detection of Depression*. Edinburgh: NHSQIS.

NHS Quality Improvement Scotland (NHSQIS) (2005a) *Working with Dependent Older People to Achieve Good Oral Health*. Edinburgh: NHSQIS.

NHS Quality Improvement Scotland (NHSQIS) (2005b) *Working with Older People towards Promoting Movement and Physical Activity*. NHSQIS.

NHS Quality Improvement Scotland (NHSQIS) (2005c) *Maximizing Communication with Older People Who Have Hearing Disability*. Edinburgh: NHSQIS.

NHS Scotland (2003) *A Partnership for Care: Scotland's Health White Paper*. Edinburgh: The Stationery Office.

Nichols, V. (2001) *Doing Research Ourselves*. London: Mental Health Foundation.

Nichols, V., Wright, S., Waters, R. et al. (2003) *Surviving user-led research: reflections on supporting user-led research projects*. London: Mental Health Foundation.

Nicholson, P. and Burr, J. (2005) Conclusions: taking a critical perspective: research methods and the role of 'users' or 'consumers', in J. Burr and P. Nicholson (eds) *Researching Health Care Consumers: Critical Approaches*. Basingstoke: Palgrave Macmillan.

Nolan, M.R. (1997) Health and social care: what the future holds for nursing. Keynote address at Third Royal College of Nursing Older Person European Conference and Exhibition, Harrogate.

Nolan, M.R. and Grant, G. (1993) Rust out and therapeutic reciprocity: concepts to advance the nursing care of older people, *Journal of Advanced Nursing*, 18(8): 1305–14.

Nolan, M.R., Grant, G. and Keady, J. (1996) *Understanding Family Care: A Multi-dimensional Model of Caring and Coping*. Buckingham: Open University Press.

Nolan, M.R., Davies, S. and Grant, G. (eds) (2001) *Working with Older People and their Families: Key Issues in Policy and Practice*. Buckingham: Open University Press.

Nolan, M.R., Davies, S., Brown, J., Keady, J. and Nolan, J. (2002) *Longitudinal Study of the Effectiveness of Educational Preparation to Meet the Needs of Older People and Carers: The AGEIN Project*. London: English National Board.

Nolan, M., Hanson, E., Magnusson, L. and Andersson, B. (2003a) Gauging quality in constructivist research: The ÄldreVäst Sjuhärad model revisited, *Quality in Ageing – Policy, practice and research*, 4(2): 22–7.

Nolan, M.R., Lundh, U., Grant, G. and Keady, J. (eds) (2003b) *Partnerships in Family Care: Understanding the Caregiving Career*. Maidenhead: Open University Press.

Nolan, M.R., Davies, S., Brown, J., Keady, J. and Nolan, J. (2004) Beyond 'person-centred' care: a new vision for gerontological nursing, *International Journal of Older People Nursing*, 13(3a): 45–53.

Nolan, M.R., Brown, J., Davies, S., Nolan, J. and Keady, J. (2006) *The Senses Framework: improving care for older people through a relationship-centred approach*. Getting Research into Practice (GRIP) Series, No. 2, University of Sheffield.

Nursing and Midwifery Practice Development Unit (NMPDU) (2002) *Nutrition for Physically Frail Older People*. Edinburgh: NMPDU.

Nussbaum, J.F. (1991) Communication, language and the institutionalised elderly, *Ageing and Society*, 11: 149–65.

O'Malley, K. (2004) *Children and Young People Participating in the PRSP Processes – Lessons from Save the Children's Experiences*. London: Save the Children.

Office for National Statistics (ONS) (2004) *Social and Economic Characteristics of the Population*. London: Office for National Statistics.

Olsson, E. and Ingvad, B. (2001) The emotional climate of caregiving in home care services, *Health and Social Care in the Community*, 9(6): 454–63.

Owen, J. (2005) Users, research and 'evidence' in social care, in J. Burr and P. Nicolson (eds) *Researching Health Care Consumers, Critical Approaches*. Basingstoke: Palgrave Macmillan.

Parker, I. (1989) 'Discourse and power', in J. Shotter and K.J. Gergen (eds) *Texts of Identity*. London: Sage.

Parr, J. (1998) Theoretical voices and women's own voices: the stories of mature women students, in J. Ribbens and R. Edwards (eds) *Feminist Dilemmas in Qualitative Research*. London: Sage.

Pawson, R. and Tilley, N. (1997) *Realistic Evaluation*. London: Sage Publications.

Pawson, R., Boaz, A., Grayson, L., Long, A. and Barnes, C. (2003) *Types and Quality of Knowledge in Social Care, Knowledge Review*. Bristol: Bristol Policy Press and Social Science Institute for Excellence.

Payne, S. and Seymore, J. (2004) Overview, in S. Payne, J. Seymour and C. Ingleton (eds) *Palliative Care Nursing: Principles and Evidence for Practice*. Oxford: Open University Press.

Pearce, A., Clare, L. and Pistrang, N. (2002) Managing sense of self: coping in the early stages of Alzheimer's disease, *Dementia*, 1(2) 173–92.

Pelchat, D., Lefebvre, H. et al. (2003) Differences and similarities between mothers' and fathers' experiences of parenting a child with a disability, *Journal of Child Health Care*, 7(4): 231–47.

Perkins, R. and Repper, J. (1998) *Choice or Control. Dilemmas in Community Mental Health Practice*. Oxford: Radcliffe Medical Press.

Pinfold, V. and Hammond, T. (2006) *Carers and Families Scoping Exercise*. London: Mental Health Research Network.

Polowycz, D., Brutus, M. et al. (1993) Comparison of patient and staff surveys of consumer satisfaction, *Hospital and Community Psychiatry*, 44(6): 589–91.

Potts, P. (1998) Knowledge is not enough: an exploration of what we can expect from enquiries which are social, in P. Clough and L. Barton (eds) *Articulating with Difficulty (research voices in inclusive education)*. London: Paul Chapman Publishing.

Proctor, I. and Padfield, M. (1998) The effect of the interviewer on the interviewee, *International Journal of Social Research Methodology*, 1(2): 123–36.

Raine, R., Sanderson, C. et al. (2004) An experimental study of determinants of group judgements in clinical guideline development, *The Lancet*, 364: 429–37.

Ramanathan-Abbott, V. (1994) Interactional differences in Alzheimer's discourse: an examination of AD speech across two audiences, *Language in Society*, 23: 31–58.

Ramcharan, P. (2006) Ethical challenges and complexities of including vulnerable people in research: some pre-theoretical considerations, *Journal of Intellectual and Developmental Disability*, 31(3): 183–5.

Ramcharan, P., Grant, G. and Flynn, M. (2004) Emancipatory and participatory research: how far have we come?, in E. Emerson, C. Hatton, T. Thompson and T. Parmenter (eds) *International Handbook of Applied Research in Intellectual Disabilities*. London: Wiley.

Ramon, S. (2000) Participative mental health research: users and professional researchers working together, *Mental Health Care*, 3(7): 224–8.

Rantz, M.J., Zwygart-Stauffacher, M. et al. (1999). Nursing home care quality: a multidimensional theoretical model integrating the views of consumers and providers, *Journal of Nursing Care Quality*, 14(1): 16–37.

Ray, L.D. and Mayan, M. (2001) Who decides what counts as evidence?, in J.M. Morse, J.M. Swanson and A.J. Kuzel (eds) *The Nature of Qualitative Evidence*. Thousand Oaks, CA: Sage Publications.

Raynes, N.V. (1998) Involving residents in quality specification, *Ageing and Society*, 18(1): 65–77.

Reed, J. (2005) The involvement of service users in care, services and policy – comments and implications for nursing development, *International Journal of Older People Nursing*, 14(3a): 41–2.

Reed, J. and Proctor, S. (1995) *Practitioner Research in Health Care: The Inside Story*. London: Chapman and Hall.

Reed, J., Cook, G. and Stanley, D. (1999) Promoting partnership with older people through quality assurance systems: issues arising in care homes, *Nursing Times Research*, 4(5): 257–67.

Reed, J., Weiner, R. and Glenda, C. (2004) Partnership research with older people – moving towards making the rhetoric a reality, *International Journal of Older People Nursing*, 13(3a): 3–10.

Reeve, P., Cornell, S., D'Costa, B., Janzen, R. and Ochocka, J. (2002) From our perspective: consumer researchers talk about their experience in a community mental health research project, *Psychiatric Rehabilitation Journal*, 25(4): 403–8.

Reissman, C.K. (1993) *Narrative Analysis*, Vol. 30. Qualitative research methods series. London: Sage Publications.

Repper, J., Newman, A. et al. (2003) *'Going the extra mile . . .' Evaluation of the Lincolnshire Assertive Outreach Service*. ScHARR, University of Sheffield. www.nimhe-em.org.uk (accessed 14 December 2006).

Roberts, B. (2002) *Biographical Research*. Buckingham: Open University Press.

Robinson, S. and Rosher, R.B. (2006) Tangling with the barriers to culture change: creating a resident-centred nursing home environment, *Journal of Gerontological Nursing*, 32(10): 19–25.

Robison, D. and Krauss, M. (2003) Lessons from the field: participatory action research in a family research project, *Mental Retardation*, 4(6): 460–4.

Roche, B., Savile, P., Aikens, D. and Scammell, A. (2005) Consumer led research? Patterns as researchers: the child health surveillance project, in L. Lowes and I. Hulatt (eds) *Involving Service Users in Health and Social Care Research*. London: Routledge.

Rodgers, J. (1999) Trying to get it right: undertaking research involving people with learning difficulties, *Disability and Society*, 14(4): 421–33.

Rodwell, M.K. (1998) *Social Work Constructivist Research*. New York: Garland.

Rolfe, G. (1999) Insufficient evidence: the problems of evidence-based nursing, *NET*, 19: 433–42.

Ronch, J.L. (2004) Changing institutional culture: can we re-value the nursing home? *Journal of Gerontological Social Work*, 43(1): 61–2.

Rose, D. (2001) *Users' Voices: The Perspectives of Mental Health Service Users on Community and Hospital Care*. London: Sainsbury Centre for Mental Health.

Rose, D. (2003) Having a diagnosis is a qualification for the job, *British Medical Journal*, 326 (14 June): 1331.

Rose, D., Fleishman, P. et al. (2002) *User and Carer Involvement in Change Management in a Mental Health Context: Review of the Literature*. Report to the National Coordinating Centre for NHS Service Delivery and Organisation R&D (NCCSDO).

Rosenwald, G. and Ochberg, R. (1992) Introduction: life stories, cultural politics and self understanding, in G.C. Rosenwald and R.C. Ochberg (eds) *Storied Lives: The Cultural Politics of Self Understanding*. New Haven, CT: Yale University Press.

Royal College of Nursing (RCN) (2003) The Royal College of Nursing Research Society: nurses and research ethics, *Nurse Researcher*, 11(1): 7–21.

Royal College of Nursing (RCN) (2004) *Research Ethics: RCN Guidance for Nurses*. London: Royal College of Nursing.

Royal College of Paediatrics and Child Health (RCPCH) (2000) Ethics Advisory Committee, *Archives of Disease in Childhood*, 82: 177–82.

Royle, J., Steele, R. and Hanley, B. (2001) *Getting Involved in Research: How to Do It*. Eastleigh: INVOLVE.

Rycroft-Malone, J., Seers, K. et al. (2004) What counts as evidence in evidence-based practice? *Journal of Advanced Nursing*, 47(1): 81–90.

Ryle, G. (1949) *The Concept of Mind*. London: Hutchinson.

Sabat, S. and Harre, R. (1992) The construction and deconstruction of self in Alzheimer's disease, *Ageing and Society*, 12: 443–61.

Sabat, S.R. and Collins, M. (1999) Intact social, cognitive ability, and selfhood: a case study of Alzheimer's disease, *American Journal of Alzheimer Disorders and Other Dementias*, 14(1): 11–19.

Save the Children (2000) *Children and Participation: Research, Monitoring and Evaluation with Children and Young People*. London: Save the Children.

Scalzi, C. (2006) Barriers and enablers to changing organisational culture in nursing homes, *Journal of Nursing Administration*, 36(5): 230.

Schein, E.H. (1985) *Organisational Culture and Leadership*. San Francisco, CA: Jossey-Bass.

Schneider, B. (2005) Mothers talk about their children with schizophrenia: a performance ethnography, *Journal of Psychiatric and Mental Health Nursing*, 12: 333–40.

Schön, D. (1987) *Educating the Reflective Practitioner*. San Francisco, CA: Jossey-Bass.

Schumacher, K.L., Stewart, B.J., Archbold, P.G., Dodd, M.J. and Dibble, S.L. (1998) Family caregiving skill: development of the concept, *Image: Journal of Nursing Scholarship*, 30(1): 63–70.

Scottish Executive Health Department (SEHD) (2001) *Caring for Scotland. The Strategy for Nursing and Midwifery in Scotland*. Edinburgh: The Stationery Office.

Scottish Intercollegiate Guidelines Network. www.sign.org.ac.uk/about/introduction.html (accessed on 28 September 2006).

Shiekh, J. and Yesavage, J. (1986) Geriatric Depression Scale; recent findings in the development of a shorter version, in J. Brink (ed.) *Clinical Gerontology: A Guide to Assessment and Intervention*. New York: Howarth Press.

Shields, G.H. and Walsh, M. (2006) Establishing the rationale for, and practice of, service user research at the Humber Mental Health Teaching Trust, *Mental Health and Learning Disabilities Research and Practice*, 3(2): 194–7.

Shields, L. and Twycross, A. (2003) Why we need ethics committees, *Paediatric Nursing*, 5(10): 19.

Shotter, J. (1993) *Conversational Realities: Constructing Life through Language.* Newbury Park, CA: Sage Publications.

Shulman, L. (1999) *The Skills of Helping Individuals, Families, Groups and Communities.* Itasca, IL: F.E. Peacock.

Simpson, E.L. and House, A. (2002) Involving users in the delivery and evaluation of mental health services: a systematic review, *British Medical Journal*, 325: 1–5.

Sloper, P. and Lightfoot, J. (2003) Involving disabled and chronically ill children and young people in health service development, *Child Care Health and Development*, 29(1): 15–20.

Small, J.A., Geldart, K., Gutman, G. and Clarke Scott, M.A. (1998) The discourse of self in dementia, *Ageing and Society*, 18: 291–316.

Smith, E., Manthorpe, J. et al. (2005) *User Involvement in the Design, and Undertaking of Nursing, Midwifery and Health Visiting Research.* Report to the National Co-ordinating Centre for NHS Service Delivery and Organisation R&D. Nursing Research Unit, Kings College London.

Steel, R. (2005) Actively involving marginalized and vulnerable people in research, in L. Lowes and I. Hulatt (eds) *Involving Service Users in Health and Social Care Research.* London: Routledge.

Steeman, E., Casterle, B., Godderis, J. and Grypdonck, M. (2006) Integrative literature reviews and meta-analyses, *Journal of Advanced Nursing*, 54(6): 722.

Sterin, G. (2002) Essay on a word: a lived experience of Alzheimer's disease, *Dementia: The International Journal of Social Research and Practice*, 1(1): 7–10.

Stevens, T., Wilde, D. et al. (2005) Consumer involvement in cancer research in the United Kingdom: the benefits and challenges, in L. Lowes and I. Hulatt (eds) *Involving Service Users in Health and Social Care Research.* London: Routledge.

Stoecker, R. (1999) Are academics irrelevant? Roles for scholars in participatory research, *American Behavioral Scientist*, 42(5): 840–54.

Surr, C. (2006) Preservation of self in people with dementia living in residential care: a socio-biographical approach, *Social Science and Medicine*, 62(7): 1720–30.

Swallow, V. (2006) *Learning to Manage Chronic Childhood Renal Disease: The Experiences of Children and Families.* Newcastle upon Tyne: School of Health, Community and Education Studies. Northumbria University.

Swallow, V., Forrester, T. et al. (2006) *Short Breaks – Big Impact: Evaluation of a Short Break Service for Children and Young People with Life Limiting Illnesses.* Newcastle upon Tyne: Northumbria University.

Tee, S.E. and Lathlean, J.A. (2004) The ethics of conducting a co-operative inquiry with vulnerable people, *Journal of Advanced Nursing*, 47(5): 536–43.

Terkel, L. 'Studs' (1972) *Working.* New York: Avon.

Thorne, L., Purcell, R. et al. (2001) *Knowing How: A Guide to Getting Involved in Research.* Exeter: Exeter University.

Thornicroft, G., Rose, D., Huxley, P., Dale, G. and Wykes, T. (2002) What are the research priorities of service users? *Journal of Mental Health,* 11: 1–5.

Tolson, D., McAloon, M., Hotchkiss, R. and Schofield, I. (2005) Progressing evidenced-based practice: an effective nursing model?, *Journal of Advanced Nursing,* 50(2): 124–33.

Tolson, D., Schofield, I., Booth, J., Kelly, T.B. and James, L. (2006) Constructing a new approach to developing evidence based practice with nurses and older people, *World Views on Evidence Based Nursing,* 3(2): 62–72.

Townend, M. and Braithwaite, T. (2002) Mental health research – the value of user involvement, *Journal of Mental Health,* 11(2): 117–19.

Townson, L., Macauley, S. et al. (2004) We are all in the same boat: doing 'people-led research', *British Journal of Learning Disabilities,* 32: 72–6.

Trappes-Lomax, H. (2004) Discourse analysis, in A. Davies and C. Elder (eds) *The Handbook of Applied Linguistics.* Oxford: Blackwell.

Tresolini, C.P. and the Pew-Fetzer Task Force (1994) *Health Professions Education and Relationship-Centred Care: A Report of the Pew-Fetzer Task Force on Advancing Psychosocial Education.* San Francisco, CA: Pew Health Professions Commission.

Trivedi, P. and Wykes, T. (2002) From passive subjects to equal partners: qualitative review of user involvement in research, *British Journal of Psychiatry,* 181: 468–72.

Turner, M. and Beresford, P. (2005) *User Controlled Research: Its Meanings and Potential.* www.invo.org.uk/pdfs/Colliding%20Worlds.pdf (accessed 14 February 2007).

UK Mental Health Research Network (2005) *Service User Involvement in the UK Mental Health Research Network.* London: MHRN.

United Nations (1989) *United Nations Convention on the Rights of the Child.* New York: United Nations.

US Census Bureau (2000) American Fact Finder: Census 2000 Summary File 3 (SF 3), Chaffee County. http://factfinder.census.gov (accessed 15 September 2006).

US Department of Health and Human Services (2000) *Health People 2010.* McLean, VA: US Government Printing Office.

User Focus Monitoring Group (2005) A hard fight: the involvement of mental health service users in research, in L. Lowes and I. Hulatt (eds) *Involving Service Users in Health and Social Care Research.* London: Routledge.

Viswanathan, M., Ammerman, A. et al. (2004) *Community-based Participatory Research: Assessing the Evidence. Evidence Report/Technology Assessment No. 99.* Prepared by RTI – University of North Carolina Evidence-based Practice Center under Contract No. 290–02–0016. Rockville, MD: Agency for Healthcare Research and Quality.

Vittoria, A.K. (1998) Preserving selves: identity work and dementia, *Research on Aging,* 20(1): 91–136.

Wallerstein, N. and Duran, B. (2003) The conceptual, historical, and practice roots of community based participatory research and related participatory traditions, in M. Minkler and N. Wallerstein (eds) *Community-Based Participatory Research for Health*. San Francisco, CA: Jossey-Bass.

Walmsley, J. (2001) Normalisation, emancipatory research and inclusive research in learning disability, *Disability and Society*, 16(2): 187–205.

Walmsley, J. (2004) Involving users with learning difficulties in health improvement: lessons from inclusive learning disability research, *Nursing Inquiry*, 11(1), 54–64.

Wang, C. and Pies, C. (2004) Family, maternal and child health through photovision, *Maternal and Child Health*, 8(2): 95–102.

Warren, L. and Cook, J. (2005) Working with older women in research: benefits and challenges of involvement, in L. Lowes and I. Hulatt (eds) *Involving Service Users in Health and Social Care Research*. London: Routledge.

Weindling, P. (1996) Human guinea pigs and the ethics of experimentation: the BMJ's correspondent at the Nuremberg medical trial, *British Medical Journal*, 313: 1467–70.

Wenger, E. (2003) *Communities of Practice: Learning, Meaning and Identity*. Cambridge: Cambridge University Press.

White, N., Scott, A. et al. (2002) The limited utility of the Mini-Mental State Examination in screening people over the age of 75 years for dementia in primary care, *British Journal of General Practice*, 52(485): 1002–3.

Whitlatch, C.J., Feinberg, L.F. and Tucke, S. (2005) Accuracy and consistency of responses from persons with cognitive impairment, *Dementia: The International Journal of Social Research and Practice*, 4(2): 171–83.

Williams, S. and Keady, J. (2005) The narrative voice of people with dementia, *Dementia: The International Journal of Social Research and Practice*, 5(2): 163–5.

World Medical Assembly (WMA) (2000) *Declaration of Helsinki: Ethical Principles for Medical Research Involving Human Subjects*. Helsinki: World Medical Assembly.

Wright, F.V., Boschen, K. and Jutai, J. (2005) Exploring the comparative responsiveness of a core set of outcome measures in a school-based conductive education programme, *Child: Care, Health and Development*, 31(3): 291–302.

Wykes, T. (2003) Blue skies in the Journal of Mental Health? Consumers in research, *Journal of Mental Health*, 12(1): 1–6.

Wyre Forest Self Advocacy (WFSA) and Tarleton, B. (2005) Writing it ourselves, *British Journal of Learning Disabilities*, 33: 65–9.

Wysocki, T. and Gavin, L. (2004) Psychometric properties of a new measure of fathers' involvement in the management of pediatric chronic diseases, *Journal of Pediatric Psychology*, 29(3): 231–40.

Yesavage, J., Brink, T. et al. (1983) Development and validation of a geriatric depression scale, *Journal of Psychiatric Research*, 17: 37–9.

Zgola, J.M. (1999) *Care that Works: A Relationship Approach to Persons with Dementia*. New York: Johns Hopkins University Press.

Index

Related books from Open University Press

Purchase from www.openup.co.uk or order through your local bookseller

---

PATIENT PARTICIPATION IN HEALTH CARE CONSULTATIONS
QUALITATIVE PERSPECTIVES

Sarah Collins, Nicky Britten, Johanna Ruusuvuori, Andrew Thompson (eds)

- How does patient participation work in practice?
- What does it look like when it happens?
- How can it be researched and how can it be taught?

This comprehensive new book provides answers to these questions by exploring interconnections between theory, research and practice. It draws on different disciplinary perspectives in the health and social sciences and invites comparisons between different health care settings.

With patient participation as the central theme, this book:

- Draws on patient, professional and academic perspectives
- Makes substantive contributions to policy, practice and professional development
- Contributes to the development of the field by offering new material and insights

The research content of each chapter is accompanied by ideas for its educational and practical application. Real examples invite comparison with academic research and health professionals' experience.

Patient Participation in Health Care Consultations takes a multidisciplinary approach and is key reading for students and academics in health and social sciences and for practising health care professionals. It will also be of interest to patients, carers and policy makers.

Contributors
Sarah Collins, Nicky Britten, Carol Bugge, John Chatwin, Rowena Field, Joseph Gafaranga, Aled Jones, Pirjo Lindfors, Anssi Perakyla, Johanna Ruusuvuori, Fiona Stevenson, Andrew Thompson, Ian Watt.

Contents
Foreword - Acknowledgements - Preface - Part I Setting the scene: Debates on patient participation and methods for studying it - Understanding patient participation - Methods for studying patient participation - Part II Participation in practice - The meaning of patient involvement and participation: A taxonomy - What is a good consultation and what is a bad one? The patient perspective - A feeling of equality: some interact ional features that build rapport and mutuality in a therapeutic encounter - Patient participation in formulations and in opening sequences - What is patient participation: reflections arising from the study of general practice, homeopathy and psychoanalysis - Nursing assessments and other tasks: influences on participation in interactions between patients and nurses - Part III A conceptual overview of participation - Components of participation in health care consultations: a conceptual model for research - An integrative approach to patient participation in consultations - Afterword - Educational supplements - References - Index of key words - Figures and tables - Appendix: Conversation analysis notation system

2007   224pp
ISBN-13: 978 0 335 21964 3 (ISBN-10: 0 335 21964 0) Paperback
ISBN-13: 978 0 335 21965 0 (ISBN-10: 0 335 21965 9) Hardback

PARTNERSHIPS IN COMMUNITY MENTAL HEALTH NURSING AND DEMENTIA CARE
PRACTICE PERSPECTIVES

John Keady, Charlotte L. Clarke, Sean Page (eds)

- What is the role of the community mental health nurse (CMHN) in dementia care?
- What knowledge and frameworks influence the way CMHNs practice in dementia care?
- How will community mental health nursing be driven forward in the future?

This exciting and long-awaited new book is a companion volume to the respected *Community Mental Health Nursing and Dementia Care: Practice Perspectives* (Open University Press, 2003, edited by Keady, Clarke and Adams). The book enhances the link between theory and practice, providing a rounded and evidence-based account of the complexity, breadth and diversity of community mental health nursing practice in dementia care.

The text is divided into three distinct sections:

- Models of community support and practice values
- Professional roles and clinical work
- Moving forward: Changing and developing CMHN practice

The book includes coverage of key contemporary issues such as service user involvement, nurse prescribing, younger people with dementia, social exclusion and vulnerability. *Partnerships in Community Mental Health Nursing and Dementia Care: Practice Perspectives* is key reading for students of dementia care at all levels. It is also of relevance to professionals within the field of community mental health nursing and all other mental health or gerontology related areas.

Contributions to this book are drawn from practising CMHNs in dementia care, researchers and commentators who are working at the forefront of their respective fields.

Contributors
Trevor Adams, Susan Ashcroft-Simpson, Caroline Baker, Diane Beavis, Catherine Brannan, Dawn Brooker, Shane Burke, Suzanne Cahill, Caroline Cantley, Peter Caswell, Charlotte L. Clarke, Vivienne Davies-Quarrell, Kenneth Day, Kay de Vries, Aine Farrell, Paula Gardiner, Sue Gunstone, Philip Hardman, Steve Iliffe, Dee Jones, Gary and Linda Jones, John Keady, Cordelia Man-yuk Kwok, Jenny Mackenzie, Mike Nolan, Simon O'Donovan, Sean Page, Emma Pritchard, Jan Reed, Jeannie Robinson, David Stanley, Fiona Wilkie, Heather Wilkinson, Kevin G. Wood

Contents

2007   312pp
ISBN-13: 978 0 335 21581 2 (ISBN-10: 0 335 21581 5) Paperback
ISBN-13: 978 0 335 21582 9 (ISBN-10: 0 335 21582 3) Hardback